Writing beyond Prophecy

Writing beyond Prophecy

EMERSON, HAWTHORNE, *and* MELVILLE *after the* AMERICAN RENAISSANCE

Martin Kevorkian

LOUISIANA STATE UNIVERSITY PRESS | BATON ROUGE

Published by Louisiana State University Press

Manufactured in the United States of America
FIRST PRINTING

DESIGNER: *Mandy McDonald Scallan*
TYPEFACE: *Minion Pro*
PRINTER: *McNaughton & Gunn, Inc.*
BINDER: *Acme Bookbinding, Inc.*

Library of Congress Cataloging-in-Publication Data

Kevorkian, Martin, 1968–
Writing beyond prophecy : Emerson, Hawthorne, and Melville after the American Renaissance / Martin Kevorkian.
p. cm.
Includes bibliographical references and index.
ISBN 978-0-8071-4760-3 (cloth : alk. paper) — ISBN 978-0-8071-4761-0 (pdf) — ISBN 978-0-8071-4762-7 (epub) — ISBN 978-0-8071-4763-4 (mobi)
1. Emerson, Ralph Waldo, 1803–1882–Religion. 2. Hawthorne, Nathaniel, 1804–1864—Religion. 3. Melville, Herman, 1819–1891—Religion. 4. Religion and literature—United States—History—19th century. 5. Literature and society—United States—History—19th century. 6. United States—Intellectual life—1783–1865. I. Title.
PS1642.R4K48 2013
814'.3—dc23

2012010391

The paper in this book meets the guidelines for permanence and durability of the Committee on Production Guidelines for Book Longevity of the Council on Library Resources. ∞

for

Colacurcio, Packer, and Wortham

active souls

the flowers placed in the sanctuary

for today's service

are in their honor

Contents

Prelude

Writing beyond Prophecy begins with a relic, preserved thanks to my colleague Douglas Bruster, and still relevant thanks to a blind spot that literary studies of the "American Renaissance" are only just beginning to rectify: "A Monument to Melville," in the form of a *Times Literary Supplement* review essay, was stamped "Rec'd" by the "Chairman's Office, Dept. of English, University of Texas" on January 25, 1972. Featured in the review is a book allegedly entitled *Progress into Science.* When the issue reached the desk of Joe Moldenhauer, he circled the word *Science,* and penned in *Silence.* Moldenhauer, the eminent Thoreauvian, was correct about the title of the Melville study under review. But thirty years later, it still seems worth noting that both the *TLS,* reverting to the default association of "progress" with "science," and the author of *Progress into Silence,* associating the later life of Melville with cessation of writing, were wrong.

Both science and silence play a role in the story to be told here of later Emerson, Hawthorne, and Melville, but neither "ence" gets the last word on how these careers progressed. Still voicing his restlessness a quarter of a century after *Moby-Dick* (1851), Melville speaks of both technological progress and spiritual silence:

> They wire the world—far under sea
> They talk; but never comes to me
> A message from beneath the stone.
> (*NN* 12:497–98)

Robert Penn Warren glosses these lines as expressing "the failure of science to solve ultimate mysteries" (*Selected Poems,* 410). As Andrew Delbanco puts it in *Melville: His World and Work* (2005): "Science, so full of promise for its insights into the processes of nature, could do nothing to satisfy what William James would soon call 'the craving of the heart to believe that behind nature there is a spirit whose expression nature is,' and *Clarel* was Melville's reproach of science for its failure to slake his craving" (282). *Clarel,* Melville's eighteen-thousand-line *Poem and Pilgrimage in the Holy Land* (1876), laments the lack of "hope" to be found through "prosing Science" (*NN* 12:113) and earnestly seeks its implicit antidote: what we might call, after Emerson, meter-making religion. In his summative study, *Emerson,* Lawrence Buell asks scholars living in our own wired world to face a fact: "Like it or not, there is no getting rid of religion as a force in human affairs. If you think it's nothing more than the opiate of others, you're likely to misunderstand yourself as well as them. Especially if you're trying to come to terms with so religio-centric a culture as the United States was in the early nineteenth century—and indeed still is" (159–60). And for those of us who are fortunate to serve in the teaching profession, the academic narrative of secular triumphalism can make it difficult to understand our students: as Joanna Brooks reminds in her 2010 *ALH* piece, "From Edwards to Baldwin," "We know, as do the undergraduates we face in our lecture halls, that religion matters, has always mattered, and will continue to matter, and that, moreover, what Edmund Morgan memorably described as 'faith lived in its proper imperfection' is capable of producing great art. It is time for new stories. How, then, shall we proceed?" (441).

The story of *Writing beyond Prophecy: Emerson, Hawthorne, and Melville after the American Renaissance* focuses on how each of these authors initially chose a self-reliant literary vocation over and against the calling of the minister, as the study traces, in the later careers, the fallout of that early prophetic confidence. Thus, to some extent, this book tells a story of these authors' relations to "organized religion." Having entered the language in 1843, contemporaneous to a romantic individualism that would tend to regard it with hostility, the phrase today bears inescapably pejorative associations. Especially when paired with "religion," "organized" has devolved from its earliest significance, in reference to something living, organic, provided with vital organs, to something systematic, mechanical, and dead. A 2001 *OED* entry typifies the contemporary usage: "He was hostile to organized religion, which he considered oppression through the fetishization of words." This twenty-first-century characterization typifies that pejorative usage precisely through concepts that Emerson forcefully articulated in 1838, in his assault on "historical Christianity" and its treatment of the figure of Jesus: "The idioms of his language, and the figures of his rhetoric, have usurped the place of his truth; and churches are not built on his principles, but on his tropes" (*CW* 1:81). Yet however vigorously Emerson pursued his thesis against verbal idolatry, did he live out his life in the belief that organized religion should die? And if not, on what terms might Emerson, and those he inspired to an aggressive literary prophecy, come to terms with the figure of the minister? As Colin Jager observes in *Varieties of Secularism in a Secular Age* (2010), "a recognizably modern notion of literariness, as something simultaneously distinct from Christianity and yet remarkably proximate to it, emerges for the first time during the Romantic era" (168). How did Emerson, Hawthorne, and Melville negotiate that proximity, and with what degree of comfort did they pursue the substitution of the distinct new discourse for the faith traditions into which they had been born?

If we are *Emerson's Ghosts,* as Randall Fuller has evocatively suggested in the 2007 publication of that title, we might wish to linger a bit, even in spite of the Sage's famously serene smile, to wonder what might have haunted him. Emerson was, as Fuller notes, in some ways markedly "unlike" the "subsequent (and largely secular) American Scholars" (*Emerson's Ghosts,* 8). And, as Michael Colacurcio reminded me on the occasion of an oral examination, Emerson concludes his critique of religious "forms" with a surprising endorsement: "Two inestimable advantages Christianity has given us; first; the Sabbath, the jubilee of the whole world; . . . And secondly, the institution of preaching" (*CW* 1:92). The Sabbath and preaching, the institutions of organized religion, provide the regular opportunity for shared spiritual instruction and "high communion" (*CW* 1:91). And it is to those possibilities that Emerson, Hawthorne, and Melville increasingly turn, after the work of prophecy, on a day we might think of as the Sunday after Emerson.

Noting the social dimension to such desires, Tanya Paull once suggested a blockbuster title and tagline for the project: *American Renaissance 2—This Time, It's Interpersonal!* The present study owes its existence primarily to scholarly community, which I here acknowledge for its many forms of fellowship. At UCLA: Luke Bresky, Laura Arnold, Maurice Lee, Lisa Gordis, John Lednicky, Jayne Devens, Willene van Blair (especially for the "Ethics" and "Religion" hats), Yair Rainer, Betty Donohoe, Emily Schiller, Joanna Brooks, Jake Martin, Bill Gleason, Ilana Nash, Jessica Brantley, Elliott Visconsi, for talking to my dad at Greg Jackson's graduation party, Rob Perrin, Thad Bower, John Dalton, Curtis Gruenler, Lezlie Gruenler, Stanley Orr, Paul Bryant, Lance Schaina, Marlo Paculdo,

Bryan Waldron, Ingrid Ruppel, Johnny Lin, Diana Chu, Jana Phifer. Kris Fresonke, Will Moddelmog, and Greg Jackson, for taking me to a Dodgers' game before it was too late. Michael Colacurcio, for *still* being the voice in my head (and thereby conveying faint echoes of Edward H. Davidson, whom I never met, and his white shoes), Barbara Packer, for making me a part of her kinship network with the gift a Parson table, Thomas Wortham, for leaping up onto a windowsill to cut a Gordian knot; and, for guidance and encouragement, Martha Banta, V.A. Kolve, Stephen Yenser, and Blake Allmendinger. At Stanford: Jeffrey Schnapp, John Freccero (also to be thanked for directing me to Jay Fliegelman), Robert Pogue Harrison, Alison Cornish, Costanza Gilson, Dina Viggiano, Corrado Vial, and Francesca Seaman, for encouraging my love of Dante. Ann Cvetkovich at UT for helping to remind me of that love. From Rinconada to the Casa Italiana: Rick Olesek, Virgilian scholar and athlete, Doug Liden, engineer and humanist. Gordon Olesek, for thoughts on Mark Twain and the limits of power, Max Braun, for questions about Queequeg's coffin. In San Diego: Doc Hansen, Bob Litchfield, and Bob Shaughnessy. I am also grateful for the opportunity to have participated in the 2010 Imitatio gathering at Stanford, led by Jean-Pierre Dupuy, Andrew J. McKenna, Robert Hammerton-Kelly, and Lindy M. Fishburne.

Representing his priceless commitment to our research community, a University of Texas at Austin Subvention Grant awarded by President William C. Powers, Jr., was of immense material benefit in the production of this book, and that same president's advocacy under fire for what we do as scholars has been a tremendous boost to morale. Also at the great university where I am fortunate to work: I would like to thank my colleague Liz Scala, for imagining the Undergraduate Research Apprenticeship; Dean Mark Musick, for supporting it; and Kevin Endres, for being the ideal student to pilot the program and for continuing to devote his intelligence to the manuscript. I owe a deep debt to Chair Liz Cullingford, especially for helping me give my summers to Melville, and former chair Jim Garrison, for bringing me aboard and remaining concerned about my well-being. I thank my comrade Roger Renwick for excellent advice on administration—you were right!—and the whole Associate Chair crew, including Mary Blockley, Wayne Lesser, and Jackie Henkel. The rest of the faculty, for the good will and commitment that make the job of Associate Chair an honor and mostly a pleasure. Susana Castillo,

Brad Humphries, Cecilia Smith-Morris for making the job possible. The 679HA trust: Dan Birkholz, for helping me daydream about the book even when there was little time to write, Cole Hutchison, for teaching me about research methods in a course we co-taught on research methods and for uncanny sartorial sense, and Janine Barchas, a steady captain in all weather. Isaac Barchas, Jim Cox, John Gonzalez, and Pat Garcia, for alert Whale-watching. Evan Carton, Phil Barrish, Gretchen Murphy, Brian Bremen, and Julia Lee, for intellectual inspiration and Americanist community. Wayne Rebhorn, for free-lance mentoring and lovable Machiavellianism, Don Rolando Hinojosa-Smith, for conversations about Johnny Depp, Tom Whitbread, for poetry, David Wevill, for the running dactyl, Dean Young, for surreal Whitmanian anaphora. In the office and its environs: Lilia Beaman, Annalise Blech Rivas, and Annelise Notzon for Powderpuff power, and Jessica Pierce, Sara Gray, Donetta Gibbs, Andrea Golden, Alyssa Martinez, Beth Rutter, and Matt Lamb for outstanding support and convivial conversation.

I thank our outstanding UT graduate students, with interesting interests of their own, who have been willing to take an instructive interest in my interests: Noah Mass, Jillian Sayre, Coye Heard, Krzysztof Piekarski, Elisabeth Sharp McKetta, Brad Saylorking, Eileen McGinnis, Cate Coleman, Ty Alyea, Jodi Relyea, Robin Riehl, Phil Leigh, Jonathan Lamb, Doug Coulson, Jessica Kilgore, Michael Quatro, Lydia French, Elizabeth Frye, David Harper, Yvette Dechavez, Anna Stewart, Jeremy Dean, Will Miller, Ousseynou Sy, Ashley Squires, Andi Gustavson, Rodney Herring, Kathryn Hamilton Warren, Tony Fassi, Tracy Wuster, Jeff Jaeckle, Zach Dobbins, Jeff Howard, Jill Anderson, Brent Winkelman, Michael Jaffe, Lacey Donohue, Christopher Hinojosa, Chuck Bradford, Nicole Harter, Alberto Varon, Julie Sievers.

I remember the many UT undergraduates who have inspired me as the project grew: Andy Uhler, for the Billy Budd program, Peter Babb, for music matters, Andrew Brummett, for considerations of the Wayside, Trevor Boehm, for tales of lightning and spirit, David Doak, for cheese straws, Duy Doan, for postcards from the Custom House, Robert Grady Rogers, for nobly bearing a resemblance to Steve Martin, Seth Park, for unlimited dialectics, Gabriel Lopez, for improvisational chalkboard diagrams, Arnold Jin, for relentless curiosity and the gift of sincerity, Nathaniel Pitoniak, for having an excellent first name and for being the first to console me upon the occasion of my death, Miguel Gonzalez, for chasing phantoms, Ashley Edwards, for Hawthornean silence, Asheley Landrum, for Hawthornean portraiture, Esther Elizondo, for taking chances, Daniel Solon, for writing the scene about the fish, Mukul Kelkar, for the Michael Jordan lunch pail ticket, Marisa Bell-Metereau, for tidings from Midwestern Manuscripts, Bobiejo Ferguson, for instructions on how to make a photo album, Mary Claire O'Banion, for being the ace among a throng of bearded men, Tom Bevilacqua, for the beatific pilgrimage, Kelsey Harmon, for the paradox of Petrarchan success, Natalie Mears, for turning the Whale inside out, Teri Krenek, for a Bonnard palette, Maxwell Stubbs, for eloquence, Ryan Walters, for timing, Johnny McElmurry, the comeback kid, Tim Pugliese, never a dull moment, Ivy Shyu, for caring, Eric Wright, for philosophical confidence, Allison Weinstein, for doubts about Hume, Rene Perez, for writing along these highways, Megan Brown, for making the trek, Philip Johnson, for tenacity, Chad Robertson, good people, Catherine Hubert, for bold claims, Nicholas Ybarra, for precise observation, Cristina Ramage, for space, Sean Reyna, for action verbs (and also for space), Brian Fonken, for Radney's sweater, Mary Beth Lickteig, for forgiveness, Caitlin Sweet, for pedagogical energy, Jessica Garcia, for steel trap structure, Hollie Neal, for entomology and the materiality of aesthetics, Robert Travis, for going Hollywood, Justin Humphries, for Your Cryogenic Tomorrow, Jeremiah McElroy, for a rhetorical blow to the rib cage, Brandon Scott Wilson, for a stirring invocation, Zane Baker, for his merry band, Alan Alexander, a stalwart, Sennett Rockers, for auditing with excellence, Chelsea Fogleman, for sugar-gliding, Georgia Moore, for identity in motion, Shane Jimenez, for the orthodontic legend of a Laker fan, Lindon Taylor Kueck, for discerning the pattern of Experience, Trisha Gutierrez, for madrigality, Ryan Powers, for the five paragraph tattoo, Scott Ramirez, for memorability, Michelle Ty, for reminding me not to be too tired to try to be one of the good guys, Erik Locascio, for raiding the tombs, Erika Arenivas, for the blue sun, Charlie Grant, for the impossible, Kulsoom Rizvi, for Emersonian success, Andrea Valdez, for study breaks and monthly Texas, Gregory Webster, for comics, Christine Ho, for leading the Milo fan club, Erika Halstead, for perseverance, Peter Beronio, for clear eyes, Beth Jones, for really getting it, Andrew Thompson, for carrying the fire, Sydney VanBerg, for playing with words, Brooke Scheyer, for theatricality, Danielle Calodney, for raising her hand, Elizabeth Munson, for a sense of calling, Heather Routt, for omnipresence, Haley Moore, for returning from monkey island, and David Eshelman, for music of the bathyspheres.

Also, I would like to thank the Reverends Ruby McNulty, Robert Luther, Bishop George McKinney, "Badveli" Shaw, Charles Smith, Dan Bauman, Mike Steiner, Mike Crooker, Dolores Nasrallah, Curt Gruber, Seda Mansour, Scott Young, Lynn Gill, Dave Hong, John Whorall, Al Heisig, Craig Barnes, John Singleton, Steve Youngdahl, Sarah De La Fuente, Sarah Allen, and Terence Sherry. Also James Parks, for a communion of fresh-squeezed carrot-beet-apple-celery-ginger juice, and for renewal, Dave Streilein, William Loven, Nathaniel Hall, Jordan Scott, Jason Booth, Joe Calabrese, Fred Schleede, Cliff Zoch, Sid Maxwell, John Borsi, Bryan Borsi, and Jerry Schmeil. Kenneth McNulty, for a liberating truth.

I'm grateful to Matt Rollins, for inscribing narrative poetry, Jeff Salamon, for editorial care and neighborhood delivery, Dave Chang, for Tales from the Secret City, James Todd Smith, for calling upon Sears shoppers to keep their dreams alive, Saul Morales, for getting things done, Tom Staley, for an excellent tip on the sequentiality of reading and writing, and to Don Davis, for books and culture and lunch.

I owe an abiding debt to John Easterly of LSU Press for reaching out to me and for guiding the manuscript through the initial phases and to Margaret Lovecraft for graciously continuing the good work with a deep understanding of the project. I am grateful to Lee Sioles for further editorial care and for shepherding the final manuscript into the capable hands of Jo Ann Kiser, whose scrupulous and sympathetic attention is a wonder, and Linda Webster, superb indexer. This book has also benefited immeasurably from the wisdom of the anonymous readings it received.

Meditation by the Sea, the anonymous painting from the 1860s that graces the cover, owes its presence here to the patient assistance of Katie Kerr at the Museum of Fine Arts, Boston. This oil on canvas, adapted from an illustration in *Harper's*, measures 34.61 x 49.85 cm (13 5/8 x 19 5/8 in.) and is a gift of Maxim Karolik for the M. and M. Karolik Collection of American Paintings, 1815–65.

I am grateful to Ed Block for permission to adapt portions of "A Pulpit of Envy" (*Renascence* 52.1: 89–104) for the subsection "Emerson, Sermons and Persons," and for his astute editorial observations about audience. I likewise thank the patient and genial Monika Elbert for permitting me to distribute significant portions of "*Septimius* and the Fate of the American Scholar" (*Nathaniel Hawthorne Review* 35.2: 84–107) to several subsections at the end of chapter 3, and I extend my gratitude to special issue editors Magnus Ullén and David Greven for their generous collaboration in the development of that piece.

I thank Leslie A. Morris, curator of modern Books and Manuscripts at the Houghton Library, for assistance with Melville's copy of Emerson's *The Conduct of Life,* and I thank Susan Halpert, reference librarian, and Dennis C. Marnon, administrative officer, for their tremendous help with the *Billy Budd* manuscript. Special thanks go out to Steven Olsen-Smith and Peter Norberg for their generosity and guidance regarding Melville's copy of Dante.

Finally, for their sustaining love and patience, I acknowledge Tanya Paull and Milo Makoto Paull Kevorkian, Tanya's extended family, Mary Kevorkian, Warren Kevorkian, and the eagle-eyed Aunt Rose Kevorkian. And all the kind and unwary souls who, in a variety of social settings, asked me how it was going.

Abbreviations

Emerson

CS *The Complete Sermons of Ralph Waldo Emerson.* 4 vols. Chief ed. Albert J. von Frank. Columbia: U of Missouri P, 1989–92.

CW *The Collected Works of Ralph Waldo Emerson.* 9 vols. Ed. Robert E. Spiller, Alfred Ferguson, et al. Cambridge, MA: Harvard UP, 1971–.

EJ *Emerson in His Journals.* Ed. Joel Porte. Cambridge, MA: Harvard UP, 1982.

EL *The Early Lectures of Ralph Waldo Emerson.* 3 vols. Ed. Stephen Whicher, Robert Spiller, et al. Cambridge, MA: Harvard UP, 1960–72.

JMN *The Journals and Miscellaneous Notebooks of Ralph Waldo Emerson.* Ed. William Gilman et al. Cambridge, MA: Harvard UP, 1960–82.

L *The Letters of Ralph Waldo Emerson.* 10 vols. Ed. Ralph L. Rusk and Eleanor M. Tilton. New York: Columbia UP, 1939–95.

LL *The Later Lectures of Ralph Waldo Emerson.* 2 vols. Ed. Ronald A. Bosco and Joel Myerson. Athens: U of Georgia P, 2001.

PN *The Poetry Notebooks of Ralph Waldo Emerson.* Ed. Ralph H. Orth et al. Columbia: U of Missouri P, 1986.

TN *The Topical Notebooks of Ralph Waldo Emerson.* Ed. Ralph H. Orth et al. Columbia: U of Missouri P, 1990–94.

W *The Complete Works of Ralph Waldo Emerson.* 12 vols. Centenary Edition. Ed. Edward Waldo Emerson. Boston: Houghton Mifflin, 1903–4.

Hawthorne

CE *The Centenary Edition of the Works of Nathaniel Hawthorne.* 23 vols. Ed. William Charvat, Roy Harvey Pearce, and Claude Simpson. Columbus: Ohio State UP, 1962–97.

Melville

NN "Northwestern-Newberry" edition of *The Writings of Herman Melville.* 14 vols. Ed. Harrison Hayford, Hershel Parker, and G. Thomas Tanselle. Evanston and Chicago: Northwestern UP and the Newberry Library, 1968–.

LCRE *Moby-Dick: A Longman Critical Edition.* Ed. John Bryant and Haskell Springer. New York: Pearson, 2007.

Writing beyond Prophecy

CHAPTER 1

Writing after the Minister

Commenting on Emerson's early nineteenth-century America, Quentin Anderson remarks, "It was as if the primal inquiry on the part of each developing consciousness was shifting from some such question as 'What role shall I be given?' to another, 'What world am I to possess?'" (4). Anderson, employing a memorable label that serves as the title for his book, calls this new Emersonian incarnation "the Imperial Self," one that has moved "beyond community" to a "post-social" sufficiency. The present project argues that later Emerson, Hawthorne, and Melville return to an inquiry more closely resembling the first question Anderson posits, as a return to the question of life's calling. This return becomes an occasion for the pursuit of religious significance in a context that questions the ideal of post-social sufficiency. The earlier Emersonian formula, "Do not seek yourself outside yourself," for all its tautological validity, ceases to supply the exclusive directive for the well-employed self. An acknowledged need for spiritual companionship troubles this ideal. One's self ceases to be the inevitable goal of the search.

The Imperial Self that Anderson describes moves away from a world of given roles. *Writing beyond Prophecy* suggests that the relation to a particular role, a particular calling, diagnoses the Emersonian trajectory most precisely: the role of the minister. In seeking not only to possess the world but to build a new one through literature (a term itself shifting from its initial usage of something read to something assertively written),[1] Emerson departs not only from the ministry but also from the framework in which the minister acted as the primary interpreter of the given world.

The minister received the word, and further words derived in community and with reference to that authority. The leader John Winthrop, for example—though surely an imperial self in his own way—models a decidedly pre-Emersonian relation to the word and the world of the minister:

> Were he now to be considered only as a Christian, we might therein propose him as greatly imitable. He was a very religious man; and as he strictly kept his heart, so he kept his house, under the laws of piety; there he was every day constant in holy duties, both morning and evening, and on the Lord's days, and lectures, though he wrote not after the preacher, yet such was his attention, and such his retention in hearing, that he repeated unto his family the sermons he had heard in the congregation.[2]

Cotton Mather reports that Winthrop does not write after the preacher: that is, he does not take notes; he does not need to. No meaning need be deferred by an act of writing; he receives the word and bears its living presence whole and unaltered into his home. To extend Mather's text, we may reach for another, more common sense of the word "after." Whatever Winthrop does write, whenever he writes it, can never be written after the minister, for by simple virtue of his historical moment, he writes during a time that belongs to the minister. In Emory Elliott's narrative of *Power in the Pulpit in Puritan New England,* Winthrop inhabits the age of the preacher patriarchs. As Elliott and others will remind us, the nature of ministerial authority and the metaphors appropriate to describe it begin to change almost immediately.[3] Without attempting to outline the many slips between the 1630s and the 1830s, one might venture to identify a single bright line distinction: prior to Emerson, one could not write after the minister. Always somewhere present at the time was a minister after whose hour one could not be said to be writing. Not that all writing had been by any means authorized by clerical dictation; simply that history had not found a way to seize those clerical figures from the relevant landscape of the present. Franklin might turn the dinner table on Whitefield as cleverly as the Enlightenment could please, but subtle guest/host reversals could not efface the cultural currency of the ministerial category.[4] After Emerson, and his somewhat lingering 1832–39 farewell to the ministry, other options emerge.

To place such initiatory emphasis upon Emerson is to borrow from a narrative most famously authorized by F. O. Matthiessen as the *American Renaissance: Art and Expression in the Age of Emerson and Whitman,* in which Emerson's "Optative Mood" strikes the opening, prophetic chord. Jonathan Arac has noted that Matthiessen's "major book, *American Renaissance* (1941), has given its name to courses taught at hundreds of institutions. More than any other single factor it enabled hundreds of Ph.D.s in English to specialize in the American literature of the nineteenth century."[5] Matthiessen's scholarly construct highlights the literary achievements of 1850–55 in terms of his authors' commitments to both symbolism and democracy. The present project draws upon this example but translates the features of Matthiessen's "Renaissance" into a religious idiom to examine these authors' relation to the practice of worship. Using a heuristic I call "Writing after the Minister," this study traces the development of the lives of the New England prophets over the long arcs of their literary careers. My initial curiosity was to wonder what happens after the period of confident symbolism Matthiessen frames. In the process of studying a cluster of later, retrospective works by Emerson, Hawthorne, and Melville, I found the content consistently drawing my attention to the troubled figure of the minister, as these works—*The Conduct of Life* (published 1860), *The Elixir of Life* mss.(begun the subsequent year, 1861, and left incomplete at Hawthorne's death in 1864), and *Clarel: A Poem and Pilgrimage in the Holy Land* (begun 1870, responding to both late Emerson and Hawthorne, and published in 1876)—enact and represent a set of shared concerns about ministry and vocation. Insofar as the three works reflect upon earlier moments in these authors' careers, they prompt the idea that the writings produced both during and after the "Renaissance" might profitably be examined as various ways of "Writing after the Minister." I employ different senses of this heuristic phrase both to describe an overarching idea of midcentury New England literary culture and to distinguish between moments of this period: first the hypercanonized period of literary production traditionally reified as the Renaissance, and then the less-studied retrospective phase. While I will discuss texts and contexts going back to the inceptions of their careers, the primary materials from their later, retrospective phases motivate the shape of the argument.[6] *Writing beyond Prophecy* traces a relay from Emerson's career up to 1860 and *The Conduct of Life,* to Hawthorne's late grappling in the *Elixir of Life* with what, for him, was this final Emersonian statement on vocation, to Melville's looking back at both in *Clarel.* Melville occupies the implicit position of a privileged reader throughout, as he acquires and comments upon Emerson's *Conduct of Life* as well as Hawthorne's *Elixir of Life* while composing *Clarel,* a work that highlights what these late texts hold in common about a need for worship and a desire for spiritual communion; thus Melville's attention makes visible, as an unfolding literary conversation, the retrospective pattern that I trace. This book examines what literature emerges when Writing after the Minister shifts from what Emerson terms a "Saturnalia" of aggressive literary prophecy to an Aftermath that reconsiders the question of calling.

First, a few words about some of the different ways of being "after": most encompassingly, Writing after the Minister uses "after" chronologically, as in After the Age of Dinosaurs, when giants ruled the earth. In *The Minister's Wooing,* Stowe frames a paradoxical scene that heralds just such a passing, in an imagined conversation between Aaron Burr, Jr., and a "Dr. H." Stowe's Dr. H. is clearly modeled on Samuel Hopkins, the spiritual heir of Jonathan Edwards, while Burr is Edwards's literal descendant: "The Doctor was soon wide awake, talking with fervent animation on the topic of disinterested benevolence,—Burr the meanwhile studying him with the quiet interest of an observer of natural history, who sees a new species developing before him."[7] The irony is that Burr witnesses not an emerging species, but (in the High Calvinist theological context invoked) the last gasp of a dying breed. Burr, the profligate grandson of Jonathan Edwards, is himself the ascendant emblem of what the Puritans would have lamented as spiritual "declension." Stowe makes clear that Burr inhabits a world quite apart from Hopkins. Stirred momentarily by "a shadowy recollection" of his grandfather's pious and celebrated encomium of Sarah Pierrepont (Burr's grandmother), Burr can sense only the faintest inklings of spiritual lack, inklings quickly dismissed by recourse to rationalism. Hopkins's Edwardsian "disinterested benevolence" gives way to Burr's worldly interests.

The story of "Writing after the Minister" does not concern primarily such bemused onlookers of the antiquation of piety, but a newer species rising to replace the fallen heroes of faith.[8] Beyond any general narrative of declension, the initiatory literary moment might be taken as Emerson's decision to break with the ministry and seek a new calling. In the first movement of this new period, the Saturnalia, "after" refers to manner of writing: in the mode of the minister; replacing, substituting for, even, at the same time, expelling the minister. Saturnalian Writing after the Minister occurs not in the weak sense of "after" connoted by the contemporary usage of "a copy after Titian" (1850) but rather as the strong response of poets usurping for themselves a privileged discourse.[9] With Emerson at its head, such writing marks the beginning of what Harold Bloom has called *The American Religion: The Emergence of the Post-Christian Nation.*[10] An incidental feature of this appropriative writing is the occasional directness with which it expresses its displacement of authority: it tends to really get after those ministers. As a material accident, some of the most important instances of this writing occurred in the place of the minister, after the minister had departed: Emerson's *Nature* and Hawthorne's *Mosses* both grew within an "Old Manse," the parsonage wherein Ezra Ripley before them had penned some three thousand sermons.[11] As the author of *Mosses* there confronts the stern visage of a pastor whose fervid eloquence had made him the friend and near equal of Whitefield, he remarks that the portrait "eyed me with an air of authority such as men of his profession seldom assume in our days." Turning to the amassed clerical library, the author finds "no living thought" in any of the venerable tomes of the mighty Puritan divines and even less of interest in the later frigid discussions on the pages of the "Liberal Preacher," which he tosses aside and feels himself "none the less a Christian for eschewing it." He finds instead a kind of "superstitious reverence for literature of all kinds" and turns, self-consciously as a "layman" in the Manse, to the task of producing an intellectual treasure of his own. This writing after the minister authorized a new mode of literary vocation, under the aspect of a democratization of spiritual language: "Let us demand our own works and laws and worship."[12]

I suggest that this outbreak of confidence entails for some an Aftermath, during which After indicates the pursuit of a lost object, a sense of felt absence. One might think of the mixed sensation of Robert Frost's "After Apple-Picking": "My instep arch not only keeps the ache, / It keeps the pressure of a ladder-round."[13] In more astringent tones than those I would apply to the inhabitants of the Aftermath, Susan Sontag has noted in her "own generation" the contradictory response of what she calls "piety without content": "It includes in differing measures both nostalgia and relief: nostalgia over the loss of the sense of sacredness and relief that an intolerable burden has been lifted."[14] Unlike the slumberers Sontag perceives, the writers who are the subject of the present study were quite well aware of the problematic nature of this nostalgia and relief. *The Conduct of Life* (1860) brings to the fore Emerson's renewed interest in the question of "Worship," a formal practice he had set aside while pursuing a course of literary and spiritual independence. Emerson's retrospective consideration sets an agenda to which both Hawthorne and Melville respond. Melville's *Clarel: A Poem and Pilgrimage in the Holy Land* (1876) dramatizes the vocational crisis of a young would-be minister desperately in need of spiritual guidance. *Clarel* also resonates with Hawthorne's two "Septimius" versions of the unfinished *Elixir of Life* manuscripts (1861–64; two early serial installments were published posthumously in the *Atlantic* 1864–65; *Septimius* appeared as a full-length serial and as a book in 1872); Hawthorne tells of a young man who abandons his preparation for the ministry under a kindly mentor to pursue a disastrous career as a mad scientist, armed only with an indecipherable recipe for eternal life and a self-reliant hermeneutics.

The present chapter serves as an introduction for the three cumulatively linked segments of this project (not to be confused with the subsections of this introductory chapter): Emerson; Hawthorne (and Emerson); and Melville (and Hawthorne and Emerson). The table of contents follows an imagined order of service for Sunday after Emerson: Emerson issues a call to worship, Hawthorne delivers a sermon, and Melville performs the benediction. In the remainder of this chapter, a discussion of some textual examples should serve to better characterize the modes of writing after the minister outlined thus far.

Writing after the Minister: Nineteenth-Century New England

> Our horizon is not very far—say, one generation, or 30 years—we all see so much. The older see two generations, or 60 years; but what has been running on through three horizons, or 90 years, looks to all the world like a law of nature, & 'tis an impiety to doubt. Thus, 'tis incredible to us if we look into the sermons &

> religious books of our grand-fathers, how they held themselves in such a pinfold. But why not? as far as they could see, through two or three horizons, nothing but ministers, ministers, ministers. (Emerson, 1861 journal entry)[15]

Within the same journal entry, Emerson goes on to call attention to the provincial limitations of his version of ministerial history, to distinguish this specific observation from the sweeping proclamations upon universal history of which he is also capable: "In other countries or districts, 'tis all soldiering, or sheep farms, or shoe-making, or Vermont cattle-driving." He speaks here of something particular. Thirty, sixty, ninety—Emerson takes the trouble to think mathematically, in precise, consistent multiplications—suppose we take his numbers literally? Such a leap might run counter to the general tendency of Emerson's habits of thought, but he does know how to draw history from key dates as well as from broad trends, as in his 1852 entry stating that "from 1790 to 1820, there was not a book, a speech, a conversation, or a thought, in the State. . . . Edwards on the Will was printed in 1754."[16] In the passage above on ministers, he speaks of grandfathers, that is, those from two generations ago. As Emerson looks back from the vantage point of 1861, the grandfathers stand at the edge of 1801. The older of these see to an additional distance of sixty years, may focus their gaze across a lifetime of consciousness upon the horizon of 1741. These grandfathers, with their incredible sermons and religious books full of ministers, ministers, ministers, write from the limit of living memory of the Great Awakening. Emerson, in the retrospective moment of 1861, writes in the knowledge of an awakening these grandfathers did not live to see, an awakening that makes their account of experience "incredible" to Emerson's generation.

Though he may have achieved incredulity at how the grandfathers had held themselves in such a "pinfold," Emerson nevertheless maintained a great reverence for the great- and great-great-grandfathers who had so convincingly put them in it. In part out of the very lack of experience of the Great Awakening was born a desire for an awakening of one's own. Born in 1803, one century after the birth of Jonathan Edwards, and in the year of Samuel Hopkins's death, Emerson wrote, from the beginning, in awareness of lapsed standards of ministerial holiness. He was deeply impressed by the liberal Christianity of William Ellery Channing, Sr. (b. 1780), and Edward Everett (b. 1794); he did choose Harvard over Andover, "the new bastion of orthodox Calvinism"—but not without thought.[17] In 1823 he recorded his sense of the "danger of a *poetical* religion from the tendencies of the age," one that could lead to resolutions not nourished by "prayer," unaccompanied by "action," and leading to "complacency"; the tendencies of the age appeared to be toward spiritual slumber.[18] Emerson's ties to the Great Awakening become clearer in Phyllis Cole's study "From the Edwardses to the Emersons," which draws upon genealogy to pluralize the names in the famous intellectual trajectory identified by Perry Miller: "An identifiable—not mystical—social entity called the Emerson family, an Eastern-Massachusetts, Harvard-educated clerical dynasty from the seventeenth century, was uniformly pro-Awakening in the era of Edwards and Whitefield."[19] And although "Harvard early declared itself against Awakening religion," Aunt Mary Moody Emerson did not. In his own early plotting to kindle a new spiritual flame, Emerson looked to George Whitefield as one model of eloquence after which to strive. Emerson's familiar 1824 journal passage on his "passionate love for the strains of eloquence" expresses both an ancient Ciceronian ideal and a sense of that passion's derivation from a grandfatherly lineage.[20] Behind the shift from father, from whom he inherited "formality," to father *or* grandfather, from whom he derived the love of eloquence, is a vote for Whitefield and against Charles Chauncy, that most notable critic of awakening; the preference appears, for example, in Emerson's evident relish in a 1823 retelling of how "the eloquent preacher" bested Dr. Chauncy in an exchange of wit.[21] Consistently, Emerson prefers Whitefield to Chauncy on the score of eloquence. Recounting Chauncy's halting and awkward eulogy for a boy drowned in Frog Pond, Emerson remarks that Chauncy "so disliked the 'sensation' preaching of his time that he had once prayed that 'he might never be eloquent;' and, it appears, his prayer was granted."[22] The very "strains of eloquence" Emerson desired were the precise laurels bestowed upon Whitefield in Phyllis Wheatley's celebrated and widely reprinted elegy:

> Thy sermons in unequall'd accents flow'd
> And ev'ry bosom with devotion glow'd;

Thou didst in strains of eloquence refin'd
Inflame the heart, and captivate the mind.[23]

Whether or not Emerson had Wheatley's poem in mind in 1824, Whitefield was an obvious eighteenth-century master of eloquence. But so, notably, was Hume, who himself had paused to consider how "the Strains of ancient Eloquence" might be made suitable "to our Age."[24] Emerson, since at least 1818, had held Hume's accomplishments as a writer in high regard, albeit a regard tempered with a skepticism of skepticism.[25] What comes of this Emersonian eloquence, potentially in the service of both piety and criticism?

Writing after the Minister: The Saturnalia

All writing comes by the grace of God. (Emerson, 1841 Journal entry)[26]

A happy thought, the fuller import of which comes from recognizing it as Emerson's not-so-innocent innocent translation of 2 Timothy 3:16. Emerson here intervenes upon a debate that had recently been summarized in Coleridge's posthumous 1840 *Confessions of an Inquiring Spirit,* in the sixth of his "Letters on the Inspiration of the Scriptures."[27] Coleridge supplies the Greek original, transliterated as "pasa graphe theopneustos kai ophelimos." Coleridge notes that the verse has attracted two distinct approaches. By supplying a hidden copula near the beginning of the sentence, one might read the verse to claim that "all Scripture *is* inspired by God and profitable [for instruction, etc.]." A translation permitting a more liberal construction would elide the "and" and defer the "is": "All Scripture inspired by God is profitable for instruction." This second reading allows for the inversion of the value criterion implicit in the first. Whereas the first posits the fact of God's inspiration as the reason for scripture's usefulness, the second proposes to measure the usefulness of a given text as a test for whether or not it comes from God.[28] Emerson makes the most radical interpretation by relying upon the most literal translation of "graphe": not merely "Scripture" but "writing" is God-breathed.

The further unspoken contrast in Emerson's decisive stroke lies in the fact that Coleridge's exegetical problematic presupposes the presence of the preacher, a key figure in his "Pentad of Operative Christianity" (fig. 1). In this diagram, Coleridge explains, "the Preacher in direct line under the Spirit but likewise the point of junction of the Written Word and the Church, is the *Synthesis.* This is God's Hand in the World."[29]

Emerson's 1838 address to the graduating Harvard divinity students had emphasized the Preacher's station "in direct line under the Spirit," as Coleridge puts it, at the distinct expense of Christ, the Scriptures, and the Church. Emerson lamented that "men have come to speak of the revelation as somewhat long ago given and done, as if God were dead. The injury to faith throttles the preacher"; the challenge at hand would be to declare "yourself a newborn bard of the Holy Ghost."[30] Such a request leaves the preacher's role itself more than a little destabilized: Emerson himself apparently felt no need (for the time being) to perform that calling of the spirit within the institution of the ministry; having left Second Church in Boston in 1832, he stopped serving even as a preacher of supply in early 1839. Not ministers narrowly defined, but "scholars are the priests of that thought which establishes the foundations of the earth."[31] And the authors of the writing that expresses that thought for the present age. Robert D. Richardson measures the height of Emerson's ambition with reference to

FIGURE 1: Coleridge's Pentad of Operative Christianity. (From *Confessions of an Inquiring Spirit. 3rd ed.* London: Edward Moxon, 1853)

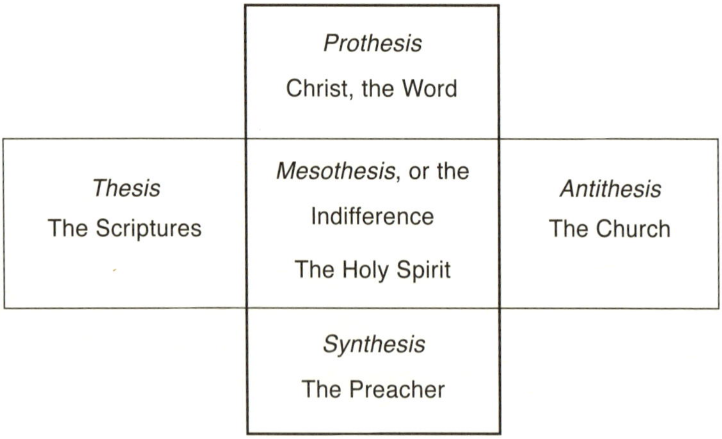

the final paragraph of *Representative Men* (1850, the Emerson book that appears within the Matthiessen "Renaissance"): "We too must write Bibles."[32]

Emerson might just be the key figure to make the substitution of public intellectual for minister, a substitution Ross Posnock finds perfectly complete in William James, who "from his pulpit at Harvard" provides for a public need formerly filled by the preacher.[33] But Emerson was not alone among his contemporaries in voicing high hopes for divine writing: Jonathan Ashley Saxton, in his July 1841 *Dial* essay, "Prophecy-Transcendentalism-Progress," applies Numbers 11:29, "Would God, that all the Lord's children were prophets," with an eye toward its broadest possible application to intuitive writing.[34] The mobilization of a new vision of the grace in all writing would require more than one hand producing gracious texts. The Emersonian project called for what Lawrence Buell has termed "literary scripturism."[35] It called for an age without belatedness, an "after" that would not be after anyone else, akin to the festive attempt imagined by Burton: "to make good musick of their own voices, and dance after it."[36]

By 1833, even rather apart from such scriptural pretense, Hawthorne was evincing his own signs of a cultural substitution already underway. Ready examples appear in the framing for Hawthorne's relinquished early experiments in short-story collection: one opposing an "itinerant novelist" to a Methodist revivalist, another setting free an aspiring "Story-Teller" from a ministerial guardian only to place him in satiric contrast to a traveling preacher. Michael Colacurcio finds that "the thematic implication is perfectly clear: according to somebody's dichotomy of spiritual culture, the literary career is being set over against the evangelical calling."[37] Somebody's: the reminder that Hawthorne works with the culturally given, as opposed to serving up autobiography, is well taken but does not diffuse the pointedness with which not only Hawthorne's panoptic narrator but also largely Hawthorne himself spends "Sunday at Home" (1837). (From one more disposed to assert the "I," we find Thoreau stridently not counting himself among the churchgoers on "Sunday" of his *Week*.) The issue is not one of simple apostasy: in "The Custom-House," after his famous moment of bearing the imagined ancestral rebuke against his writing of "story-books!" Hawthorne permits himself a compensatory thought: "And yet, let them scorn me as they will, strong traits of their nature have intertwined themselves with mine."[38] He finds himself in possession of what he calls the "moral quality" of his Puritan ancestors, but perhaps has found a way of expressing it that they would not recognize.

Thoreau in 1849 petitioned Jared Sparks for borrowing privileges from Harvard Library and justified his eligibility for this privilege above all "*because I have chosen letters for my profession,* and so am one of the clergy" (emphasis his).[39] Others, though equally attuned to what they might be up to, were less sanguine about what entitlements such a calling might bring: in an 1851 letter to Hawthorne, Melville groused, "Though I wrote the Gospels in this century, I should die in the gutter." In an earlier letter of the same year, Melville apologized for "falling into my old foible,—preaching."

Also under the Saturnalia heading, we may locate examples of an aggressive writing after the minister that "gets after" the minister: "after" syntactically precedes and designates a target of criticism, a target perhaps receding or in flight. Frederick Law Olmsted, architect of Central Park, writes in an 1846 letter, "I am beginning to have a horror of ministers. They are such a set of conceited, dogmatical, narrow minded, misanthropic, petty mind [*sic*] tyrants."[40] By 1870, Olmsted could proudly describe his parks as "the only places in those . . . cities . . . where . . . you will find a body of Christians coming together . . . all classes largely represented, with a common purpose."[41] His writing after the minister had been written large in the heart of New York, with Olmsted assuming the role of architect as invisible high priest. His achievement, as he saw it, was spatially to constitute a body of believers without making recourse to a central human figure. Yet others would note replacement modes of public expression, no less humanly centralized, which acted to move those park-going crowds. James Russell Lowell, the son of a preacher, imagines one Parson Wilbur voicing his unhappiness at cultural encroachments on the power of the pulpit: "Indeed, the position which [the editor] now holds is that which the clergyman should hold even now. . . . So it has come to pass that the preacher, instead of being a living force, has faded into an emblematic figure at christenings, weddings, and funerals. . . . Meanwhile, see what a pulpit the editor mounts daily."[42] Thoreau senses the tension involved in both shunning tyrannical influence and seeking access to the press, but he rationalizes his vocation with the thought that though the essayist could possibly sway a larger audience, the potential for harm would be much less than in the case of the minister, whose power is "almost despotic."[43] If preachers were becoming emblematic, it was none too soon for him.

For a clear contrast we might recall the Mather text with which the present chapter opens: Mather proposes Winthrop as "greatly imitable." Winthrop himself perfectly parrots the preacher for his family's edification: he is imitable because he faithfully imitates. To state the obvious, the distance between Mather's model of Christian Winthrop and the Divinity School Address approaches something like a theoretical limit on the issue of emulation. Emerson's doctrine—"to refuse the good models"—though most ambitiously directed against the practice of *imitatio Christi,* could readily be applied to remove the need for exemplary ministers. And if Emerson admonishes refusal of the good models, Hawthorne and Melville suggest we refuse the bad ones too, and while we're at it, not to be too sure we can tell the difference. Their most well-known novels dramatize the dangers posed both by and to an influential ministerial center. *The Scarlet Letter* finds a troubled and troubling Reverend Dimmesdale as the central figure of community desire and expectations. Of *Moby-Dick,* Ann Douglas points out that "Ahab, damned as he is, will convert the entire crew, with the exception of Starbuck. . . . Ahab is probably the greatest orator, the finest preacher in American literature."[44] This achievement would not seem to argue for more and better preachers in American life; rather only for something like great art. To anticipate an issue that recurs in each chapter of this project, I hypothesize that *The Conduct of Life, The Elixir of Life,* and *Clarel* collectively register a shift from the *problem* of a ministerial center to a retrospection on the *need* for such a role model: unecstatic Emerson's reaching out in "Worship" for a divinized other with a moral sentiment in working order, for "those who can help in counsel or conduct . . . who were appointed by God Almighty";[45] Septimius Felton's disregard of his clerical mentor and his fatal creative misprision of a text offering eternal life; Clarel, adrift, unable to lead, unable to find a guide, desiring counsel from fellow pilgrims. For these authors, the question of conduct remained significantly religious, and tutelary models were again acknowledged as desired.

In the 1842 address "The Transcendentalist," Emerson offers a rich definition of the so-called "*new views* here in New England": "Shall we say, then, that Transcendentalism is the Saturnalia or excess of Faith."[46] This January lecture alludes to the Roman festival of December 17: a day of reversed hierarchy; traditionally, of master and servant. Emerson speaks of a Saturnalia of Faith; one analogous reversal to be imagined would be that of pastor and flock. In reminding his audience at the Masonic Temple that the views attending such reversals are "the very oldest of thoughts" he outlines a history: "This way of thinking, falling on Roman times, made Stoic philosophers; falling on despotic times, made patriot Catos and Brutuses; falling on superstitious times, made prophets and apostles; on popish times, made protestants and ascetic monks, preachers of Faith against the preachers of Works; on prelatical times, made Puritans and Quakers; and falling on Unitarian and commercial times, makes the peculiar shades of Idealism which we know." Again, we by now need hardly remark that the last high water mark on the list before his own belongs to the Puritans and Quakers. The Saturnalias Emerson mentions had sufficient impact and tenure to problematize their association with a mere day's game instituted by the powers-that-be precisely not to challenge the status quo. Yet the idea of Saturnalia as a temporary reversal remains in the progressive concatenation of the revolts, lapses into formalism, new revolts (a common Emersonian series). Similarly, an "excess of Faith" suggests the possibility of hangover and corrective motion to follow.

Writing after the Minister: The Aftermath

My pride is superior to any feelings I have yet experienced: my affection is strong admiration, not the necessity of giving or receiving assistance or sympathy. When disappointed, I do not ask or wish consolation,—I wish to know and feel my pain, to investigate its nature and its source; I will not have my thoughts diverted, or my feelings soothed; 'tis therefore that my young life is so singularly barren of illusions. I know, I feel the time must come when this proud and impatient heart shall be stilled, and turn from the ardors of Search and Action, to lean on something above. But—shall I say it?—the thought of that calmer era is to me a thought of deepest sadness; so remote from my present being is that future existence, which still the mind can conceive. I believe in Eternal Progression. I believe in a God, a Beauty and Perfection to which I am to strive all my life for assimilation. From these two articles of belief, I draw the rules by which I strive to regulate my life. But, though I reverence all religions as necessary to the happiness of man, I am yet ignorant of the religion of Revelation. Tangible promises! well defined hopes! are the things of which I do not *now* feel the need. At present, my soul is intent on life, and I think of religion as its rule; and, in my opinion, this is the natural and proper course from youth to age. What I have written is not hastily concocted, it has a meaning. . . . I have here given you all I know, or think, on the most important of subjects—could you but read understandingly![47]

Margaret Fuller writes with a tone that promises rare insight: "I have given to you, in this little space, the substance of many thoughts, the clues to many cherished opinions. 'T is a subject on which I rarely speak." The space, by quotational standards, is not so very little, but I find her words sufficiently prophetic to warrant full inclusion. From the perspective of the early 1840s, she gives a forthright description of the "Saturnalia of Faith" and intimations of what might follow. Her text exhibits, in a word, self-reliance; a self-reliance that moves along a continuum from limiting the nature of interpersonal relations to limiting the use of religion—she allows for no dependence upon authority in either persons or revelation. Yet she senses that age might change that; her view of the subject might be called psychological.

She did not live to see what truth these intimations might hold for her personally; the conclusive accuracy of other intimations intervened. In her famous journal entries just before the voyage on which she drowned, she expresses her "fear of the voyage" and her sense that her "future upon earth will soon close" (338). At forty, old age has no part in this fear, and her self-reliant saturnalia has not faded, but rather waxes toward a climax to arrive in the near future: "But it has long seemed, that, in the year 1850, I should stand on a plateau in the ascent of life, where I should be allowed to pause for a while, and take more clear and commanding views than ever before" (338–39). According to the Matthiessen tradition, her survivors did indeed effectively express such "clear and commanding views" over the next few years, with Whitman's 1855 *Leaves of Grass* often cited as the ripe culmination. In subsequent years, a changed mood sets in with the New England generation born 1800–1820 (to borrow Lewis Mumford's convenient *Golden Day* criterion for membership in what he calls the "New World Renaissance"). It is a mood well evoked by Longfellow (b. 1807) in "Aftermath" (1873), which picks up on the agronomic etymology of that word:

When the summer fields are mown,
When the birds are fledged and flown,
  And the dry leaves strew the path;
With the falling of the snow,
With the cawing of the crow
Once again the fields we mow
  And gather in the aftermath.

Not the sweet, new grass with flowers
Is this harvesting of ours . . .[48]

Mortality becomes a big issue, not just in the massive numbers of casualties of war but also in the inevitable mortality of a generation. That is, it was a time in which Whitman might hear not only "Drum Taps" but also "Whispers of Heavenly Death."

In an 1860 letter, a fifty-six-year-old Hawthorne noted of his fifty-seven-year-old neighbor that "Emerson is unchanged in aspect—at least, he looks so, at a distance, but, on close inspection, you perceive that a little hoar-frost has gathered on him. He has become earthlier during these past seven years."[49] Hawthorne would shortly take up his *Elixir of Life* project, in which a quasi-Emersonian One Man seeks to reverse the "curse" of human mortality. Of Thoreau's late natural history projects, ambitiously under way in 1860, Emerson observed that "the scale on which his studies proceeded was so large as to require longevity."[50] Despite his stated aversion to the church, Emerson would renew his interest in the pulpit around 1847, giving a discourse called "Worship" (considered by some observers and critics to be a sermon) periodically on Sundays until its appearance as a key chapter in *The Conduct of Life;* beginning 1861, the topic of worship shifts focus slightly as his favorite Sunday lecture becomes "Immortality."

Of the primary figures I examine, Melville seems to raise the question of the extent to which my project is properly a pursuit of individual biographies rather than an experiment in literary historical simultaneity. Notably the youngest of the three, not until 1876 does Melville offer his version of a young minister obsessed with death. An appeal to biological clockwork is tempting, if we accept before proof the hypothesis that *The Conduct of Life, The Elixir of Life,* and *Clarel* belong together: Melville is sixteen years Emerson's junior, and his inventory of discourse—with a questing, questioning divinity student in the midst—appears sixteen years after the Concord sage publishes the results of his endeavor to find a "private solution" to "the riddle of the age" by the "method of taking up in turn each of the leading topics which belong to our scheme of human life";[51] Melville is fifteen years younger than Hawthorne, and he puts the finishing touches on Clarel's pilgrimage more than twelve years after Hawthorne abandons Septimius. But in fact, Melville's presence in the grouping is still attributable to a logic of literary order. Hawthorne may take as his text Emerson's 1860 body. Melville takes up Emerson's 1860 text and leaves notes in the margins, with a keen eye for Emerson's returning tendency to "leap into the pulpit." Melville's poem "Monody" may or may not point to Hawthorne as the "cloistral vine" often identified as Vine in *Clarel,* but we do know that he owned Hawthorne's *Elixir* (as published in Boston in unfinished form as *Septimius Felton,* 1872).[52] Melville thus affords us a second-order observation, as he responds to Emerson's and Hawthorne's documents of the aftermath of renounced ministerial vocation. *Clarel* of course arises also out of Melville's own prewar travel experiences in the Holy Land (as recorded in the 1856–57 journals) and undergoes an extended composition process as he continues to educate himself in the recent history of religious debate; for these reasons as well *Clarel* bears upon the onset of a ministerial aftermath.[53]

Sometime in the late 1850s the age that Emerson had accused in 1836 of being "retrospective" became self-reflexively so. The shift of attention was not from "the sepulchres of the fathers" to "an original relation to the universe" but more nearly toward shaping the imminent epitaphs of the now-aged children. James Morris Whiton received a Ph.D. for the study of language and literature from Yale in 1861 for a dissertation entitled *Ars Longa, Brevis Vita.* The fact that this was the first year that an American institution granted a Ph.D. says something about available modes of discourse, of a receptivity to scholarly views of literature, a capacity for cultural retrospection.[54] In his exposition of the "Consciousness" of "Art and Expression in the Age of Emerson and Whitman," Matthiessen praises Emerson's "Historic Notes of Life and Letters in New England" as "probably the most illuminating account of the intellectual movements of our eighteen-thirties and -forties which has yet been written"; he goes on to note that "other comparable narratives which supplement Emerson's are

Theodore Parker's *Experiences as a Minister* (1859) and Orestes Brownson's *The Convert* (1857)."[55] These recollections represent the first books about the "American Renaissance": lives had been lived and something had happened.[56] It is no accident that neither of these latter two revelatory accounts are literary histories: the something that had happened had everything to do with the unsettling of the traditional role of the New England minister, and these spiritual autobiographies sharply reflect that: in Parker's reminiscences, occasionally uneasy ones, on the nature of a liberal ministry whose primary authority derived from the strength of its oratory; in Brownson's tempestuous Transcendentalism and final haven in the authority of the Catholic tradition.

An 1860 commemoration for James Freeman Clarke on his fiftieth birthday, given by his Church of the Disciples, makes explicit the potential congruence between retrospective biography and narrative history:

> I suppose that you will hardly realize that now twenty years have almost fled away, since our Pastor, then but three-fifths of his present age, began to preach to us. . . . I thought it was but yesterday we began to gather in this fold, until just now I was reminded that a young man before me, now in the opening bloom of his manly age, was born after this church was organized, and was the first infant who received baptism at its altar.
>
> Twenty years . . . have identified James Freeman Clarke not only with this single organization, but also with the Unitarian body itself; with the ideas, progress, history, and character of liberal Christianity.[57]

The act of memory turns upon the chance physical presence of the young man: his figure serves as a reminder that something once happened that now has a life of its own. Such a view of living history, of decisions that grow up, may provide some insight into why the older Hawthorne and Melville were writing about young protagonists: to measure the distance between then and now, to consider consequences.

Such speculation aside, I would argue for the retrospective quality of the three main texts to be studied. Perhaps this is not so bold a claim, as we already know Emerson, for instance, to be quite self-allusive throughout his career. My claim is for perhaps a greater intensity of self-allusion:

Emerson explicitly opens "Fate" (1860) with a reflection upon an 1841 lecture series (that he gave, as it happened, at the same time that others were also lecturing on "The Times"), so that the exercise the book promises to perform occurs under the sign of retrospection, as it were. In particular, I'm interested in the way these later texts appear to reflect on early decisions in these writers' careers, especially to underscore religious and vocational implications. *Writing beyond Prophecy* pauses to ask, What were the later careers of the prophets? Much scholarship seems to be written as if, once Emerson turned his back on the church, literary America breathed a sigh of relief and never looked back. *Writing beyond Prophecy,* attending to Emersonian inspiration *and* its aftermath, suggests otherwise.[58]

CHAPTER 2

Emerson's Call to Worship

THE YEAR AFTER resigning from his pastorship, Emerson records this solitary observation of the Sabbath: "I kept Sunday with Milton & a Presbyterian magazine. Milton says, 'if ever any was ravished with moral beauty, he [Milton] is the man.'" Reflecting upon Milton's pious boast, Emerson cannot refrain from adding, with grave, emphatic brevity: "He did not love it more than I" (1833). This love Emerson so insistently claims may well be a quality he seeks in and of itself, but in the later essay "Worship" (1860), Emerson declares that a heart filled with devotion serves as the source of much else besides, and beyond, armchair spirituality:[1]

> 'Tis certain that worship stands in some commanding relation to the health of man, and to his highest powers, so as to be, in some manner, the source of intellect. All the great ages have been ages of belief. I mean, when there was any extraordinary power of performance, when great national movements began, when arts appeared, when heroes existed, when poems were made, the human soul was in earnest, and had fixed its thoughts on spiritual verities, with as strict a grasp as that of the hands on the sword, or the pencil, or the trowel. It is true that genius takes its rise out of the mountains of rectitude; that all beauty and power which men covet, are somehow born out of that Alpine district; that any extraordinary degree of beauty in man or woman involves a moral charm. (*CW* 6:115)

Power and beauty hang in the balance—high stakes indeed, then, to lay claim to a superior love of spiritual verities; but in "Worship" (1860) Emerson temperately, almost self-mockingly, edits the resistant boast of his younger self: "Thus, I think, we very slowly admit in another man a higher degree of moral sentiment than our own,—a finer conscience, more impressionable, or, which marks minuter degrees; an ear to hear acuter notes of right and wrong, than we can. I think we listen suspiciously and very slowly to any evidence to that point" (*CW* 6:115). The suspicions here entertained no longer lead ineluctably to outright dismissal—to an invidious rebuttal that "he [does] not love it more than I." Moreover, after allowing that such suspicions might be overcome, however slowly, by the worshipful skeptic, Emerson evinces a willingness to reconsider worship as a more than private matter:[2] "But, once satisfied of such superiority, we set no limit to our expectation of [another person's] genius. For such persons are nearer to the secret of God than others; are bathed by sweeter waters; they hear notices, they see visions, where others are vacant. We believe that holiness confers a certain insight, because not by our private, but by our public force, can we share and know the nature of things" (*CW* 6:115).

One overall goal of the present chapter will be to trace the shift from Emerson's imperious 1833 journal rivalry with Milton to the modulated admissions of "Worship"—in particular as this shift touches upon the questions of religion and vocation. The chapter opens here with a brief glimpse at the genesis of "Worship" at a moment of return to ministerial concerns; the intermediate sections retrace the development of Emerson's treatment of the topic of worship leading from his 1832 departure from the pastorship to the later public "return"; the concluding sections examine the essay "Worship" in its final published setting. "Worship" will be treated within the context of its rhetorical occasion as a lecture/sermon, within the context of a career logic, and within its compositional context in the completed book of *The Conduct of Life.*

Here Emerson "jumps into the pulpit"

In Emerson's career as a lecturer, the transition from *Representative Men* to *The Conduct of Life* presents one occasion for reading the aftermath of the American Renaissance. Though a decade separates the print publications of these series, a single moment in 1847 may be taken to stand for a shift to a new, renewed mode of writing after the minister. On Sunday, May 9, 1847, Emerson delivers a lecture—or is it a sermon?—entitled "Worship." For the preceding week (according to William Charvat), he has been lecturing from the *Representative Men* series: Plato, Swedenborg, Shakespeare, Napoleon, Goethe, Montaigne. (As it happens, *Representative Men* is the only volume Emerson publishes during the period Matthiessen will later identify as the classic American Renaissance years, 1850–55: and it earns its stripes as Emersonian prophecy with such audacious avowals of scripturism as, "With each new mind a new secret of nature transpires, *nor can the Bible be closed* until the last great man is born" [*CW* 4:12; my emphasis]). The lecture with which he usually concludes this series has been "The Uses of Great Men." But on this Sunday, he sets "Great Men" aside: Carlylean hero worship gives way to "Worship."

Emerson's use of the verb "to believe" indexes this shift, from *Representative Men* to *The Conduct of Life,* toward the question of worship as such. "The Uses of Great Men" opens, not surprisingly, with a note of the humanistic: "It is natural to believe in great men. . . . Our religion is the love and cherishing of these patrons" (*CW* 4:3–4). In its finished form, "Worship" retains a degree of continuity with these sentiments on the nature of belief. But in ways more and less subtle, it points to the possibility of *something else.*[3] "Worship" reminds us, both more simply and more equivocally, of a prior inevitability: "We are born believing" (*CW* 6:108). Here endeth the sentence. Great men or no, and not even necessarily believing *in,* we worship.

The precise contents of the 1847 lecture/sermon have not been determined.[4] Thanks to cross-referencing work by Merton Sealts, Jr., we can speculate that it presented part (though not all) of "Worship" as it appears in *The Conduct of Life.* (Sealts, in *Emerson on the Scholar,* notes that the finished text of the essay draws substantially from 1847–48 journal entries.) Much of the remaining material in the *Conduct* series first reached the public in 1850–51 lectures. Given this chronology, the 1847 occasion may be viewed as a groundbreaking for that later lecture series and book project, and "Worship" viewed as something of a cornerstone.

At the very least, we can assert that the gesture of explicitly addressing the topic of worship for a Sunday discourse fits closely with changing concerns expressed in Emerson's journals and letters of the time. Robert Richardson reports that "during the first two-thirds of 1847 Emerson was more restless and dissatisfied than he had been for many years" (436). David Robinson, underscoring Emerson's "waning" experience of the ecstatic, similarly points to the 1847–48 period as one of personal "change arguably as significant as his . . . [1833–34] transition from preacher to lecturer and essayist" (112).[5]

In 1847, some six weeks prior to his delivery of the "Worship" lecture/sermon at Nantucket, Emerson gives voice in his journal to what sounds rather like another crisis of vocation: "A Scholar is a candle which the love and desire of men will light. Let it not lie in a dark box. But here am I with so much all ready to be revealed to me as to others if only I could be set aglow. I have wished for a professorship. Much as I hate the church, I have wished the pulpit that I might have the stimulus of a stated task" (March 25, 1847).

The call of the pulpit involves the desire for a "stated task." Wesley T. Mott's work on Emerson's sermons can help us answer the question of what Emerson might have supposed that task to be. For Emerson the minister, assuming the pulpit has meant offering one's self, through speech, as a model for conduct: "Emerson's minister is meant to be representative in this high sense . . . in his prophetic role, as a model to which the goodness in all people might be drawn."[6] Mott identifies Emerson's concept of the minister as one inherited from his early spiritual hero, William Ellery Channing. Preaching at the dedication of Divinity Hall in 1826, Channing proclaimed that "this edifice is dedicated to the training of ministers, whose word, like their Master's, shall be '*with power,*' . . . that strong action of the understanding, conscience, and heart, on moral and religious truth, through which the preacher is quickened to awaken the same strong action in others" (Mott, *Strains of Eloquence,* 47).

Such a concept of the minister's task apparently suited the young Emerson well: "Emerson fancies himself 'the believer (if not the dupe) of brilliant promises, and can respect myself as the possessor of those powers which command the reason & passions of the multitude.' This fantasy of power and control suggests that Emerson did *not* approach the ministry with reluctance" (Mott, *Strains,* 5). The more mature Emerson may have, as Mott suggests, moderated his "fantasy" of commanding the multitude; but by 1847, certain aspects of his youthful pulpit ambition look attractive once more.

One might think of Emerson's poem "Days" (first published 1857) as describing the contours of a call renewed.[7] In "Days," the speaker laments forgotten "morning wishes." Whatever these unspecified wishes may have been, their higher purpose has been lost in the shuffle, as the speaker belatedly settles for "hastily" gathering a few herbs and apples. In a journal entry from May 24, 1847, Emerson summarizes the same argument: "The days come & go like muffled & veiled figures sent from a distant friendly party, but they say nothing, & if we do not use the gifts they bring, they carry them as silently away." His earliest morning wish had been to preach: "In divinity I hope to thrive" (1824). And the Days had brought him the gift of opportunity—above all the day known as "*the Sabbath,* the jubilee of the whole world," along with the "*institution of preaching*" (as he will acknowledge these two "inestimable" blessings in "The Divinity School Address," *CW* 1:92). As of his 1832–39 lingering departure from the ministry, this gift was one he had decided not to use. But by 1847, he stood prepared to reconsider the practical application of this gift anew, in wishing for the stated task of the pulpit.[8]

For Emerson, the moment of 1847 brings together the concepts of a new mode of "writing after the minister" and that of an "aftermath of the American Renaissance." "Writing after the minister" has shifted to its later mode of writing in pursuit of a lost object: "I have wished the pulpit." At the same time, a period of prophetic scripturism is approaching a cusp point. Though the writers whom Emerson had inspired were just coming into what Matthiessen called the "heady confidence" that made possible "the renaissance of those years," Emerson himself "was more conscious, in his journal of 1847, of the precarious balance of such periods" as he sensed the "great moment" was about to be followed by the onset of a "moment of transition,—the foam hangs but a moment on the wave; the sun himself does not pause on the meridian; literature becomes criticism, nervousness, and a gnawing when the first musical strain has waked the echoes" (*American Renaissance*, 373). Emerson has waked echoes aplenty; and he is the first to recognize them as such and change the tune. New scripture ceases to provoke newer scripture and now instead becomes the object of exposition. Literature becomes commentary, and prophecy becomes preaching.

A brief journal entry from later in 1847 captures this impulse: "The secret of life is to preach, you think" (*JMN* 10:164). Emerson's shift of vocational inclination shows up in both the form and tone of the *Conduct* series.

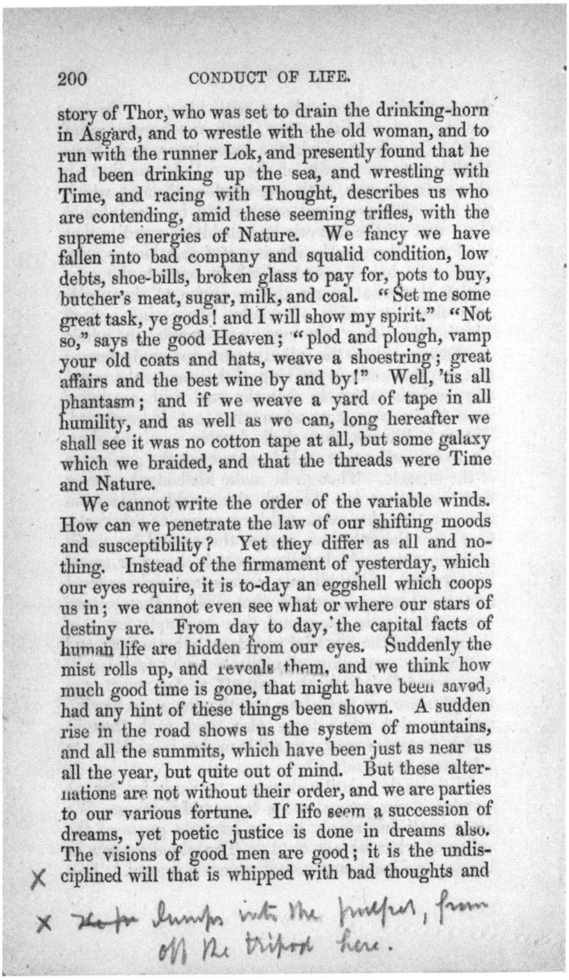

200 CONDUCT OF LIFE.

story of Thor, who was set to drain the drinking-horn in Asgard, and to wrestle with the old woman, and to run with the runner Lok, and presently found that he had been drinking up the sea, and wrestling with Time, and racing with Thought, describes us who are contending, amid these seeming trifles, with the supreme energies of Nature. We fancy we have fallen into bad company and squalid condition, low debts, shoe-bills, broken glass to pay for, pots to buy, butcher's meat, sugar, milk, and coal. "Set me some great task, ye gods! and I will show my spirit." "Not so," says the good Heaven; "plod and plough, vamp your old coats and hats, weave a shoestring; great affairs and the best wine by and by!" Well, 'tis all phantasm; and if we weave a yard of tape in all humility, and as well as we can, long hereafter we shall see it was no cotton tape at all, but some galaxy which we braided, and that the threads were Time and Nature.

We cannot write the order of the variable winds. How can we penetrate the law of our shifting moods and susceptibility? Yet they differ as all and nothing. Instead of the firmament of yesterday, which our eyes require, it is to-day an eggshell which coops us in; we cannot even see what or where our stars of destiny are. From day to day, the capital facts of human life are hidden from our eyes. Suddenly the mist rolls up, and reveals them, and we think how much good time is gone, that might have been saved, had any hint of these things been shown. A sudden rise in the road shows us the system of mountains, and all the summits, which have been just as near us all the year, but quite out of mind. But these alternations are not without their order, and we are parties to our various fortune. If life seem a succession of dreams, yet poetic justice is done in dreams also. The visions of good men are good; it is the undisciplined will that is whipped with bad thoughts and

FIGURE 2: Melville's marginalia in Emerson's *Conduct of Life:* here Emerson "jumps into the pulpit" (AC85.M4977. Zz860e, by permission of the Houghton Library, Harvard University)

Frederick Henry Hedge, in an 1861 review of *The Conduct of Life,* speaks of Emerson's book as a piece of virtual pulpit evangelism: "Though his voice is no longer heard in Christian pulpits, yet what preaching can be more practical and evangelical than this?" (Hutchinson, *Transcendentalist Ministers,* 192). William R. Hutchinson interprets Hedge's review—ministerial approval granted to an apostate—as evidence of the slippage of liberal religion in its embrace of transcendentalism and reinstatement of the "heresiarchs" Emerson and Theodore Parker (193). But Hedge's latitudinarianism, though an important factor in the positive nature of the review, does not account for the specific attributes he celebrates. Hedge may well have detected something more preacherly, more evangelical, in *Conduct* than in previous volumes of Emerson's essays. Hedge, as we will see below, was not entirely accurate about the absence of Emerson's voice from Christian pulpits. In the main, his comments are insightful: though Emerson's literal occupation of Christian pulpits would never again be frequent, Hedge was certainly not the only observer to find in *Conduct*'s pages a figurative ascent to the minister's post.

In supporting witness to Emerson's ministerial conduct, Herman Melville casts a dart as the essayist leaps into preacherly prose. In a telling bit of marginalia in his copy of *The Conduct of Life,* Melville catches Emerson in the ministerial act as, with a stern turn of phrase and an elevation of moral tone, the former preacher "jumps into the pulpit" (fig. 2). Later readers have independently confirmed this impression in a variety of registers. In his study of *The Conduct of Life,* Richard Lee Francis notes a "return to a more sermonic approach." What Melville and Francis respond to in part is Emerson's tone in the *Conduct* essays, as experienced, for instance, by Edwin Arlington Robinson: "In the essay on Power he takes me over his paternal knee and wallops me with a big New England shingle for about three-quarters of a New England hour."[9]

The passage to which Melville responded packs just such a moralizing wallop: "The visions of good men are good; it is the undisciplined will that is whipped with bad thoughts and bad fortunes" (*CW* 6:172). Walker Cowen has performed the invaluable service of transcribing the comment Melville scribbled in the margin of his copy: "~~The p~~ Jumps into the pulpit, from off the tripod here" (*Melville's Marginalia V,* 11). Whether we take the tripod to be the surveyor's instrument (more famously wielded by Thoreau) or the mystical device of the Delphic Oracle (the passage does refer to visions), the "jump" described by Melville translates Emerson from a position of privileged *observation* to one of *exhortation,* from (transparent?) eyeball to embodied voice. Francis's critical ear detects a parallel transformation that is borne out, not just in this passage, but in the book of *Conduct* as a whole. Francis notes that "the return to a more sermonic approach [in *Conduct*] affected Emerson's angle of vision. . . . If we appropriate a theological term, the method of *Nature* was transcendent. In returning to certain characteristics of the sermonic method with *The Conduct of Life,* Emerson also returned to the ascendant angle of vision."[10] In alignment with Melville's terms, the visionary tripod had been transcendent—a site of Olympian observations, but the hortatory pulpit is ascendant—a platform for pushing listeners toward moral improvement.

Gertrude Reif Hughes's subtle analysis of the form of *Conduct* might also be enlisted to point toward a sermonic quality of these essays. Hughes takes as her point of departure the method implied in "The American Scholar": "The scholar of the first age received into him the world around; brooded thereon, gave it a new arrangement in his own mind, and uttered it again. It came into him life; it went out from him truth" (*W,* I, 87). But the Emerson Hughes finds at work in *The Conduct of Life* does not follow the model of "the scholar of the first age" (6). Hughes discusses "Behavior" from *The Conduct of Life* as a good example of an essay that proceeds "far more deductively than the formula from 'The American Scholar' suggests" (6).[11]

Hypothetically, Hughes supposes, "such an essay on behavior might be expected to begin with examples of all kinds of behavior . . . and then to evaluate these by way of articulating a concluding abstraction about behavior. . . . Such an essay would have started, progressed, and ended very differently from the one Emerson actually wrote" (6). One might, based upon the "American Scholar" model, have expected this *Conduct* essay to have been more inductive . . . *unless* the essay happens to be a sermon. If it is a sermon, the expectation of moving from examples to a distillation of truth would be inverted: a standard sermon might begin with doctrine, then move through proofs and finally on into applications; the progress would be from definitive general statement to explanation and examples. It would, as Hughes notes that it does, precisely violate the expectations raised by "The American Scholar" and its inductive life-to-truth formula: this essay, as sermon, begins in truth and ends in life.

Hughes does not explicitly address the essays in *Conduct* as sermonic, but her reading opens the way for such a conclusion: "The Emersonian essay is an exercise in the sublime as Emerson defines it in 'Worship': 'To make our word or act sublime we must make it real' (*W,* VI, 226). The important thing . . . is to see that the Emersonian essay ends with power and to recognize as fully as possible the ramifications of that fact. . . . It is an end designed to create its readers" (7).[12] The sermon, and above all the evangelical sermon, seeks as its end to (re)create, or convert, its listeners.

Amid such potentially slippery formal considerations, one additional testimony may be in order: the report of a firsthand, visceral experience of the "Worship" lecture as delivered in the *Conduct* series. A skeptical British-born listener—tentatively identified as John Ross Dix[13]—who had heard a portion of the incipient *Conduct* series found the least "satisfaction" in Emerson's "concluding Lecture on Worship." The critic concludes that on the whole Emerson "'sermonizes' too much" in his delivery.

One last preliminary consideration should help contextualize the importance of Emerson's call to worship: Emerson's turn (in vocational concerns and presentational form) breaks a silence of sorts. In *Virtue's Hero: Emerson, Antislavery, and Reform,* Len Gougeon has referred to 1838–44 as "The Silent Years." While Gougeon refers to Emerson's silence on the issue of slavery, I would note that this period includes rather precisely the years during which Emerson was silent on Sundays. His last sermon as a preacher of supply was January 20, 1839. He did not speak again on a Sunday until 1844, when he spoke on March 3 about "NE Reformers," on March 10 about an unidentified subject, and on August 1 about "Emancipation in the British West Indies."[14] A renewed interest in the question of public worship and preaching corresponds strikingly with his conversion to public antislavery activity; for instance, in 1851, the very last lecture he gives before his address on the "Fugitive Slave Law" (which he gave on a Sunday) is "Worship."

I have discussed above the March 25, 1847, journal passage in which Emerson confesses that "I have wished the pulpit that I might have the stimulus of a stated task." The continuation of this passage asserts a potential alliance between this wish and an engagement in abolitionist activity. Gougeon also gives selective emphasis to this passage, citing it as a turning point in Emerson's emergence from the silent years: "'But here I am with so much already to be revealed to me as to others if only I could be set aglow.' While wishing for 'the stimulus of a stated task' and 'a sense of direction,' Emerson pointedly notes that 'N.P Rogers spoke more truly than he knew, perchance, when he recommends the Abolition-Campaign to me. I doubt not, a course of mobs would do me much good'" (*JMN* 10:28, Gougeon, 129). Given the focus of his study, Gougeon omits Emerson's reference to the "pulpit." The present study seeks, in part, to restore that dimension as a subtext for the narrative Gougeon tells; and conversely, though it will receive little subsequent mention in what follows, Gougeon's exhaustive work on Emerson and antislavery can be read as an important context for the religious concerns of the present project.

"Worship" bears indications of these merging concerns. "The highest virtue is always against the law" (*CW* 6:126), Emerson announces, in a statement whose sting increases within the context of the Fugitive Slave Act (of which Emerson had sworn, "I will not obey it, by God.").[15] Surveying the sad state of faith "in this country," Emerson asks, "What proof of infidelity, like the toleration and propagandism of slavery?" (*CW* 6:111; Melville, "who always abhorred slavery as an atheistical iniquity" [*NN* 16:186] would make a similar connection between an absence of effective faith in the divine and the practice of dehumanization). As "slave-holding and slave-trading religions" reveal, "the fatal trait is the divorce between religion and morality" (*CW* 6:110). Emerson seeks to reconcile these estranged parties through his Sunday preachings on worship and antislavery.

The confluence of these projects bespeaks a reinvestment in the power of hortatory language to engage religious and moral sentiments. Ralph Rusk has described Emerson's "Conduct of Life" lecture years under the heading, "Down from His Ivory Tower." Part of this descent involved a renewed willingness to make use of Sunday pulpit venues and thus to avail himself of the twin advantages he had identified in the Divinity School Address:

> Two inestimable advantages Christianity has given us; *first; the Sabbath,* the jubilee of the whole world; whose light dawns welcome alike into the closet of the philosopher, into the garret of toil, and into prison cells, and everywhere suggests, even to the vile, the dignity of spiritual being. Let it stand forevermore, a temple, which new love, new faith, new sight shall restore to more than its first splendor to mankind. *And secondly, the institution of preaching,*—the speech of man to men,—essentially the most flexible of

> all organs, of all forms. What hinders that now, everywhere, in pulpits, in lecture-rooms, in houses, in fields, wherever the invitation of men or your own occasions lead you, you speak the very truth, as your life and conscience teach it, and cheer the waiting, fainting hearts of men with new hope and new revelation? (*CW* 1:92; my emphasis)

Emerson would continue to deliver "Worship" as an occasional Sunday discourse over a number of years, and Charvat ventures to identify an 1854 delivery of it as part of a "Sunday sermon." These Sunday discourses sometimes featured a church venue, including at least one additional instance not identified by Charvat: on February 19, 1860, Emerson delivered "Worship" on a Sunday at the Unitarian Church in Detroit.[16] That year, the lecture would assume a new place of importance as a published essay in *The Conduct of Life.*

This survey of Emerson's career began with a moment from 1847, viewed from several angles as Emerson's return to a ministerial role and as the genesis of "Worship." Before proceeding to examine the essay "Worship" in its final setting, taking a look back over some of the moments that led up to the "silent years" may enable a better understanding of the return to worship that stands behind that essay's appearance.

Emerson, Sermons, and Persons

The particular occasion of Emerson's departure from the ministry in 1832, his refusal to administer the elements to his congregation in the celebration of communion, is sometimes dismissed as an arcane matter. It has been suggested that Emerson somewhat arbitrarily selected this act of rebellion, the so-called "Lord's Supper Controversy," as an expedient way to terminate his ministry. In this view, the point of the "Lord's Supper Controversy" is simply to be done with the confines of the pulpit and to get on with the literary ambitions. Certainly any discussion of young Emerson would be amiss that discounted his ambition. But perhaps it would be instructive to view the controversy from the perspective of Emerson the young minister rather than that of Emerson the not-yet famous essayist. One might attempt to join in the critical discussion that has attempted to understand his departure from the ministry by reading the farewell sermon within the context of a series of sermons that led up to it, with a particular eye to what these reveal about the young minister's emotional and religious life. It is this line of questioning that I wish to pursue in the present section.

In sermon 76 on "the authority of Jesus," Emerson describes and *praises* the authority of Jesus, taking as his text the verse which says of Jesus that "He taught them as one having authority and not as the scribes" (Matthew 7:29). Emerson declares that Jesus "taught more truth, and (if I may say so) more truly; he expressed with unexampled force, the great laws to which the human understanding must always bow."[17] In sermon 162 on "The Lord's Supper," Emerson *objects* that "the service does not stand upon the basis of a voluntary act, but it is imposed by authority. It is an expression of gratitude to Christ, enjoined by Christ."

At stake in both sermons is the status of authority and exemplarity. "Jesus was exemplary: he taught with authority" saith the first text. But, read tendentiously, the second text raises a conflict: "We need not follow Jesus' example: to do so would be to bend to authority." Possible arguments might show that no strictly logical contradiction need exist between these two 1832 sermon statements, even apart from the fact that they are not delivered upon precisely the same occasion. For instance, we might draw, with Emerson (and in anticipation of Theodore Parker), a distinction between the legitimate authority of eternal verity and the waning command of transient forms. But such arguments cannot entirely dissipate the tension Emerson's sermons express. What frame of mind might explain Emerson's apparently conflicting feelings on authority as admirable and inadmissible?

Part of the answer may lie in the sermons leading up to "The Lord's Supper" farewell in which Emerson so dramatically inverts the believer's relation to the authority of Jesus. Sometime in early June 1832, Emerson mails his definitive valedictory letter to the Second Church committee stating his new views on the Lord's Supper. Maurice Gonnaud has pointed to a cluster of key sermons from around this time which lay the intellectual groundwork for Emerson's discontinuance of eucharistic observation: "In May and June of that same year, Emerson preached three sermons that when joined together constitute a formidably coherent attack against the scheme of redemption which was indispensable to the idea of communion" (102). In sermon 155, Emerson "throws off the notion of sin"; in sermon 157 "Emerson argues that the discovery of interstellar space made null and void not only Calvinism but also all other forms of anthropomorphic religion"; in 158 "Emerson begins by positing that divine unity subsists across time like 'one law, one nature, one truth, one goodness,' and he draws from this concept an argument against the federal theology" (102).

Of the "subversive" three Gonnaud identifies, sermon 157, with its denial of a personal God (continued in the subsequent sermon's attack on historical Christianity), presents the greatest departure from Unitarian doctrine. The denial of the innate depravity of man in sermon 155 and the rejection of the federal theology of fall and atonement in sermon 158 both sound rather like standard Calvinist-bashing.[18] Emerson's controversial assertion of an impersonal God in sermons 157 and 158 merits further attention; but first, a word about the sermon that immediately precedes these. Those keeping score at home may have noticed a skip in the series—155, 157, 158—what about sermon 156? Gonnaud mentions in passing that sermon 156 was "a sermon on envy, oddly isolated amid the subversive triad." In the remainder of this section, I hope to make some sense of Emerson's "oddly" situated discourse on envy.

Of envy, Emerson observes that "it is set down among the foremost sins and threatened with the sorest condemnation. Yet it sounds to some as if it were only written in books. Envy—men say—Who envies? and will almost deny the existence of such an old world vice" (148).

A more recent analyst of metaphysical desire, René Girard, writes,

> We often brag that no word can scandalize us anymore, but what about 'envy'? Our supposedly insatiable appetite for the forbidden stops short of envy. Primitive cultures fear and repress envy so much that they have no word for it; we hardly use the one we have, and this fact must be significant. We no longer prohibit many actions that generate envy, but silently ostracize whatever can remind us of its presence in our midst. Psychic phenomena, we are told, are important in proportion to the resistance they generate toward revelation. If we apply this yardstick to envy as well as to what psychoanalysis designates as repressed, which of the two will make the more plausible candidate for the role of best-defended secret?[19]

Girard suggests that envy, no less than sex, is the true repressed "thing." Such repression might be evident in Gonnaud's account of the "subversive" sermons, as he brushes envy aside as if it were a topic hardly appropriate to a serious mind like Emerson's at a time of formative intellectual challenge. Suffice it to say that Emerson does not repress the subject: "In short if envy be the hatred of superiority—then, I had almost said, there is none without it" (*CS* 4:148). Emerson catches himself—why had he only "almost" said it? A pious interpretation might see Emerson stopping short of what would be heretical (but not blasphemous) even to Unitarians: the implication that even Jesus, exemplar of moral perfection, was not free of envy. But also of course, for Emerson to say that "none are without it" would be implicitly to confess his own experience of envy.

Melville's narrator in *Billy Budd* asks, "Is Envy then such a monster? Well, though many an arraigned mortal has in hopes of mitigated penalty pleaded guilty to horrible actions, did ever anybody seriously confess to envy? Something there is in it universally felt to be more shameful than even felonious crime. And not only does everybody disown it, but the better sort are inclined to incredulity when it is in earnest imputed to an intelligent man. But since its lodgment is in the heart and not the brain, no degree of intellect supplies a guarantee against it" (*Billy Budd, Sailor* (1984), 1385). René Girard explains further: "Envy subordinates a desired *something* to the *someone* who enjoys a privileged relationship with it. Envy covets the superior being that neither the someone nor the something alone, but the conjunction of the two, seems to possess. Envy involuntarily testifies to a lack of *being* that puts the envious to shame. That is why envy is the hardest sin to acknowledge." Emerson speaks in his sermon on "the authority of Jesus," expressly of the "superiority of Jesus over other teachers . . . we have the very words of Jesus, yet how ineffectual they prove from so many lips as utter them" (*CS* 2:362). Emersonian envy is the hatred of superiority; Jesus's superiority to other teachers is that his words are effectual: they have power. The desired something is authority; Jesus is the someone who possesses it.

Emerson's sermon 156 employs a personification for envy and, via this slight displacement of outright personal confession, allows Envy to speak in the first person: "What right has this man, [Envy] says, to be more courted or better served than I? I don't like it that he should be drawn in his carriage whilst I walk afoot. I don't like to have his opinion quoted when mine is not. . . . I am tired, like the Athenian, of hearing Aristides called the Just" (*CS* 4:149).

This last complaint by Envy, of the irksomeness of hearing about someone else's virtue, finds resonance in Emerson's 1833 journal. In the journal passage, Christ and authority have been nominally replaced by other variables of envy. Emerson first reports without further comment that "Milton says, 'if ever any was ravished with moral beauty, he [Milton] is the man.'" But, as already noted, Emerson cannot let this claim go unchallenged. On the next day, Emerson returns to this point: "Milton describes himself in his letter to Diodati as enamoured of moral perfection. He did not love it more than I" (*EJ* 117). An earnest profession of piety, no doubt—but in his very earnestness, Emerson gives himself over to perhaps more than a touch of envy.

If we return to the preceding sermon complaint spoken by the figure of Envy—"I don't like to have his opinion quoted when mine is not"—we find yet another sentiment quite close to Emerson's heart. Writing about the anxiety of influence experienced by Emerson himself, for whom Harold Bloom supplies no clear precursor, Michael Colacurcio has noted that "from one point of view, the missing term is quite probably Jesus, that strongest of all the prophets who, though he wrote no text, was nevertheless, according to Emerson's early reading of his own tradition, always being given credit for absolutely everything truly thought and said" ("The Corn and the Wine," 3). For example, in a journal passage Whicher includes from 1832, Emerson laments (somewhat testily) that "every teacher, when once he finds himself insisting with all his might upon a great truth, turns up the ends of it at last with a cautious showing how it is agreeable to the life and teaching of Jesus, as if that was any recommendation" (Whicher, 10). The hints of rancor in these passages suggest that Emerson's sermon on the fearsomeness of envy may hold some personal truth: "This evil is still alive; this snake has bitten us; the disease creeps in our vitals" (*CS* 4:148).

One way to expel envy might be to downgrade or deny the envied someone's relation to the desired something. To present the most irenic face, one might claim that such a denial would be just what the person wanted, a strategy we have noticed in "The Lord's Supper": "I fear it is the effect of this ordinance to clothe Jesus with an authority which he never claimed." Emerson may have been "tired, like the Athenian, of hearing Aristides called the Just"; he was perhaps even more tired, as a young American, of hearing Jesus called the Christ.

Yet this diminishment of Jesus does not quite exhaust Emerson's religious animus as expressed in the sermon foreground to the "Lord's Supper." Emerson's preoccupation with the "*person* of Jesus" (a preoccupation he would call "noxious" in the Divinity School Address) is linked to his concern with the personhood of the Unitarian God. Emerson in sermon 157 condemns an historical anthropomorphizing practice that persists in his church: "Even God himself, the infant religion of all nations has clothed in human form, and idolatry imputed to him the passions as well as the person of man" (*CS* 4:155). Here Emerson's sermon anticipates his statement in the Divinity School Address that the "soul knows no persons."

Emerson's Second Church partner, Henry Ware, Jr., in a sermon on "The Personality of Deity" defending the idea of a personal God two months after Emerson delivered the Divinity School Address, provides some thoughts that may shed light also on Emerson's related 1832 sermons:

> The person, the conscious, intelligent, active, enjoying, suffering being, is foremost in importance and honor; principles and laws operate for its support, guidance, and well-being; and therefore are secondary. Some of these principles and laws have their origin in the relations which exist amongst intelligent, moral agents; most of them come into action in consequence of the previous existence of those relations. If there were no such agents, there would be no such principles, or they would have no operation. Thus, for example, veracity, justice, love, are sentiments or obligations which spring up from the relations subsisting between different beings, and can exist only where there are persons. (435)

Take away persons and "sympathy, friendship, love, all social enjoyment, all social life, are annihilated" (436). Ware's tally of "social" losses leaves some things unspoken: not just the virtue vanishes—also, we might add, envy. By eliminating the personal God from his mind, Emerson can banish God-envy. It may be true that, as Ware suggests, one cannot worshipfully love the abstract laws of the universe; it is possibly truer that one cannot envy them. Emerson speaks of the challenge of envy, the hatred of superiority. By way of a solution, he diminishes Jesus and dissolves God.[20]

On the Impersonality of the Deity

In "Religion" (1837), Emerson delivers an impersonal formulation of what otherwise might be recognized as an Edwardsian metaphysics and ethics. The anchoring term of being in Jonathan Edwards's famous declaration, "Absolute sovereignty is what I love to ascribe to God" (*Basic Writings*, 83), becomes diffused in a tribute not to any personal God but rather to what Emerson in this Philosophy of History lecture series calls "the Universal mind" (*EL* 2:84). "Its highest attribute is its selfexistence. It looks to no higher source. It admits of no essence prior to itself"; this ultimate term, the Universal mind, supplies the unifying concern of the entire lecture series, as Emerson announces in his "Introductory" lecture. Subsequent lectures define their topics with reference to the Universal mind: "Religion is its self-respect" (2:12). Henry Ware, Jr's, assertion about the unlovability of such an impersonal abstraction notwithstanding—at least for the moment—Emerson appears to maintain his reverent love for the religious only insofar as he preserves an impersonal idea of worship. Three superlatives, placed at the beginning, middle, and end of the lecture, form a sort of new Emersonian trinity: "the mind of the mind" (2:83–84), "the soul of the soul" (2:89), and "the law of laws" (2:95–96).

"The mind of the mind" gives the individual access to the dictates of the Reason, that higher faculty that—according to the familiar Transcendental distinction which identifies Reason's attributes as "intuition and eternity"—claims absolute authority over the mere Understanding, grasped by "the Hand of the mind" (83). In acts of true virtue, Reason discerns a universal duty which takes precedence over the individual, nonuniversal interests that appear to the Understanding. Elsewhere, Emerson calls this faculty of discernment the "moral sentiment." "Religion" is the sentiment that allows the individual to obey the nature of true virtue with love and joy: "Virtue is the adopting of this dictate of the Universal mind by the individual Will. And religion is the accompanying emotion, the emotion of reverence which the presence of the Universal mind always excites in the individual" (2:84).

Emerson attributes three features to those actions undertaken out of intuitive religious obedience. The first is "Universality," the sense of Duty beyond one's private satisfaction. Though this sentiment inevitably seeks the "public good," Emerson makes clear that discerning the claim of a universal duty does not involve a utilitarian moral calculus: "The authority of that sentiment [of universal duty] is the simplest insight into the intrinsic quality of actions and has *no reference to advantages nor to disadvantages, nor to persons few or many*" (my emphasis). Far from appealing directly to the greatest good for the greatest number, universality finds that "the multitude is the worst argument. And in fact the only way of arriving at the universal mind is to quit the whole world and take the counsel of the bosom alone. The representative of the universe is total solitude" (2:86). This lesson Emerson and Margaret Fuller shared, separately, together. Fuller's "Great Lawsuit" (1843) had pitted "Man versus Men, Woman versus Women"; the "new revelation" would not reveal itself through "the numerous party."[21]

The second attribute of the religious action, which sanctifies the authority born in the counsel of solitude, is the "sign" of the "Profitable." Again, Emerson takes care to indicate that profitability supplies *only* a sign and "never the motive" (2:87). The motive consists in nothing other than "the awful *I ought.*" Well, the Yankee heart might say, dollars are only signs, and I ought to have a fair number of those signs of my virtue. The doctrine of sanctification had long indexed such signs; as Thomas Shepard had hinted in the seventeenth century, "the sealed of heaven are ever prosperous men" (McGiffert, *God's Plot,* 147–48). Some passages of Emerson, particularly later Emerson, do lend themselves quite readily to that sort of calculation, but Emerson in no way espouses a gospel of "Wealth" at this juncture. In "Religion," his list of worthies who exemplify the sign of the "profitable" reveals, on the contrary, how little evident may be the profit to the "fortunes and life of the doer." Socrates, Peter, Paul, More, Russell, Sidney, Vane—martyrs of conscience every one—were servants of profitability on "the largest scale."

Finally, the religious action exhibits "the power to exalt" (*EL* 2:87); this ecstatic confirmation stands apart as "the most excellent property of the sentiment." Though not utilitarian, the criterion is experiential and pragmatic. This third attribute reveals the self-dependence of the "soul of the soul" (2:89)—that is, the middle, animating, term of Emerson's impersonal trinity. Emerson cites the Brahmin formula, "All that depends on another gives pain; all that depends on himself gives pleasure" (2:89); access to the self-dependent soul of the soul yields exalting pleasure. Emerson's construction of an impersonal deity becomes unmistakable here: earlier in the lecture series, he had proclaimed that "nothing but God is self-dependent" (*EL* 2:17). To complete the syllogism: for Emerson, "God" and "the soul of the soul" are one. He continues in a vein that once again brings to mind Edwards: "Every being in nature has its existence so connected with other beings that if set apart from them it would instantly perish" (2:17). Edwards finds "God Glorified in Man's dependence" and everywhere asserts that "the God who alone saves is the same as He who alone exists" (Colarcurcio, *Doctrine and Difference,* 98). For Emerson, the foundational attribute of "selfexistence" (*EL* 2:84) belongs to the Universal mind, glorified in religious exaltation.

Emerson does preserve for Jesus Christ a status somewhat distinct from the other examples of religious ecstasy he cites under this third, exalting, attribute of the religious sentiment. Of those who bear witness to "the soul of the soul," Emerson lists Jesus, Socrates, Plotinus, Luther, George Fox, Böhme, and Swedenborg and points to Moravian and Quietist "rapture," Calvinistic "revivals," and Methodist "experiences." But Jesus is not quite just "another enthusiast" (the almost dismissive tag line Emerson uses for Jacob Behmen or Böhme, *EL* 2:92). Others on the list are seen primarily to *experience* the exaltation or "ravishment," passively received: Socrates "was repeatedly the subject of a Trance or Rapture" and once "fell . . . into a deep contemplation" that rendered him motionless an entire day; Plotinus "was entranced repeatedly" and thus obtained "an ineffable energy"; George Fox underwent "convulsions" as well as suspended animation; Emanuel Swedenborg "was affected in a singular manner" to be granted visions (*EL* 2:90–92). By the time we work our way down to the "less striking" examples of group experience, Emerson's language signals a sense of diminishing returns, even distaste: "Every where, the history of religion betrays a tendency to enthusiasm" (*EL* 2:92). Jesus, at the head of the list, admonishes, *preaches* the way of glory. On the one hand, this delivers him into a different category, but on the other hand we might say Emerson assigns him a role with regard to religion closest to Emerson's own:

> Jesus Christ was a minister of the pure Reason. The beatitudes of the Sermon on the Mount are the utterances of the mind contemning the phenomenal world. "Blessed are the righteous poor, for theirs is the kingdom of heaven." "Blessed are ye when men

> shall revile you and persecute you and say all manner of evil against you falsely on account of the truth in you. Rejoice and be exceeding glad."—This is falsehood and nonsense, says the Common Sense.—I can make nothing of it, says the Understanding. The Reason affirms its immutable truth. He has filled the world with the music of words which only Reason can interpret. All that emphatic reference to his divine nature, which has distracted the Church into how many sects, clears itself, the moment the busy understanding suffers the Reason to read, which sees that he speaks of itself. (*EL* 2:90)

We may note Jesus Christ was "*a* minister"—a minister without, necessarily, a difference from other such ministers. This nondifference coincides with the assertion that he was a minister "*of* the Pure Reason." This preposition might pass as neutral had not Emerson so clearly stated at the outset that in any consideration of Reason, "We belong to it, not it to us" (*EL* 2:83). That is, although Emerson omits the deliberate grammatical markers of passivity that accompany every other example, the philosophical hierarchy, in which all serve the authority of reason, remains intact. Granted grammatical agency, Jesus Christ "has filled the world with the music of words," but words which are intelligible only from an impersonal vantage point without need of recourse to a privileged personal intentionality (cf. Daniel, 20). To underline a few key phrases from Emerson's anti-utilitarian explanation cited above, the words of virtue possess an "authority" that "has no reference . . . to persons few or many."

We may discern at work here a version of what Stephen H. Daniel has termed "divine semiotics" in his philosophical study of Jonathan Edwards. Daniel locates his *Philosophy of Jonathan Edwards* within a Stoic-Ramistic tradition, in which "the task of reading the Book of Nature or the Scriptures is not concerned with the attempt to interpret the mind of God as the author of Nature or Scripture, for that would imply that the notion of God as a self is intelligible independently of the system of signs in which the notion is embedded. Instead the centrality of signs in the Renaissance mentality undercuts the need to interpret these texts in terms of authorial intention by denying that such a tactic provides a clearer notion of their meaning" (19). With Emerson's "Religion," we encounter a version of Edwards's ultimately Christocentric "divine semiotics" dissolved toward a "universal semiotics."[22] Emersonian semiotics might here be thought of as reconfiguring the map of signification, with impersonality taken to a leveling extreme.

In supplanting Jesus Christ the minister with the universal principles of his ministry, Emerson stages an imagined dialogue between the music of the beatitudes and the various faculties that resist or receive it. Three faculties register responses: "—This is falsehood and nonsense, says the Common Sense.—I can make nothing of it, says the Understanding. The Reason affirms its immutable truth." Again playing Reason against the stolid Understanding, Emerson enlists another deaf philosophical ear to make a pair with the latter: the truth likewise falls ineffectually upon the hard soil of the "Common Sense." The Common Sense most likely referred to here is that of Scottish Common Sense philosophy, that favorite grounding strategy of the "Unitarian Conscience."[23] Emerson liked the idea of an intuitive moral sense, as posited by the Common Sense school imported to Harvard from Scotland, but in this passage he is after something more exalted than a provincially popular response to skepticism. He does not speak here with the Unitarians or with the *sensis communis* of any interpretive community that would seek to conserve a traditional, theistic reading of revelation.

Even given this insistence upon impersonality, Emerson's system still makes room for a ministering agent and the expository preaching of the word, but not by the authority of any synod or magisterium. Reason, the only qualified interpreter of Scripture, affirms only the "immutable." This goal requires a reading that excludes distracting emphasis—emphasis implying exclusivity—on the divine nature of Jesus Christ. Emerson foregrounds what he hopes to be the antisectarian pragmatics of this theory of pure Reason: he claims that the emphasis on divine nature has "distracted the Church into how many sects." He echoes a prime concern from his "Introductory" lecture that "all false views, sects" stem from an elevation of the particular over the "Whole" (*EL* 2:5).

Hawthorne's "The Man of Adamant," also from 1837, expresses a similar concern with sectarianism, as the central character clings to a "plan of salvation so narrow, that, like a plank in a tempestuous sea, it could avail no sinner but himself" (*CE* 3:564). The tragedy of Hawthorne's sectarian Man of Adamant is his ultimate rejection of all communion: "He is acting in accordance with that least fortunate impulse of the Reformation by which in the search for authenticity one is likely to find oneself at last in a church of one" (Jeffrey, *People of the Book*, 306); as Melville's Clarel will later lament, the Reformation has left every pew a sect. Emerson, on the contrary, projects his antisectarian vision from a lecture in which he has just suggested that "the only way of arriving at the universal mind is to quit the whole world and take the counsel of the bosom alone. The representative of the universe is total solitude" (*EL* 2:86). For him, the Reformation and even those forgers of "An American Reformation," the Unitarians, have not gone far enough. At the precise moment in the lecture that he opens himself up to accusations of sectarian subjectivism, Emerson claims to achieve a unifying universalism through elimination of the last vestiges of an embodied external authority.

Reason, in order to see that Jesus Christ speaks not of himself but of Reason "itself," has already made the necessary adjustments to the Scriptures cited. A comparison with the original should make clearer the import of Emerson's revised beatitudes.

The Gospel according to Matthew:

> Blessed are the poor in spirit: for theirs is the kingdom of heaven.
>
> Blessed are ye, when men shall revile you, and persecute you, and say all manner of evil against you falsely, for my sake. Rejoice, and be exceeding glad: for great is your reward in heaven: for so persecuted they the prophets which were before you. (KJV 5:3.11–12)

The Gospel according to Reason:

> "Blessed are the righteous poor, for theirs is the kingdom of heaven." "Blessed are ye when men shall revile you and persecute you and say all manner of evil against you falsely on account of the truth in you. Rejoice and be exceeding glad."

Of the beatitudes, Emerson adapts the first and the last. These may be taken to stand for the whole list, but the two selected do serve well as examples of "utterances of the mind contemning the phenomenal world." Particularly as edited: the original of the first does not contain quite so resounding an endorsement of material poverty. Surely the Gospels offer no shortage of such endorsements, or corollary warnings about enslavement to material riches. But the source in this case speaks of "the poor in spirit." Now it is no accident that this beatitude has been embraced by, for example, the Franciscans, who literalize the *beati pauperes* in their holy poverty. But they do so not by glossing over the humility implied by "poor in spirit." Emerson, though perhaps not explicitly opposed to humility, would seem to want no part of being "poor in spirit": especially insofar as this kind of poverty would imply a lack of spirit or of spiritedness or of inspiration. His address to the Harvard Divinity School notably decries just such a lack. Being "poor in spirit" is not Emerson's idea of participation in the Universal mind.

Most crucially, Emerson's version of the last beatitude elides the emphatic reference to divine incarnation. Persecution earns blessing when suffered not "for my sake," not for Christ, but rather "on account of the truth in you." The truth becomes incidentally embodied to the extent that it resides "in you," but its importance lies solely in its Reason-able universality. One ought not to dwell upon the way the truth reveals itself through the phenomenality of a particular body in the world. Apart, perhaps, upon one's own ecstatic experience. "Rejoice and be exceeding glad." Period. Emerson, who will go on to write "Compensation," does not bother to repeat the bit about a reward in heaven.

Which is not to say that Emerson might not be interested in the rest of the affirmation: "for so persecuted they the prophets which were before you." To stand with the prophets is to be persecuted—or even, to be persecuted is in some sense to achieve the status of prophet. We can connect this concern with prophecy to the words Emerson *does* use. For the substituted words, the truth that is "in you," are not without their own biblical resonance. Later in Matthew, Jesus continues the sentiment of the beatitude upon the persecuted faithful:

> And ye shall be brought before governors and kings *for my sake*. . . . But when they deliver you up, take no thought how or what ye shall speak: for it shall be given you in that same hour what ye shall speak. For it is not ye that speak, but the Spirit of your Father which speaketh *in you*. (10:18–20; cf. also John 14:17, 20; 15:4; 1 John 2:24, etc.)

This text promises divine inspiration, prophecy; it is a promise Emerson's testimony embraces. What Emerson's lecture refuses is the characterization this text gives to the source of truth. Not that Emerson insists upon an individual truth, but rather that the truth "in you" is impersonal, not personified to the extent of having a locatable external source, the spirit of an anthropomorphic Father.

The name given to this impersonal truth is "Revelation"; once received, it immediately becomes susceptible to the threat of formalism:

> The effort to embody these truths and laws in some outward form, for the sake of preserving . . . remembrance of [the] vision, and of provoking all men to efforts after this beatitude, makes the Church.
>
> But the Revelation and the Church both labor under one perpetual disadvantage. They need always the presence of the same spirit that created them to make them thoroughly valid. All attempts to confine and transmit the religious feeling of one man or one sect to another age, by means of formulas the most accurate or rites the most punctual, have hitherto proved abortive. . . . The truest state of thought rested in, becomes false. Thought is like manna, that fell out of heaven, which cannot be stored. It will sour if kept; and tomorrow must be gathered anew. (EL 2: 92–93)

With this axiom, Emerson's lecture makes a turn. Up to this point, he has elaborated a philosophy of religion, using historical examples. As he moves toward his conclusion, he subsumes this theory into a philosophy *of the history* of religion, in accordance with the overall design of the lecture series. "In the preceding lectures," Emerson reminds his listeners, "I have aimed to show how deep and beneficent a Necessity underlies everything human. . . . Let us now see how this same force acts in reference to the religious element" (2.94).

History reveals the philosophical Necessity that governs the religious sentiment: "In actual history it will be found that its more illustrious exhibitions are periodical" (2:96). This periodicity of ages of Belief follows from the axiom stated above, that religious truth must ever be gathered anew. The "law of laws" that creates true beliefs "consists in a perpetual substitution of Being for Seeming and with the sublime propriety God is described as saying *I am*" (2:95). This self-existent "law of laws," that remains at the core of religion "when all forms are taken away," crowns Emerson's impersonal trinity. But inevitably, a substituting counterstroke betrays the influx of truth.

The great enemy of religion in Emerson's vision is not difficult to discern. The religious sentiment "must yield always to that obstinate tendency to personify and bring under the eye-sight what should be the contemplation of Reason alone" (2:96). The "obstinate tendency to personify" recurs as a bugbear in much of Emerson's religious thought, which may be thought of as an array of responses to this problem in all its guises. Here he tags personification with a harsh and traditional name: "In proportion to a man's alienation from wisdom and goodness do they seem to him another and not himself; that is to say the Deity becomes more objective, until finally flat idolatry appears" (2:96). In the farewell sermon cluster discussed earlier, we saw how the problem of persons became associated with the sin of envy. Here, Emerson makes the link to idolatry.

The effects of this "obstinate tendency" dominate what Emerson can see of the current scene: "Something like this has been the recent condition of Christendom" (2:97). Even so, the periodic contours shaped by a beneficent Necessity determine that the religious sentiment cannot languish "ossified" indefinitely: "Unbelief never lasts long" (2:97). As he will assert at various points of his career, including "Worship" in *The Conduct of Life* (1860), he finds that the world has entered into a stage of "transition" ("The Present Age," *EL* 2:158, 169–70).

Emerson finds his optimism enlivened by a new "call." The worthies who now uphold the "law of laws" form a group markedly dissimilar from those adduced earlier in the lecture. The "new communities of faith" spring up not around religious thinkers per se, but voices crying out for "moral education": "Pestalozzi, Coleridge, Owen, Degerando [Joseph Marie de Gérando], Cousin, Bentham, Spurzheim, and Wordsworth" (2:97). The poets on the list do not surprise, but we find also reformers (some with decidedly utilitarian leanings) of pedagogy, of labor, of prisons, eclectic systems-building philosophers, and a phrenologist for good measure. With this final catalog, we see Emerson's interest moving away from religion and religious practice as such and toward the manifold functioning of the religious sentiment in society: "The hope of society resides in the omnipotence of Reason alone." The visionary final words of the lecture underscore Emerson's broader interest in the workings of power: when the melodious, thunderous, new call of Reason shall go forth, all "shall hear with joy and with joy obey."

The Power of Holiness and the Hero's Retreat from Religion

In the Human Culture lecture series, first delivered January 1838, Emerson's preoccupation with power has become even more stark than in the previous season's *Philosophy of History* series (1837). "Religion" (1837) had identified the traits of religious action as universality, profitability, and the power to exalt. The lecture on "Holiness" from Human Culture pares back the ultimate trait. In "Religion," Emerson had claimed of religious action that its most excellent property is its power to exalt. In "Holiness" (1838), its most excellent property is its power.

"Holiness," in effect, expands on point two from "Religion," that religious acts are accompanied by the sign of the profitable. "Religion" glossed rather quickly over this point, as if, though profitability might give valid indications of an action's fidelity, such considerations might be construed as an embarrassment to true virtue. Emerson expended more space anxiously clarifying what profitability was *not* than in expounding its positive (if nonmaterial) value. Beyond and above the sign of the profitable lay the promise of exaltation: the ecstatic would in no way be eclipsed by functional concerns. Not so in "Holiness." The thrust of this lecture in some ways anticipates Theodore Parker's later sermon "What Religion Can Do for You," with its unabashed focus on the payout. Saith the pious American to such notions: Ask not what your religion can do for you. Saith Emerson: What you can do for your religion, if anything, is to ask precisely that question. For Emerson, as he will make especially plain in the lecture on "Holiness," the primary index of holiness is not piety but power. "Power was Emerson's True Grail," as Barbara Packer observes, invoking the terms of the hero's quest ("Ralph Waldo Emerson," 389). Here, power becomes the heroic expression of true belief.

To achieve the true belief of "Holiness," one must chart a course to escape "the two sad extremes, Superstition and Atheism, between which our being oscillates" (*EL* 2:343). Allowing ourselves to slip toward either of these extremes saps us of power. To fall into Superstition is to kneel in confusion and fear, to submit to the compulsion of tradition.

In so kneeling out of "imported faith," one forsakes "the God with us that vaticinates ever to the listening soul"; "God with us" glosses the traditional name Emmanuel; to "vaticinate" is to prophesy. Superstition is thus the abandonment of prophecy, but what occupies Emerson in this lecture is not the loss of prophecy as such, but rather the chief effect that accompanies this loss: a loss of power. The powerlessness of the superstitious position appears as a lack of heroism: "We miss in the devotee all the heroic, sprightly, intrepid motions of the soul." Such a devotee has lost the power of "his life, his thinking" (2:342).

But the swirling void of Atheism menaces those who flee the false foundation of Superstition: "Meantime, as unlovely, nay frightful is the solitude of the soul which is without God in the world" (2:342). The atheistic wanderer forfeits the power to animate creation, to *make* sense of the world: "To him, it is not creation. To him, these fair creatures are hapless spectres. He knows not what to make of it" (2:342). The "Introductory" lecture to this series similarly lays out the stakes of the appeal of "Religion to my Reason." The soul must make the "great step" of faith in feeling at home "in the world which exists for it."[24] All the things of the world are "chaos until he come like a creator and give them light and order" (2:223). In atheism, one cannot sustain and enjoy the reciprocal power of creation: "I cannot keep the sun in heaven if you take away the purpose that animates him. The ball is indeed there, but his *power* to cheer, his *power* to illuminate the heart as well as the atmosphere is gone forever" (2:342; my emphasis). Hermeneutics lapses into poststructuralism, a semiotics without divine or even universal cheer: "Every thought loses all its depth and has become mere surface" (2:342). The ultimate risk of Atheism thus replicates the ultimate risk of Superstition, as both imperil active thinking, thoughtful action, or thought as action.

Emerson wants to think the middle course of belief and to present such a course in its fullest appeal. To do so, he chooses to emphasize the power of "Holiness"; but this emphasis puts his religious category into competition with "Heroism," the topic he has treated in the preceding lecture from the series. Emerson recognizes such a competition presents an uphill battle: "Heroism is very attractive. Holiness is unattractive" (EL 2:341). We tend to associate the latter with a "mean, cowering, and dependent attitude." (Issues of class distinction may intrude upon this judgment: in "our age" there exists an "aversion of men of taste to Evangelical religion" [2:341]; but Emerson finds the root of the aversion in the question of attitude.) Emerson wants to redefine Holiness, not as the unattractive opposite of Heroism, but as a more powerful, more universal quality with affinities for Heroism.

In establishing these heroic-holy affinities, Emerson first clarifies his position on Heroism itself. In "Heroism," Emerson had allowed of the titular property that "there is somewhat [that is, "something"] not holy in it: it seems not to know that other souls are of one texture with it; it hath pride; it is the extreme of individual nature. Nevertheless, we must profoundly revere it" (331). Somewhat not holy or not, "there is somewhat in great actions, which does not allow us to go behind them." The hero's "highest deed" is "not open to the censure of philosophers or divines" (331). But the deed's immunity to censure does not exempt the hero's awareness; the heroic consciousness might yet benefit from ministerial or philosophical instruction. In "Holiness," Emerson repeats his earlier qualification that "somewhat not holy" clouds Heroism, and amplifies the idea that Heroism suffers from a confusion about the status of the Individual: Heroes "have never discriminated between their *individual* and what philosophy denominates the *universal* nature, and, really resting on this last, have esteemed it their private property" (2:341; emphasis in original).

To achieve Holiness, then, one ought to be freed from the hero's delusions. But, paradoxically, to be "holy" is also to avoid the mentality of "the saint": "The saint, on the other hand, is a man who accustomed to revere the moral sentiment as a law discriminates it in his thinking from his private self; cuts it off; puts it far from him; calls it by another name . . . and so, is divided" (2:341). He calls this law by that other name, "God—and worships it" (2:341). But in Emersonian holiness, a heroic holiness: "I command myself" (2:344).

Emerson provides several pages of examples of what he means by Holiness and how it enables one to operate from a position of power, an unimpeachable "superiority" (2:347). If Heroic action stood immune to the censure of divine or philosopher, the same applies here to Holiness: "when I burn with pure love, what can Calvin or Swedenborg say?" (2:346). Holiness "is that invincible spirit,"

> Whom unarmed
> No strength of man or fiercest wildbeast could withstand;
> Ran on embattled armies clad in iron,

> And weaponless itself;
> Made arms ridiculous; useless the forgery of brazen shield and spear. (2:347)

Emerson has just asserted that Holiness "is . . . readily discriminated from Heroism" (2:346), but the battlefield bravery trumpeted in this passage, his first literary sample of Holiness, scarcely seems adapted to aid such a discrimination. Emerson does introduce the fearsome agent portrayed in the lines of poetry as a "spirit," thus distinguishing holy power from brute strength; introduced in this manner, the poetry goes on to show holy power as superior to brute strength; as, in fact, "invincible." In the realm of power, Holiness trumps Heroism. Holiness may be distinguished from Heroism by the former's proper humility, but it is also distinguished by the results it obtains.

The poetry Emerson selects comes from Milton's *Samson Agonistes* (ll. 126ff). If we go back one line to read Milton's lead-in, we discover that Milton is rhetorically positing "That *Heroic,* that Renown'd / Irresistible Samson" (l. 125). Emerson, to portray what he calls Holiness, selects a passage containing Milton's description of the "Heroic."

In the Biography lecture series of 1835, Emerson had paid tribute to Milton for instituting a holy heroism, a spiritualized revision of Roman militarism: "To this antique heroism, Milton added the genius of Christian sanctity. Few men could be cited who have so well understood what is peculiar in the Christian ethics, and the precise aid it has brought to men, in being an emphatic affirmation of the omnipotence of spiritual laws, and, by way of marking the contrast to vulgar opinions, laying its chief stress on humility" (*EL* 1:156). Milton "celebrates in the martyrs, 'the unresistable might of weakness'" (1:156).

But in "Holiness," Emerson's appropriation of Milton is further complicated by the fact that the passage describes not a final spiritual triumph for Samson, not a celebration of his holy, heroic martyrdom, but rather the full strength of Samson's youth. Moreover, the description takes place at a time when Samson no longer possesses this strength: Finding the blind Samson before the prison at Gaza, the Chorus addresses his state with wonderment and pity—"Can this be hee . . .?"—contrasting his languished condition with reminiscences of previous exploits. Milton's passage recalls the brute heroism Samson has lost, a loss that serves as a step on his path to spiritual illumination. Milton's blind Samson becomes a holy hero, but Emerson seems to want to rescue the earlier vision of undiminished heroism and project this vision of strength onto true holiness.

Emerson caps his adapted quotation with a proclamation on the dynamics of holy invincibility: "This principle feels that it is the inviolable mistress of its own honor. . . . Nothing but humility is a match for pride. Humility puts it out of countenance" (*EL* 2:347). The superiority of humility rests not merely on some internal spiritual principle, but on what it *does to* its prideful adversary. In this final sense, the example of Samson is not so ill-adapted after all. But Emerson would still seem to prefer a story in which the hero is not obliged to share in his adversaries' bad end.[25]

Emerson follows with a second literary example of Holiness, this time cleaving more closely to the letter of original context, which he cites explicitly: "I know no more agreeable illustration of the superiority of this principle to the vulgar sentiment, than occurs in the novel of Manzoni, called *I Promessi Sposi,* a story in which the interest is drawn from the source of these higher sentiments" (2:347). Emerson goes to the trouble of not merely quoting but actually translating from the Italian some four pages from the novel, to restore what he finds to be "the most significant passages" which had been omitted from the English translation available to him.[26]

Emerson sets the scene: a "virtuous citizen" kills a "turbulent nobleman" during a street brawl; the citizen is struck with remorse, seeks sanctuary in a convent, and resolves to become a monk; as Father Cristoforo [bearer of Christ], the citizen-monk gains an invitation to the house of the slain nobleman's brother "to express his anguish and to entreat forgiveness" (2:347). The slain man's brother has elaborately staged the moment of apology as a public spectacle to "enhance his credit with the family and the world" (2:348). Cristoforo "penetrated the motive" of this staging, but accepts it.

Such is the friar's comportment, indeed, that he turns the public nature of the event to his advantage: his bearing is an example of "such an effusion of the inmost mind that in a whole crowd of spectators but one opinion shall be formed of what that mind is" (2:348), that is, an example of religious action that attains universality, commanding rather than swayed by the crowd. On the day of atonement, Cristoforo's countenance makes plain that he has not taken the steps of becoming a friar and seeking forgiveness "out of any fear of man. And this impression began to conciliate all parties" (2:348). Faced with the friar's humble confession and regret, the nobleman, who had initially stood "in an attitude of great disdain and compressed wrath," concedes that his brother "was a man a little choleric. But everything happens by the will of God. But speak no more of it" (2:349). He then interrupts the friar's repeated pleas for pardon:

> "Pardon," said the nobleman, "You have no need of it: But since you ask it, surely surely I pardon you with all my heart and all of us—"
>
> "All! All!" cried the bystanders with one voice. (2:349)

Emotional exclamations and embraces ensue. The following page, after the crowd has departed carrying the friar "as it were in triumph to the gate of the city" (2:350), finds the nobleman in a moment of solitary reflection:

> The master with emotion he had never before known thought over by himself the strange scene he had witnessed and the part he had himself acted and muttered between his teeth; "That devil of a Father!" (for we must needs recite his precise words) "that devil of a father! if he had remained there one moment longer on his knees, I verily believe I should have been down myself on the floor and asked his pardon for killing my brother." (2:350)

These are the final words from the lengthy passage of Manzoni's that Emerson reproduces, and he makes no further comment upon the example—these are the words it was his purpose to restore.[27] By leaving us with the proud nobleman's retrospection, Emerson emphasizes the dramatic results that the heroic power of Holiness can achieve. As a speech act, the holy man's humble petition performs with remarkable perlocutionary effectiveness.

He follows the Manzoni with a "real life" literary example that likewise "illustrates the ineffable *power* of the devout sentiment" (my emphasis); in this case, the holiness of a prisoner serves to "charm down" a jailer (2:350). Emerson had led into these examples with a definition reminiscent of "Religion" (1837): "The self-surrender to [the] moral sentiment, the acceptance of its dominion throughout our constitution as the beatitude of man, is Holiness" (2:346). In the examples, the self-surrender by the holy tends to bring about the surrender of others. These others may be rendered somewhat more holy through the encounter (though the nobleman is left cursing under his breath), but the unmistakable trend reveals Holiness as netting its practitioner both an internal and an external gain. One can, it appears, get away with murder—and be the better for it.

Building upon the above definition, Emerson declares Holiness the crown jewel of the lecture series: the self-surrender to the moral sentiment "is Holiness. And as students of Human Culture, I call your attention to the fact, that, the highest state of which we have any experience, is the act of adoration, the state in which, with perfect lowliness, we aspire. It is thus readily discriminated from Heroism" (2:346). But a curious circumstance of Emerson's presentation of the Human Culture lecture series problematizes this declaration.

Emerson sometimes concluded the series with "Holiness": the inspiring send-off, the pinnacle of Human Culture. Yet on other occasions, notably at Concord, he omitted this lecture (textual note, 2:340). What can it mean for Emerson to have made the claim that holiness is the "highest state"—and then sometimes not to have included this lecture in the series? End the series with "Heroism," with its "somewhat not holy," and the overall message changes considerably.

Holiness may be the highest state of which we have any experience, but life on the heights is evidently a bit precarious. A schematic look at the space Emerson reserves for Holiness may illustrate the fragility of the state as defined. It resides between the "two sad extremes" of Superstition and Atheism. Emerson begins by defining the baseline of Superstition—the lowest state of Human Culture, the zero point of fearful credulousness and no power. Atheism is likewise sad, but Emerson portrays it as not quite so powerless: it may miss out on the beauty of creation, but at least it does not lie supine before the idol of Tradition (2:342). The pathway from Superstition to Atheism leads toward increasing skepticism—but so does the pathway from Superstition to Holiness, up to a point. The desiderata:

FIGURE 3: Emersonian Power as a function of Skepticism. (Author's diagram)

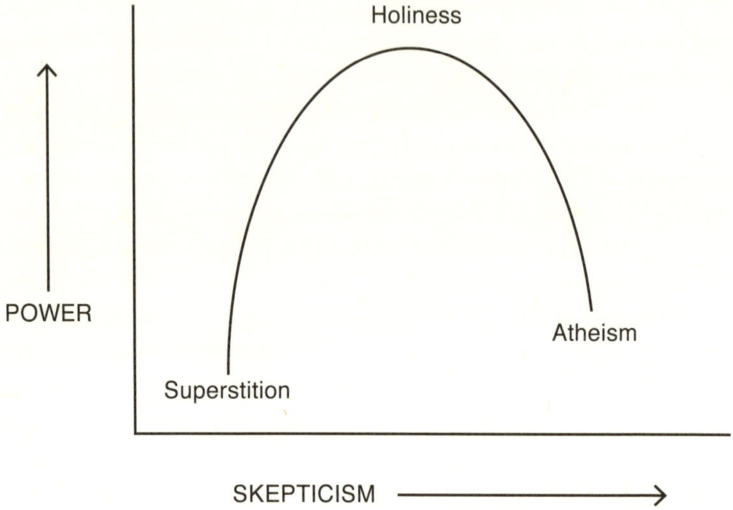

to maximize power but to moderate skepticism. The later criterion is more delicate than the former.

If we imagine a Cartesian plane with increasing skepticism corresponding to increasing horizontal values, and increasing power corresponding to higher vertical values, we can plot the positions of Superstition, Holiness, and Atheism (fig. 3).

The practitioner of Holiness must maintain a balanced skepticism to avoid slippery slopes on either side of this apex of power.

In Emerson's view of humanity, the slide into Superstition presents the more grievous and treacherous descent, the one to which human susceptibility most frequently falls victim. A familiar tendency rears its anthropomorphizing head: the root temptation of Superstition matches the tendency he had identified in "Religion" (1837). The danger lies in the propensity to personify or personate, and Emerson underscores this danger to frame the lecture on "Holiness."

In the first description of Superstition, Emerson observes that "the established religion of every people is always representing the divine agency as *personated* in a God quite external to the soul and the world; and, again, as *personated* in particular men, and particular actions" (*EL* 2:341). Toward the lecture's end, Emerson posits another impersonal formulation of the divine agency, this time as "the Cause of Causes" (2:352). In proper speech this "Essence" "refuses to be defined or personified" (2:353). But Emerson laments "the weakness which tends ever to degrade and falsify the religious sentiment by our importunate craving that it should be a *person* as an individual man is" (2:353; my emphases on "person" and "personated"). Emerson notes that to even begin to speak of this Essence with a third-person grammatical marker initiates the danger of personifying, and thus "I unsay as fast as I say my words" (2:353).

Persons dominate the sayable at all levels of society: "The talk of the kitchen and the cottage is exclusively occupied with persons" and with "the fortunes of persons"; "Go to the parlor and into fashionable society; the persons discussed are more conspicuous and graceful but the fact is the same." This habit of mind to dwell on persons (a habit which Emerson seems increasingly to find offensive in and of itself) infects the religious discourse of all classes. Even the "cultivated," though capable of contemplating the sublime "impersonality" of Beauty, fall into this trap: when they "speak of God they demand a biography of him as steadily as the kitchen and the barroom demand personalities of men" (2:354). Some of the most positive religious affirmations will thus betray, to "the devout mind," a "frozen unbelief." In comparison to the mild description of periodic belief in "Religion" (1837), Emerson's language grows more severe in "Holiness": "God will not make himself manifest to cowards" (2:355).

Though he ends with a prophetic call for "true culture" to "rid itself of superstition" (2:355), what has preceded this call all but guarantees the impossibility of its coming to fruition. The words "all" and "always" echo through Emerson's litanies on the personating reflex. Talking about holiness is playing with fire, a fire fueled by human proclivity. Though the highest state, holiness is a dangerous state. In this ambivalence, one suspects, lies the explanation for why Emerson only sometimes sees fit to provide his case for a careful "Holiness," and why at other times he might think best to omit this lecture when delivering his course on

Human Culture. By analogy, the original Human Life series opens with "The Doctrine of the Soul," which was given once in 1838 but probably not (says Spiller) in the abbreviated Human Life series as it was given in 1840. The view from the top is precipitous: avoiding the slippery slope to supine, personated superstition, Emerson dives for the relative haven of increased skepticism.

A later lecture also entitled "Religion" (January 1840), from the Present Age series, makes this preference for skepticism clear. Emerson again loudly laments that we can't escape superstitious personification. But he eliminates the cautions against atheism which "Holiness" maintained as a guardrail against unrestrained skepticism. As he discusses religion here in the context of "the present age," Emerson is perhaps more focused on the present moment of "transition" (*EL* 3:274, 275) than on any general loss of spiritual possibilities; but he may be speaking more directly from his current feelings on the topic. And the language has become positively vehement.

Whereas "Holiness" presented Superstition as one unfortunate state into which religion may lapse, "Religion" (1840) subsumes virtually all religious practice into this debased category. Emerson equates the superstition of the carnival sideshow with current established faith: "The idea of a revelation—see how degraded it is! The idea of a revelation which obtains in modern Christendom is, that, it is a telling of fortunes" (*EL* 3:276-77).

Whereas the first "Religion" (1837) lecture reported with joy the sounding of a "new call," in the 1840 reconsideration Emerson finds, sadly, "We are born too late for the old and too early for the new faith" (3:274). The new call as it is now audible can perform only the work of the negative:

> I see in those classes and those persons in whom I am accustomed to look for tendency and progress . . .—I see in them both skepticism and character; a clear enough perception of the inadequacy of the popular religious sentiment to the wants of the heart and intellect, and explicit declarations of this fact. They have insight and truthfulness; they will not mask their convictions; they hate cant; but more than this I do not readily find. The gracious motions of the soul, piety, adoration, I do not find. (3:274–75)

The two "positive" qualities Emerson discerns are "skepticism and character," and the latter quality consists simply of a willingness to express the former. To the religious question, as presently posed, the answer is skepticism. In "Holiness," Emerson sought to moderate skepticism and warned of skepticism's sad extreme. In "Religion" (1840), no such warning exists: "If this age is skeptical, it is because it loves the truth" (3:285). Though Emerson scarcely heralds the call to skepticism with joy, neither does he seek to keep it in check.

Religion by Other Means

The Problem

I like a church; I like a cowl;
I love a prophet of the soul;
And on my heart monastic aisles
Fall like sweet strains, or pensive smiles;
Yet not for all his faith can see
Would I that cowled churchman be. (ll. 1–6)[28]

The trajectory traceable from "Religion" (1837) to "Religion" (1840) brings Emerson to a religious halting point. In actions (and inactions) that correspond with these lectures, he completes, in several senses, a lingering vocational farewell. Emerson composes "The Problem" in 1839, drawing upon journal entries from the previous year, and he publishes it in *The Dial* in 1840. The poem bespeaks a mind prepared to put behind conclusively the labor of the pulpit.

We have previously considered his departure from the Second Church pastorship in 1832. Between 1839 and 1841, several other aspects of Emerson's ministry come to an end. He ceases to occupy the space of the minister, to speak at the time of the minister, or to address formally the topic of the minister. In January 1839, he delivers his last church sermon as a preacher of supply (though no longer a pastor of a particular congregation, he had continued to fill in for other ministers in the intervening years, often recycling his old sermons). By 1841, he ceases to speak publicly on Sundays, even in lectures apart from any official ministerial function. And, beginning the same year, the formal topic of "Religion" drops out of his repertoire. That he still loves the "sweet strains" of "a prophet of the soul" presents a problem. His sworn hatred of superstitious personation generates a few ingenious intermediate solutions.

The fate that befalls the Human Culture lecture series at Concord finds its way into book form. In *Essays: First Series* (1841), we get "Heroism," but nothing called "Holiness." In the essay version of "Heroism," Emerson retains the lecture's reminder that there is "somewhat not holy in it" (*CW* 2:148), the statement that opened the way for the subsequent consideration of "Holiness" in the lecture series. In the table of contents for the *Essays*, "The Over-Soul" (essay IX) appears to replace the latter in a sequential pairing with "Heroism" (essay VIII). Textually, "The Over-Soul" contains many long passages from "Religion" (no. 2, 1840), and also long passages from "Religion" (no. 1, 1837), but relatively little of "Holiness" (1838), most of which, as the editor of the *Early Lectures* notes, appears never to have been published under Emerson's auspices. The religious topics of the lectures, traditionally denominated, have vanished into transcendental entities. "Spiritual Laws" also gathers from both "Religion" lectures; "Self-Reliance," tellingly, gathers from the vehement second "Religion."

But the essay which, in some ways, does more of the work of "Holiness" is "Friendship." Emerson signals the topic's function in a passage on correspondence: "To my friend I write a letter, and from him I receive a letter. That seems to you a little. It suffices me. It is a spiritual gift worthy of him to give, and of me to receive. It profanes nobody. In these warm lines the heart will trust itself, as it will not to the tongue, and pour out the prophecy of a godlier existence than all the annals of heroism have yet made good" (*CW* 2:124). Friendship, then, replaces holiness, as a practice "godlier" than "heroism" (2:124). Compensatory to not-holy heroism (the not-holiness of which, after all, consisted of its seeming "not to know that other souls are of one texture with it" [2:148]), "Friendship demands a religious treatment" (2:123). At this juncture, Religion evidently does not. Though it may seem but "a little," Friendship may pick up the slack and perform some of the work of Holiness, but not *as* Holiness.

Friendship acts as an antidote to spiritual ills, for cheerless skepticism that has lapsed into the deadliest mortal sins: "O friend . . . Me too thy nobleness has taught / To master my despair" (*CW* 2:111). In the wake of the demoralized note of "Religion" (no. 2,1840)—"The gracious motions of the soul, piety, adoration, I do not find" (*EL* 3:275)—this proximity to nobleness "suffices" (*CW* 2:124).

In the context of a retreat from religion as such, the logic of "Friendship" appears to follow a path of compromise: if humanity persistently exhibits the fatal tendency to personify divinity, perhaps this impulse might be less noxiously channeled into the divinization of persons. That is, in friendship (outside of any formal religion and thus free of traditional superstition), one may retain in good faith a portion of the religious sentiment: this friendship "treats its object as a god, that it may deify both" (*CW* 2:127). But the friendly object enjoys only a precarious status as a person, as subsequent essays in the series refine the concept.

The essay on "Love" (which precedes "Friendship") similarly participates in the compromise inversion, in which the divinization of persons replaces the personation of divinity. It does so with the provision that the divinization of persons must ultimately impersonalize: "love, which is the deification of persons, must become more impersonal every day" (*CW* 2:108). In a two-word sentence Emerson suggests a religion-like practice that, ideally, would act toward no particular object: "Love prays" (2:108).

"The Over-Soul" distills this process of impersonalization and emphasizes the antisocial structure of nature: "Space is ample, east and west, / But two cannot go abreast, / Cannot travel in it two" (*CW* 2:157). Two may, perchance, shout across space to one another, but any conversation depends upon reference to a "third party." This (quasi-Leibnizian) third party that guarantees communication is not in any sense a third *person:* "that third party or common nature is not social; it is impersonal; is God" (2:164).

Again, the possibility of spiritual instruction, of ministry, is weak: "It is of no use to preach to me from without" (2:170). Although "all men stand continually in the expectation of such a teacher" as would preach from "within," *expectation* is the (quasi-Beckettian) key here, and the essay concludes that the soul "is no follower" (2:174). "The Over-Soul" accords with the impersonality of "Spiritual Laws" in which Emerson strategically utilizes an impersonal construction: "There is guidance" (*CW* 2:81).

"Circles," immediately following "The Over-Soul," continues the trend of impersonalization by renouncing even the desirability of a divinized other as posited in "Friendship" and "Love": "I thought, as I walked in the woods and mused on my friends, why should I play with them this game of idolatry? I know and see too well, when not voluntarily blind, the speedy limits of persons called high and worthy. . . . Every personal consideration that we allow costs us heavenly state" (*CW* 2:182).

With this renunciation of the personal as idolatry, Emerson comes out the other end of friendship's enchantment. "Friendship" had intimated the possibility of such a disenchantment, also by raising the specter of idolatry. Though "we pursue persons," we finally discover that "the persons are such as we." Why then should we overvalue their portion of divinity? "Let us drop this idolatry. . . . Let us even bid our dearest friends farewell, and defy them, saying, 'Who are you? Unhand me: I will be dependent no more'" (*CW* 2:126). He goes on to state that "I do then with my friends as I do with my books. I would have them where I can find them, but I seldom use them" (2:126). More frequent use, it seems likely, more speedily reveals "limits of persons" (2:182).

Infrequent use (as an aid to voluntary blindness), though perhaps the only prescription, is not the only condition for disenchantment's deferral. "Circles" declares as inevitable the discernment of "limits" in the other; prior to such revelations of the friend's finitude, Emerson describes how a rather agonistic model of "Friendship" may be sustained. Seek out, in your friend, that "great, defying eye, that scornful beauty of his mien and action"; "let him be to thee for ever a sort of beautiful enemy, untamable, devoutly revered, and not a trivial conveniency to be soon outgrown and cast aside" (*CW* 2:124). In the Human Life (1839) lecture series, Emerson averred that "a true man can never feel rivalry. All men are ministers to him" (*EL* 3:107). In "Friendship," Emerson further suggests that a taste of what untrue men experience as rivalry might do you some good, if viewed from a worshipful angle: "Worship his superiorities; wish him not less by a thought, but hoard and tell them all. Guard him as thy counterpart" (*CW* 2:124).

With an insight into the principles of mimetic desire, Emerson sees that it is the superior model/obstacle who is not to be "soon outgrown and cast aside" (2:124). The dark side of the Emersonian "true man's" acceptance of tutelage under the "beautiful enemy" is Dostoyevsky's "underground man," who perversely idolizes the superior who scorns him. Emerson explains that a friend reaches the point of being discarded when the "scornful beauty" (2:124) loses status: "If he were high enough to slight me, then could I love him, and rise by my affection to new heights" (2:182). The underground man tells another possible story that obeys the same dynamic: If he were high enough to slight me, then could I make him my obsession, and sink by my resentment to new depths.

Emerson has answered the question that Jean-Michel Oughourlian once posed to René Girard: "You are always referring to a subject who never gets the upper hand in his struggles with his rival. But the opposite can happen. What happens if the subject successfully gains possession of the object?"[29] Girard replies that once the object is obtained, "the subject sets off in search of a new model and a new object that will not let him down so easily. From this point, desire seeks only to find a resistance that it is incapable of overcoming" (*Things Hidden*, 297).

In the case of "Friendship," the object and the model are in a sense one, as the subject pursues friends out of a metaphysical desire: "I will receive from them, not what they have, but what they are" (*CW* 2:126). Emerson's desire for the friend is metaphysical in the technical sense that it is a "desire without object," a desire for "the *being* of the other." And once the Emersonian subject perceives that that being has been exhausted, a new friend, a new model of desire, must take the stage.

"Circles" presents the stronger theorization of transient, serial Emersonian friendship: "How often must we learn this lesson? Men cease to interest us when we find their limitations. The only sin is limitation. As soon as you once come up with a man's limitations, it is all over with him. Has he talents? has he enterprise? has he knowledge? it boots not. Infinitely alluring and attractive was he to you yesterday, a great hope, a sea to swim in; now, you have found his shores, found it a pond, and you care not if you never see it again" (*CW* 2:182-3). And again, the fuller statement of a friendship dependent upon the possibility of scornful insult: "The sweet of nature is love; yet, if I have a friend, I am tormented by my imperfections. The love of me accuses the other party. If he were high enough to slight me, then could I love him, and rise by my affection to new heights. A man's growth is seen in the successive choirs of his friends" (2:182). Emerson here expresses a key ambivalence: on the one hand, a sort of exasperation at the predictability of the dynamic—"How often must we learn this lesson?"; on the other hand, an optimistic formulation of the dynamic's coldest consequences—"growth" indicated by "successive" friendships.

Oughourlian expands on this point: "In effect, whether he succeeds or fails, the subject always courts failure. Rather than conclude that desire itself is a cul-de-sac, he can always find pretexts for coming to more favourable conclusions and giving desire one last chance. He is always ready to condemn the objects he has once possessed and the desires he has already experienced—the idols of yesteryear—at the very moment when a new idol or a new object comes over the horizon" (*Things Hidden*, 298). In light of the desperate optimism of this compulsive repetition, Girard remarks that "desire has its own logic, and it is a logic of gambling. Once past a certain level of bad luck, the luckless player does not give up" (298).

At this turn, Oughourlian brings Girard's reflections into an explicitly theological register: "People always refer to Pascal's famous wager about the existence of God as if it were the only one of its kind. What you have been saying amounts to what Pascal perceives when he theorizes about *divertissement*. Desire is also a kind of wager, but it is always a losing wager. Betting on the existence of God is therefore betting on a God radically other than the God of desire, a non-violent and benevolent, rather than a violent and perpetually frustrating, divinity" (298). The Unitarians, notably Channing, bet on a certain sort of nonviolent God. How does Emerson place his bets?

Unlike the puppet of desire, who stumbles inexorably onward "without being able to recognize" the serial pursuit of model/obstacles "as the pursuit of failure," Emerson recognizes the precariousness of the pursuit of religion by other means. Which is not to say that he counts this pursuit a pure "failure"—as a series of experiments, successive friendships are not devoid of edification; and a certain precariousness is not inappropriate for the author who announces in this same essay that he is an "endless seeker" resolved to "unsettle all things" (*CW* 2:188).[30] But he is willing to make a wager on the existence of a God beyond the dynamics of alternately frustrated and disillusioned desire: "O my brothers, God exists" (*CW* 2:81). It is a wager with careful stipulations; Emerson refers to this God as "it": "It has . . . infused its strong enchantment into nature" (81). These credos appear in the same paragraph of "Spiritual Laws" in which Emerson offers that most impersonal of assurances: "there is guidance."

In the midst of his rejection of idolized persons, Emerson interjects a fervid confession: "O blessed Spirit, whom I forsake for these, they are not thou!" (*CW* 2:182). In the acknowledgment of what is forsaken in the substitution of friendship for holiness, Emerson verges on personation. His apostrophe to the blessed Spirit takes a "whom," not a "which." Human language ever threatens to betray true holiness. Of which topic (*as* a topic), it would consequently appear, the less said the better.

This discussion has brought us into the midst of what Len Gougeon calls "The Silent Years"—years which we can now understand to have been silent in another sense. Consider the table of contents for *Essays, Second Series* (1844): The Poet, Experience, Character, Manners, Gifts, Nature, Politics, Nominalist and Realist, New England Reformers—not even an "Over-soul" in this gathering. We are now in a position to consider, from the perspective of the earlier career, what happens when Emerson breaks the silence with "Worship." We will make our final approach by calculating the stakes Emerson lays down in preparing the way for "Worship" within *The Conduct of Life.*

The Place of "Worship" in The Conduct of Life

In 1859, Emerson records intimations of a terminus: "[I] sometimes believe that I have no new thoughts, and that my life is quite at an end." Around this same time, Emerson is putting the finishing touches on *The Conduct of Life* (1860). If Emerson indeed senses that he has no new thoughts to set down—that "Fancy departs" (as he writes in the poem "Terminus")—we might do well to look all the more carefully at the work he does to arrange the given thoughts he finds before him as he shapes the Conduct lecture series into a *book,* a finished expression of the end of a life.

Robert Spiller finds that "*The Conduct of Life* marks the culmination of Emerson's work" ("Ralph Waldo Emerson," 385). By "culmination," Spiller means more than a sense of ending or completion, as he also expressly praises Emerson's literary accomplishment: *Conduct* and *English Traits* are "his two ripest and roundest books" (384), and "never up to the moment of his death did he equal the achievement of *The Conduct of Life*" (386). Gertrude Reif Hughes, concurring with Lawrence Buell, also finds the book to be a culmination in terms of both life and literature:

"*The Conduct of Life* is 'Emerson's most sophisticated book in terms of literary structure,' and the last one composed by Emerson himself without the editorial assistance of James Elliot Cabot" (2). We have, in our survey of the career, perhaps given some sense of the ripening process that produced the "unfallen fruit" ("Terminus") he gathers for this work. But we also need to consider the roundness of it, that is, the shape Emerson gives to it as a complete, polished book.

Richard Lee Francis urges that "we need to take more seriously than we have in the past the fact that most of Emerson's essays are contained in volumes that were arranged with some care in their ordering" ("Necessitated Freedom," 73). Francis cites two other notables whose judgments of *Conduct* corroborate the high opinions cited above, judgments that point to a basic flaw in the history of its criticism: "Despite the fact that Carlyle called it the 'best of all' Emerson's books, and more recently Josephine Miles saw it as his 'most coherent work,' *The Conduct of Life* has suffered from enlarged attention to its opening essay, 'Fate.' Such an approach has tended to distort not only the balance and weight of the essay in relation to the whole but to disrupt the total coherence of the work" (73–74). As Francis (and, subsequently, Lopez and Newfield) have noted, this distortion is due in no small part to Stephen Whicher's *Freedom and Fate,* but perhaps even more so, it can be traced to Whicher's influential "organic anthology," which concludes with the essays "Fate" and "Illusions." Joel Porte's 1983 Library of America edition made the remainder of the essays more accessible, and a continued enlargement of scholarly attention to the book as whole should eventually follow from the 2003 appearance of *Conduct,* edited by Barbara Packer, Joseph Slater, and Douglas Emory Wilson, as a volume in the ongoing standard Harvard edition.[31]

Though "Fate" may no longer stand as *the* inevitable locus of critical attention, *The Conduct of Life* remains a big, dense work, and scholars tend to privilege a key passage or two in narrowing their studies to a manageable scope. Even Francis, who provides the most thorough and balanced study of the book's architecture, does not deny himself a vantage point for reading the whole from the perspective of a "pivotal" moment: "Since others [Whicher and Bishop] have devoted themselves to rhetorical analysis, I should like to examine the hierarchical structure. Such an approach begins with the definition of 'Fate' as the ground from which the next five essays evolve, culminating in the pivotal essay with the misleading title, 'Considerations By the Way'" (74).

Others have nominated "Behavior" as the key essay: Gertrude Reif Hughes calls it "the neglected central chapter of *The Conduct of Life*. . . .The essay is neither resigned nor homely but rather central in both the arithmetical and Emersonian senses" (2, 5; Hughes here alludes to the fact that "Behavior" appears as fifth in a series of nine essays, and thus its "arithmetical" centrality happily coincides with its Emersonian importance in advancing the challenges of a demanding optimism). Julie Ellison also makes "Behavior" central, a logical move in a study that helpfully locates Emerson's *The Conduct of Life* within the tradition of "conduct literature," and in particular within the American strain, which conceives of its task as addressing " 'behavior' or 'manners' as the problem of social difference in a republic" (Ellison, "Transparency," 601, 587).[32] Ellison's contextualization within the book-of-manners genre is compelling, though one might also note that "the conduct of life" (not incompatibly) appears to have been a traditional sermon title of some long standing.

The present study claims no exception to this tendency to grant the spotlight to a particular essay. one hopes, nevertheless, to justify the choice as something other than arbitrary. Our particular focus will be "Worship," an essay critics have praised, while nevertheless intimating that it may indeed contain, as Emerson feared, "no new thoughts." Francis calls Emerson's "Worship" "one of his most searching explorations. . . . 'Worship' is an essay which . . . harks back to an earlier Emersonian concern (most notably in the Divinity School Address): religion and its particular manifestation" (*"Necessitated Freedom,"* 82).[33] So if we hope to learn something new from an essay that may contain very little new material, our tack might be to consider the way Emerson shuffles the deck. Happily in this regard, Emerson wears his dealing strategy rather plainly on his sleeve.

Though Francis finds "Considerations by the Way" to be "pivotal," he does not miss the weight Emerson grants to "Worship": "Within the structure of *The Conduct of Life*, this essay is particularly important because its opening paragraph pauses to acknowledge the strategy that is essential to the series: that dialectical structure in which Emerson has frequently played the 'devil's attorney'" (82). But the beginning of

"Worship" is only one of several important points at which Emerson pauses to discuss his strategy; most of the other pertinent structuring passages have gone unremarked in the criticism. Taken together, these passages make quite clear Emerson's intentions about the structure of the book leading up to "Worship."

Acknowledging its origins on the lecture circuit, "Fate" rapidly contextualizes the motivating impulse behind the entire book. Emerson launched the project at a time when a variety of famous personages had been speaking and writing on "the Spirit of the Times."[34] To Emerson, "however, the question of the times resolved itself into a practical question of the conduct of life. How shall I live?" (*CW* 6:1). Emerson proposes a method for approaching this "riddle": "If one would study his own time, it must be by this method of taking up in turn each of the leading topics which belong to our scheme of human life, and, by firmly stating all that is agreeable to experience on one, and doing the same justice to the opposing facts in the others, the true limitations will appear. Any excess of emphasis, on one part, would be corrected, and a just balance would be made" (6:2). In this opening passage, Emerson gives one example of this balancing act that will be played out first in the first and second essays, "Fate" and "Power":

> If we must accept Fate, we are not less compelled to affirm liberty, the significance of the individual, the grandeur of duty, the power of character. This is true, and that other is true. But our geometry cannot span these extreme points, and reconcile them. What to do? By obeying each thought frankly, by harping, or, if you will, pounding on each string, we learn at last its power. By the same obedience to other thoughts, we learn theirs, and then comes some reasonable hope of harmonizing them. We are sure, that, though we know not how, necessity does comport with liberty, the individual with the world, my polarity with the spirit of the times. (*CW* 6:2)

So far, the dialectical method is quite clear. But what principles might structure the "leading topics" that make up the table of contents of the whole book: "Fate," "Power," "Wealth," "Culture," "Behavior," "Worship," "Considerations by the Way," "Beauty," "Illusions"?[35] The simplest and most direct clues come from Emerson's asides to the reader, as in the essay "Power": "I have not forgotten that there are sublime considerations which limit the value of talent and superficial success. We can easily overpraise the vulgar hero. There are sources on which we have not drawn. I know what I abstain from. I adjourn what I have to say on this topic to the chapters on Culture and Worship" (*CW* 6:42). This rhetorical cue of adjourning begins to reveal that the dialectic transpires not only between individual essays (though it often does) but also between groups of essays. In the midst of the second essay, Emerson adjourns remarks of another kind until essays 4 through 6, looking beyond essay 3. Though "Power" opposes "Fate" in the first accounting, there may be another reckoning whereby "Fate" and "Power" along with "Wealth" (presented by Emerson as a means of power, as well as a product) all reside on the same side of the ledger, to be countered by a second list.[36]

Two passages from "Worship" bring this scheme more sharply into focus. The first of these passages identifies (and then discounts) the skeptical grouping on the ledger:

> I see not why we should give ourselves such sanctified airs. If the Divine Providence has hid from men neither disease, nor deformity, nor corrupt society, . . . let us not be so nice that we cannot write these facts down coarsely as they stand, or doubt but there is a counter-statement as ponderous, which we can arrive at, and which, being put, will make all square. The solar system has no anxiety about its reputation, and the credit of truth and honesty is as safe; nor have I any fear that a skeptical bias can be given by leaning hard on the sides of fate, of practical power, or of trade, which the doctrine of Faith cannot down-weigh. The strength of that principle is not measured in ounces and pounds: it tyrannizes at the centre of Nature. We may well give skepticism as much line as we can. The spirit will return, and fill us. It drives the drivers. It counterbalances any accumulations of power. (*CW* 6:107)

Emerson has begun by "pounding" on the strings of skepticism, "leaning hard on the sides of fate, of practical power, [and] of trade": these are the first three essays, "Fate," "Power," and "Wealth."[37] But the "doctrine of Faith" counters these calculations. This doctrine emerges through essays

4 and 5, "Culture" and "Behavior," then culminates and receives its proper name in the sixth essay, "Worship": "In the last chapters, we treated some particulars of the question of culture. But the whole state of man is a state of culture; and its flowering and completion may be described as Religion, or Worship" (*CW* 6:108). "Worship" then, marks the pinnacle of Emerson's topical survey. This leaves open the question of what work the final three essays will perform, though it does clarify what they are not: "Considerations by the Way," "Beauty," and "Illusions" do not correspond to higher topics in a continuation of the series; nor are they needed to correct any balance—the first six essays achieve "completion" (108) as far as the "whole state of man" is concerned. Though a careful examination exceeds the bounds of the present study, I would suggest that essays 7 through 9 represent three distinct types of inquiry that Emerson, having ascended the highest peak, finds himself in a position to view. They correspond, respectively, to the three transcendental categories: the good, the beautiful, and the true. "Considerations" considers practical reason, "Beauty" examines judgment (in a rather scientistic vein), and "Illusions" critiques (not purely in the negative sense) pure reason. But all proceed from the vantage point gained in "Worship" (perhaps here we find an inversion of the Kantian trajectory of reason's critique making room for faith: in *Conduct,* faith makes room for an assessment and affirmation of the limits of reason).

Another return to the lecture record reaffirms the climactic importance of "Worship" in Emerson's conception of the Conduct series. As Merton L. Sealts, Jr., has noted, "Worship" was the lecture with which Emerson most frequently concluded the series while on the lecture circuit. Other titles changed or were shuffled in the order, but "Worship" remained almost constantly in the final slot. "Worship" was the final message Emerson sent audiences home with in the most complete (and most completely documented) instances of the series, as in Pittsburgh (March–April 1851), Boston (December 1851–January 1852), Cincinnati (December 1852), and St Louis (December 1852–January 1853) (Sealts, *Emerson on the Scholar*, 234–35, 241; Charvat, "Chronological"). The new chapters he adds for the book could scarcely be called afterthoughts, but they are thoughts that come after, reflections that Emerson finds himself qualified to make in the light of the series that precedes them.

In writing—and in fact preaching—a series on the "conduct of life" that works its way up gradually to the high point of "Worship," Emerson fulfills one model of the ideal minister as envisioned by Harriet Beecher Stowe in her 1859 novel *The Minister's Wooing.* Though Stowe displays obvious admiration for the protagonist Dr. H (modeled upon Samuel Hopkins, theological successor of Jonathan Edwards), she also notes his limitations. Some scholars' presentations of the novel have eagerly overemphasized Stowe's criticism of stern, puritanical religion. But Dr. H also serves as an important model for Stowe, as his high theological seriousness undergirds his uncompromising condemnations of slavery, which he persists in voicing despite the threat of alienating wealthy members of his congregation.[38] His unwavering approach to this moral topic holds clear appeal for Stowe, yet in other ways, Dr. H's failure to consider his audience leads to an inadvertent and unnecessary alienation of his flock. Stowe's narrator observes that the good-hearted Dr. H might be more successful in reaching his congregation were he to address a wider scope of topics from the pulpit, working his way upward toward the spiritual. But, the narrator laments, Dr. H was interested only in leaping directly to the "top rung" of worship, not in working his way through the entire "conduct of life" (53). Emerson, writing after any such rung-leaping minister, self-consciously adopts, in his stepwise *Conduct of Life,* precisely the neglected course that Stowe prescribes. Though, as we have heard, some listeners still faulted Emerson for "sermonizing" too much in "Worship," they cannot claim that he has leaped to this spiritual topic (and its attendant moral concerns with slavery) without preparation.

We have noted the accumulation of explicit cues in *Conduct* that point to a special purpose for "Worship": how Emerson declares, in "Fate," that he will consider the topics of life in order; how he hints, in "Power," that he is keeping something up his sleeve that will later astound us; how he affirms, in "Worship," that the principle of faith completes culture and counterbalances all that has come before. But what issue is "Worship" supposed to settle, exactly; and in what way and to what extent might it be said to settle it?

"How shall I live my life?"

The Conduct of Life: the title of the book itself provides the first riddle. The most conventional meaning of the title is the one people usually have in mind when buying a "conduct" or "self-help" book: in this sense conduct refers to "the action or manner of conducting, directing, managing or carrying on any business, performance, process, course, etc." and is said "of the business or the thing" (OED, 6a). That is, "the conduct of life" would be expected to provide a program for carrying out the business of life. The OED finds Emerson's title to be sufficiently unambiguous as to list his "*The Conduct of Life* (1860)" as the prime example of this definition of "conduct."

But this pragmatic meaning is not the only possibility Emerson's book offers. Another meaning of "the conduct of life," most evident in the catalogs of woe and misfortune that "Fate" unflinchingly reports, is an *evaluative* one. In *The Conduct of Life,* Emerson has written out a report card for Life's conduct, with demerits duly noted: life has been exhibiting disturbing and disruptive behavior lately—counseling may be necessary.

A third meaning, like the second, also animates or attributes agency to this thing called "Life." This meaning depends upon the definition of "conduct" as "guidance" or "leading" and is said "of the person or the thing that leads" (*OED,* 1a). A useful example comes from a simile penned by Spenser: "As a ship, that through the Ocean wyde, By conduct of some star, doth make her way" (*Amoretti* XXIV). The conducting star Spenser has in mind appears in an 1852 (conduct) book by Louisa Payson Hopkins, *The Guiding Star; or, The Bible, God's Message,* a volume owned by Emerson (Harding, 140):

> "Would it be consistent with benevolence for God to leave men without a revelation?"
>
> "I should think not," said James.
>
> "Why not?"
>
> "Why, if men cannot be happy without doing right, it must be necessary to their happiness to know what *is* right. And a benevolent being would give them whatever was necessary for their happiness."
>
> "But, then," said Fanny, "could they not have found out what was right, and what was wrong, for themselves? I thought conscience was given for that."
>
> "So it is, my dear; but conscience, since man has fallen, is not an infallible guide. It needs to be enlightened by the word of God." (*Guiding Star,* 16–17)

In the passages of *Conduct* that grant the most weight to fate, the scripture Emerson substitutes for this guiding authority is a text authored by life: "We must accept an irresistible dictation" ("Fate," 943). Like Luther's *sola scriptura,* it is a self-interpreting document: "if there be irresistible dictation, this dictation understands itself" (943). In this third meaning, the terms of the conventional "conduct book" expectations have been reversed. "The Conduct of Life" is not, in this account, about *how to lead your life.* It is about *how life leads you.*

Even the simple question Emerson sets out early as the keynote of the text echoes this divergence: "How shall I live my life?" This question does not necessarily answer to the expectations of "conduct books" either. In the choice of "shall," one might discern the invisible hand of fate. "How shall I live my life?" is not quite the same as the less-predetermined "How will I live my life?" and certainly not as simply ethical as "How should I live my life?"[39] To ask how I *shall* live my life is not necessarily to undertake a program of deciding between options; it may be to inquire about individual destiny, as the passages that follow observe with some irony: "We can only obey our own polarity. 'Tis fine for us to speculate and elect our course, if we must accept an irresistible dictation" (943). With these meanings put into play, Emerson proceeds to oscillate throughout the book on the question of life's "conduct," between leading and being led: "This is true, and that other is true" (943).

If this issue were to receive a resolution, the architecture of the book would suggest that we might find it in "Worship." "Does Emerson," asks O. W. Firkins of "Worship," "finally succeed in writing the lofty chant which the opening of the essay had foreshadowed? Yes and No" (220). The first words of "Worship," looking back upon the earlier essays (in fact, looking back upon their earlier setting as parts of a lecture series), seem to herald the arrival at a higher platform:

> Some of my friends have complained, when the preceding papers were read, that we discussed Fate, Power, and Wealth, on too low a platform; gave too much line to the evil spirit of the times; too many cakes to Cerberus; that we ran Cudworth's risk of making, by excess of candor, the argument of atheism so strong, that he could not answer it. I have no fears of being forced in my own despite to play, as we say, the devil's attorney. I have no infirmity

> of faith; no belief that it is of much importance what I or any man may say: I am sure that a certain truth will be said through me, though I should be dumb, or though I should try to say the reverse. Nor do I fear skepticism for any good soul. A just thinker will allow full swing to his skepticism. I dip my pen in the blackest ink, because I am not afraid of falling into my inkpot. (*CW* 6:107)

Emerson completes this boldly self-deprecating disclaimer with a confident flourish: "We are of different opinions at different hours, but we always may be said to be at heart on the side of truth" (6:107). The invocation of the lecture context invites us to associate each of these "hours" with one or another of the occasions within the series "when the preceding papers were read." A new hour, the worship hour, has rolled around, so we might now think it would be time for something "different," a more affirming side of the truth. But as Firkins observes, something curious happens: "We anticipate a counterblast to the negations, but no, we are shortly served with a diatribe on the faithlessness and godlessness of our own time, in which the iconoclasm and the energy of the sinning essays on Fate, Power, and the like are only too faithfully reproduced. Cerberus has had another cake; one begins to fear that the surliness of that ill-conditioned animal may speedily be augmented by dyspepsia" (220).

But further reports of life's poor conduct are not all that "Worship" contains, nor is this sometimes darkly satiric catalog of infidelities the only feature of the essay to have attracted mention.[40] The concluding stroke of "Worship," not altogether unjustly, has drawn the most attention, in its solemn celebration of paradox. Emerson finally offers up not different news, but a different perspective on the news: "And so I think that the last lesson of life, the choral song which rises from all elements and all angels, is, a voluntary obedience, a necessitated freedom. Man is made of the same atoms as the world is, he shares the same impressions, predispositions, and destiny. When his mind is illuminated, when his heart is kind, he throws himself joyfully into the sublime order, and does, with knowledge, what the stones do by structure" (*CW* 6:128). Emerson calls this "the last lesson of life"—it seems we can stop holding our breath, waiting for the big payoff. The lesson actually quite closely resembles the solution hit upon by the much-maligned Cudworth: in his *True Intellectual System of the Universe*, the Cambridge Platonist's response to the challenge of materialistic determinism was to propose what he called a "willed necessity."[41] The first lesson of *The Conduct of Life*, in the conclusion of "Fate," calls for praise of the "Beautiful Necessity" (*CW* 6:26–27). In "Worship," Emerson gives this concept a philosophical twist: necessity is not merely held up as beautiful but may also be seen as wedded to free will. Emerson's "necessitated freedom" and "voluntary obedience"[42] complete his Cudworthian synthesis of the freedom/fate oscillation in *Conduct*.[43] Each pairing approaches the mixed concept by modification from a different pole. "Freedom" becomes necessity; "Obedience" becomes will. By conduct of such terms, necessity becomes beautiful.

But before this grand stroke, along the way in "Worship," an overlooked dynamic emerges. A complementary oscillation briefly appears within, before vanishing back into, the freedom versus fate antinomy. Before moving to his resolution of freedom and fate, Emerson considers the problematic question of self versus other in the determination of conduct. It is the possibilities of this secondary dynamic that the final section of the present chapter will attempt to preserve, against the philosophical tendency of *The Conduct of Life* to subsume its own interest in this "practical question" (*CW* 6:1). Though not given ultimate emphasis, the question of the other bears centrally on the book's status as "conduct" literature, while also touching on the larger freedom/fate complex. Somewhat unexpectedly, self bears the stamp of fate, while other may offer a kind of liberation. "We can only obey our own polarity": this obedience to our "own polarity" is fate (6:1–2). But someone else's polarity might change everything.

"My best gift from God"

In 1859, when Emerson records his fear that he has "no new thoughts," he finds this condition relieved only by the chance presence of a person who acts upon him (and his polarity) with a force of "magnetism." Why should he depend upon encounters with such persons? "Because in my bones is none of the magnetism that flows in theirs. They inundate all men with their streams." These persons recall the acknowledged moral exemplars of "Worship": "such persons are nearer to the secret of God than others;

are bathed by sweeter waters; they hear notices, they see visions, where others are vacant" (*CW* 6:115).

The above passage is the second point in the essay at which the counsel of blessed *persons* appears as an antidote to the infidelity of the times. The first instance prepares the way a few pages prior. After the introduction, followed by the streak of more bad news, the first relief from the litany comes at the following key juncture: "Even well-disposed, good sort of people are touched with the same infidelity, and for brave, straightforward action, use half-measures and compromises. . . . Only those can *help in counsel or conduct* who did not make a party pledge to defend this or that, but who were appointed by God Almighty, before they came into the world, to stand for this which they uphold" (6:113; my emphasis). This passage in "Worship" is about as close as Emerson gets to directly answering the book's opening "practical question of the conduct of life" (6:1): only those with a divine calling can "help in counsel or conduct." Though not the traditional ministers—those found among the "dead men of routine" or "official men" (6:113) to which Emerson opposes the appointees of "God Almighty"—these uncompromising counselors fulfill a ministerial vocation on a personal level.[44] In commenting upon this passage, William Scheick supplies a useful working definition: "Emerson understands the function of the prophet in the Old Testament sense; they do not predict the future, but rather they are preaching men of action who believe themselves to be the mouthpieces of Yahweh and the instruments of his creative design."[45] But his further commentary, that "everyone latently possesses the gift of prophecy in some form" (98), though generally true to the Emersonian spirit, somewhat obscures what I find distinctive about this turn. What stands out here is not another assurance of the capacity for self-authorization, but the idea that one would seek guidance from a preacher, that one would no longer refuse a good model. Overall, though, I concur with Scheick's insight that "Emerson, in the later phase of his career reflected in 'Worship,' realizes more than ever before the difficulty the prophet faces in trying to erect his church" (101). The Emersonian self on display here is willing both to preach and be preached to, but seems less than confident about independent acts of prophetic founding.

The very fact and circumstances of Emerson's public performances of this text further testify to the significance of this passage. As we have already noted, this essay derives from a lecture, the delivery of which was an occasion for Emerson's return to the Sunday pulpit. We should not be surprised that this text, however briefly, theorizes a space for a ministerial calling. That space begins to open up with the ebb tide of transcendental self-sufficiency.

Emerson confesses, "'Tis remarkable that our faith in ecstasy consists with total inexperience of it" (*CW* 6:113). David Robinson has usefully emphasized this passage in reading an Emersonian turn toward pragmatism and ethical purpose. As one consequence of this lack of individual ecstatic religious experience—the waning sense of which characterizes what I am calling the "aftermath" of the American Renaissance—faith seeks to replenish itself through a desire with an external dimension. This external motion of self toward other intrinsically acknowledges "the superiority that has no superior; the redeemer and instructor of souls, as it is their primal essence, is love" (6:116). As a corollary, a "loss of faith" will be marked by a corresponding "loss of attraction to other minds" (6:116).

In our survey of Emerson's writings on the topic of religion, we noted a problematic with "persons" and divinity that leads up to a period of silence on the topic: "Religion" (1837), with its insistence upon the impersonality of the deity, proceeds to "Holiness" (1838), with its emphasis on power and warnings against a personating superstition that would sap that power, and gives way to "Religion"(no. 2; 1840), with its unrestrained skepticism toward a current state of belief seemingly incapable of evading such superstition. The importance given to "Worship" in *The Conduct Of Life*, and the prominence given to the consideration of persons within that essay, suggests a softening of the logic that led up to the break of 1839 when Emerson ceased all preaching activities and the break of 1840 when he dismissed the topic. Michael Colacurcio, citing Barbara Packer, observes that "none of Emerson's fablings of the Universal Plot can find any part for a personal God; nor can his mature, self-trusting soul find much sympathy for those which can. We do, Emerson appeared to feel, grow out of that."[46] In particular, Colacurcio reads the Divinity School Address (1838) as working toward Emerson's "sense of what worship might mean in a world where God no longer figures as a person" (22).[47] But in a later trajectory that ends in "Worship," it may be that Emerson himself outgrows his lack of sympathy for souls wanting in absolute self-trust. Emerson may have "appeared to feel," in 1838, that we could outgrow the need to personify when thinking about worship. Yet in his successive lectures on "Religion," Emerson seems to notice that although *he* has outgrown what he called the "noxious exaggeration" of the personal, "we" stubbornly seem constitutionally unfit to do so when we turn to worship. This realization leaves Emerson quite bitter on the topic for a while; his bitterness comes through most vehemently in the second "Religion" lecture (1840), in which he tends to lump all religion into the category of idolatrous superstition. How can he, in good faith, continue to encourage the pursuit of religious experience when that pursuit so tends to betray us? A few intermediate compromises to accommodate our weakness appear in *Essays, First Series* (1841)—a shift of emphasis to a human scale, to a divinized friend as a surrogate minister, a surrogate deity—but the consideration of religion as a proper topic drops out of his repertoire for several years.

By *Representative Men* (published 1850, from lectures given as a series beginning in 1845 and continuing virtually up to the time of the first delivery of the sermon called "Worship" in 1847), Emerson is still not ready for a full-fledged broaching of the topic, but he is ready to reconsider compromise, as he moves from disparaging personhood to provisionally allowing for the less-than-ideal fact that we do inevitably personify. The anthropomorphizing tendency reveals itself, as Emerson has previously noted, in the history of religion: "Our colossal theologies of Judaism, Christism, Buddhism, Mahometism, are the necessary and structural action of the human mind. . . . Our theism is the purification of the human mind. Man can paint or make or think nothing but man" ("The Uses of Great Men," *CW* 4:4).

Here acknowledgment of the fatal tendency does not kill the discussion entirely, even if the religious dimension formally falls out. If we can think nothing but persons, is there not some use to which we can put this necessary and structural action of the human mind? In a passage from "The Uses of Great Men" that anticipates the social aspects of "Worship" (*CW* 6:113–16), Emerson looks to the possibilities of the other:

> If now we proceed to inquire into the kinds of service we derive from others, let us be warned of the danger of modern studies, and

> begin low enough. We must not contend against love, or deny the substantial existence of other people. I know not what would happen to us. We have social strengths. Our affection towards others creates a sort of vantage or purchase which nothing will supply. I can do that by another which I cannot do alone. I can say to you what I cannot first say to myself. Other men are lenses through which we read our own minds. Each man seeks those of different quality from his own, and such as are good of their kind; that is, he seeks other men, and *the otherest.* (*CW* 4:4; emphasis in original)

Even so, "the addressing to a human being thoughts out of a certain height, and presupposing his intelligence" is rare in the extreme, "possible in *personal* intercourse scarcely twice in a lifetime" (*CW* 4:10; my emphasis). And the problem is not just the infrequency of opportunity: "Direct giving [of "metaphysical aid" from "superior" persons] is agreeable to the early belief of men. . . . The boy believes there is a teacher who can sell him wisdom" (*CW* 4:5); Emerson here implies the immaturity of those who seek such personal guidance. Moreover the nature of things militates against the success of such instruction: "In strictness, we are not much cognisant of direct serving. . . . Gift is contrary to the law of the universe" (4:5–6).

With direct personal inspiration effectively ruled out, "indirect service is left. Men have a pictorial or representative quality, and serve us in the intellect" (4:6). And even with the compromise of inspiration through representation, the old danger lurks: "Our delight in reason degenerates into idolatry of the herald" (4:11).

Moving beyond such inhibitions, passages from "Worship" in *The Conduct of Life* (1860) feature an even greater acceptance of this risk of turning to the other, not merely as removed and representative, but as a personal guide "appointed by God" and "nearer to the secret of God" who might "help with counsel or conduct" (*CW* 6:113, 115). At some point, the experiment of turning to persons has become an acceptable one for the endless seeker.

The position of a possible other-reliance entertained in "Worship" corresponds to an insight passed down by his Aunt Mary Moody Emerson, a memory that resurfaces in 1867, beyond the end of *Conduct:* "Social affections also are part of Nature & being, and the delight in another's superiority is, as M.M.E. said, 'my best gift from God.' For here the moral nature is involved, which is higher than the intellectual" (October–November 1867).

Such a gift the younger Emerson had felt obligated to reject: at base, he could not accept it to be true. Another moment from 1833, the year of Emerson's spiritual face-off with Milton, points up the sense of impossibility: "It occurred with sad force how much we are bound to be true to ourselves—(the old string)—. . . . The truth is, you can't find any example that will suit you, could not, if the whole family of Adam should pass in procession before you, for you are a new work of God" (September 16, 1833; *EJ* 117). In all its absolutism ("you can't find any example"), even this declaration of independence contains the seeds of a desire for something else: the revelation of a necessary self-reliance strikes him with "sad force." A more joyful insight might be the discovery of an exemplary other.

By "Worship" he is willing (albeit "suspiciously and very slowly" [CW 6:115]) to receive such a gift. But he finds, as he discloses in the essay's conclusion, that the gift is most often withheld. In his final, stark hymn of worship, he must find a way to make do without it:

> There will be a new church founded on moral science. . . . Was never stoicism so stern and exigent as this shall be. It shall send man home to his central solitude, shame these social, supplicating manners, and make him know that much of the time he must have himself to his friend. He shall expect no coöperation, he shall walk with no companion. The nameless Thought, the nameless Power, the superpersonal Heart,—he shall repose alone on that. (*CW* 6:128)

The practical crux drives home the lesson that "much of the time he must have himself" as his only companion. Stern as this passage is, its obedience to necessity is not quite so voluntary as to claim this lonesome state of affairs as optimal.

If this be self-reliance, it does not quite settle for the no-exceptions advice to "insist on yourself; never imitate" (*CW* 2:47).[48] "Worship," in the conjunction between its conclusion and its earlier statement of desire for the help of a spiritual exemplar, offers a more contingent directive:

Find role models if you can, but sometimes, kid, you're all you've got. Waiting to lead a life, our lonely mortal finds only life to lead him: "The Laws are his consolers. . . . They animate him with the leading of great duty, and an endless horizon" (*CW* 6:128). This guide to conduct, this "leading of great duty," is ultimately an impersonal leading: "The religion which is to guide and fulfill the present and coming ages, whatever else it be, must be intellectual. The scientific mind must have a faith which is science. . . . Let us not be pestered with assertions and half-truths, with emotions and snuffle" (6:128). Emerson here insists that, above all, religion must be "intellectual"; in the name of this priority, "emotions" are banished, and, in the subsequent passage (cited earlier) about the new church to be founded on moral science, the "social" is shamed. To some extent this "stern" stoicism aligns with the strained masculinity of his stated distaste for a contemporary religion that, twice in the course of "Worship," he criticizes as "unmanly and effeminating" (6:110) or as a practice that "effeminates" (6:127). But his later reflections on the wisdom of Aunt Mary Moody Emerson, as well as the interpersonally oriented passages earlier in "Worship" itself, tell a different story: "Social affections also are part of Nature & being . . . here the moral nature is involved, which is higher than the intellectual." In those passages of "Worship" where Emerson finds himself inclined to accept "my best gift from God," "the delight in another's superiority," he does so on a personal level, inverting the hierarchy in which persons have primarily a "representative quality, and serve us in the intellect" ("Uses of Great Men," *CW* 4:6). In "Worship," the possibility surfaces that a person might minister to him through loving counsel (*CW* 6:113, 115–16).

Over *The Conduct Of Life* as a whole, nevertheless, the concluding move of "Worship" prevails again at the end of the final essay, "Illusions":

> There is no chance, and no anarchy, in the universe. All is system and gradation. Every god is there sitting in his sphere. The young mortal enters the hall of the firmament: there is he alone with them alone, they pouring on him benedictions and gifts, and beckoning him up to their thrones. On the instant, and incessantly, fall snow-storms of illusions. He fancies himself in a vast crowd which sways this way and that, and whose movement and doings he must obey: he fancies himself poor, orphaned, insig-

> nificant. The mad crowd drives hither and thither, now furiously commanding this thing to be done, now that. What is he that he should resist their will, and think or act for himself? Every moment, new changes, and new showers of deceptions, to baffle and distract him. And when, by and by, for an instant, the air clears, and the cloud lifts a little, there are the gods still sitting around him on their thrones,—they alone with him alone. (*CW* 6:174)

The young mortal, at the limits of what may be known, encounters "the gods" who constitute the "system" of the universe; in the conclusion of "Worship," similar entities traveled under the name of "the Laws" (*CW* 6:128). Personified or not, these laws or gods remain impersonal; indeed, the interfering illusions come from an excessive presence of persons—though these are impersonal as well, moving madly, tyrannically as an undifferentiated multitude. The rare individual person who might "help with counsel or conduct" does not attend this scene. Though this final scene portrays a moment free of illusions, the final word of *The Conduct of Life* produces a haunting echo: "alone."

For Emerson, the view from Stowe's "highest rung" is finally this solitude at the end of both "Worship" and "Illusions." Among other considerations, it is a solitude that might be seen to correspond with biographical developments during the period Emerson was writing much of the material for the Conduct series. In *Emerson among the Eccentrics,* Carlos Baker devotes a series of poignant later chapters to "The Absentees," treating in turn the departures or deaths of Emerson's closest confidants: "Emerson's hopes for a permanent community of writers and thinkers in Concord suffered a series of blows between the fall of 1845 and the summer of 1850. The Hawthornes were the first to leave, after three years and three months in the Old Manse" (280).[49] In November of 1848, the Alcotts were next to join the trend of Absenteeism: "One by one, Emerson's good companions were falling away—Hawthorne to Salem, Margaret Fuller to Rome, and the Alcotts to Boston" (302).[50]

The absence with the largest textual presence in "Worship" is Margaret Fuller's. Her absence may be detected primarily in one of the series of impassioned sentences with which Emerson exposes the need for a new call to worship. We have already noted the foremost indicator Emerson adduces: "What proof of infidelity, like the toleration and propagandism of slavery?" (*CW* 6:111). His tirade builds to the following oratory:

> What proof of skepticism like the base rate at which the highest mental and moral gifts are held? Let a man attain the highest and broadest culture that any American has possessed, then let him die by sea-storm, railroad collision, or other accident, and all America will acquiesce that the best thing has happened to him; that, after the education has gone far, such is the expensiveness of America, that the best use to put a fine person to, is, to drown him to save his board [that is, the expense of feeding; Emerson in the next paragraph decries the belief of solid society "that life is an affair to put somewhat between the upper and lower mandibles"]. (6:111–12)

If the reference to Fuller seems a bit oblique in the finished essay (someone who has attained highest and broadest culture of any American ever dies by sea storm), the parallel journal passage makes the source of Emerson's discontent plain:

> It is a bitter satire on our social order, just at present, the number of bad cases. Margaret Fuller having attained the highest & broadest culture that any American woman has possessed . . . perished by shipwreck on the rocks of Fire Island, off New York; and her friends said, "Well, on the whole, it was not so lamentable, & perhaps it was the best thing that could happen to her. For, had she lived, what could she have done? How could she have supported herself, her husband, & child?" And, most persons, hearing this, acquiesced in this view that, after the education has gone far, such is the expensiveness of America, that the best use to put a fine woman to, is to drown her to save her board. (1853; *JMN* 13:139)[51]

The published essay disguises Fuller's story amid masculine pronouns and multiplied hypothetical means of death, but the circumstances of her loss stand unmistakably behind Emerson's sense of outrage. Fuller's absence, here so clearly marked, remains a presence in the essay's end. The fact of her loss may be read as one facet of the conclusion of "Worship," with Emerson's hard lesson that "much of the time he must have himself to his friend" and "he shall walk with no companion" (*CW* 6:128).

In happier times, Emerson had testified how Fuller's presence had offered an effective antidote to low skepticism: "Beside her friendship, other friendships seem trade, and by the firmness with which she treads her upward path, all mortals are convinced that another road exists than that which their feet know."[52] As Robert Richardson characterizes her effect on Emerson, simply, "She inspired faith."[53] Soon after her death, he eulogized, "I have lost in her my audience" (1850).[54] Fuller had been one in whose magnetic presence new ideas flowed; she was preeminent in that personal category Emerson provisionally addressed in "The Uses of Great Men": "I can say to you what I cannot first say to myself" (*CW* 4:4).

In *Sources of the Self,* Charles Taylor proposes that the self emerges from "webs of interlocution."[55] At times, Emerson approaches a similar conclusion, and in portions of *The Conduct of Life,* Emerson turns to his sense of this interpersonal construction project as a basis for action. But Emerson also finds (as at the end of "Worship" and "Illusions") that for company the individual has, many times, only one's "central solitude." It is this instability that will provide the animating tension for Hawthorne's *Elixir of Life* manuscripts and, even more powerfully, for Melville's *Clarel: A Poem and Pilgrimage in the Holy Land.*

CHAPTER 3

Hawthorne's Sermon

HAWTHORNE'S CAREER AS a preacher was somewhat shorter than Emerson's; understandably, the collected sermons of Nathaniel Hawthorne have received considerably less critical attention. Of course, depending upon how broadly one might define the "sermon" genre, Hawthorne's sermonic output might be deemed quite substantial. In one sense, much of his writing may be said to belong to the "art of prophesying," as the New England divines once termed their craft, but Hawthorne's parables and allegorics tend to exceed the bounds of this technical category. For the traditional ministers, to "prophesy" had meant to expose biblical truth for the benefit of the flock. Hawthorne instead claims for his fiction an inspired status as "a new revelation."[1] And even in those instances when his writing might be brought into didactic alignment with the preexisting biblical record, he could not literally be said to have preached any of his tales or sketches. Unlike Emerson, he did not cultivate a public audience of listeners to complement his readership.[2] In the narrower sense of nonfictional sermon making for oral delivery, Hawthorne himself appears to have mentioned only one instance of giving a sermon—and the content of that performance he preserved only indirectly. But he did in fact preach, and he testified to the act in the last book published in his lifetime.

In *Our Old Home* (1863), he recounts among his "Consular Experiences" in England having received a visit from one reverend doctor of divinity, "a perfect model of clerical propriety, scholar-like, yet with the air of a man of the world rather than a student, though overspread with the graceful sanctity of a popular metropolitan divine" (*CE* 5:25). Hawthorne learns of this American preacher that "he was somewhat distinguished in his own region for fervor and eloquence in the pulpit, but was now compelled to relinquish it temporarily for the purpose of renovating his impaired health by an extensive tour of Europe" (5:25). Hawthorne makes plans to dine with this gentleman, but a collision (intimated by Hawthorne's layered description) between the man's "sanctity" and "the world" intervenes. The appointed hour comes and goes with no sign of the minister; the subsequent day passes without word of explanation or apology. Within a few days Hawthorne has put the matter out of mind, until he receives a concerned visit from a Captain Emerson, upon whose ship the minister had arrived from America.[3] No one has heard from the minister, his personal belongings seemingly abandoned aboard ship.

Despite the captain's state of alarm, Hawthorne decides not to go to the police. To a large degree, his decision is one of patriotic diplomacy: "At home, in our native country, I would have looked to the Doctor's personal safety and left his reputation to take care of itself. . . . But in scornful and invidious England, on the idea that the credit of the sacred office was measurably entrusted to my discretion, I could not endure, for the sake of American Doctors of Divinity generally, that this particular Doctor should cut an ignoble figure in the police-reports of the English newspapers" (5:26). As this explanation suggests, the question of American honor is but one dimension of Hawthorne's sense of loyalty. In determining to handle the manner with all due discretion, Hawthorne also begins a process of identifying himself with the clergy: "The clerical body, I flatter myself, will acknowledge that I acted on their own principle" (5:26).

This acting upon clerical principle connects loosely with a self-consciously constructed "hereditary" (5:28) Puritanism that recurs throughout *Our Old Home*. For example, in a gesture toward filiopiety, Hawthorne makes a pilgrimage to England's "Old" Boston, where he imagines himself in the place of John Cotton: "The tower of Saint Botolph's looked benignantly down; and I fancied it was bidding me farewell, as it did Mr. Cotton, two or three hundred years ago, and telling me to describe its venerable height, and the town beneath it, to the people of the American city" (*CE* 5:166). In this reverie, Hawthorne's imagined identification with Cotton in England becomes projected, somewhat whimsically, into the responsibility of bearing witness to a New England audience. But the dramatic scene that follows the mysterious disappearance of the latter-day American preacher provides the occasion for Hawthorne's much more clear-cut performative identification with the clergy.

A full week after the minister had vanished, there appears at Hawthorne's office a man who "looked disreputable to the last degree, but still had a ruined air of good society glimmering about him" (5:27). Given the narrative frame, the true identity of the "dissipated" individual, despite the red herring of his "shabby" blue military surtout, will surprise few readers. But Hawthorne cannot recognize the man: "'Am I then so changed!' he exclaimed with a vast depth of tragic intonation. . . . If I had meditated a scene or a *coup de théâtre,* I could not have contrived a more effectual one than by this simple and genuine difficulty of recognition. The poor Divine must have felt that he had lost his personal identity through the misadventures of one little week" (5:27). Hawthorne fits this precarious, destructured sense of identity to a Calvinist hypothesis: "And, to say the truth, he did look as if, like Job, on account of his especial sanctity, he had been delivered over to the direst temptations of Satan, and proving weaker than the Man of Uz, the Arch Enemy had been empowered to drag him through Tophet, transforming him, in the process, from the most decorous of metropolitan clergymen into the rowdiest and dirtiest of disbanded officers" (5:27). On this final detail of the transformation, Hawthorne permits himself a further hypothesis: "I never fathomed the mystery of his military costume, but conjectured that a lurking sense of fitness had induced him to exchange his clerical garments for this habit of a sinner" (5:28). For Hawthorne—the "PEACEABLE MAN" of *Chiefly about War Matters*—the martial accoutrements are indeed marks of lost piety (even if, as his continuing exploration of the cleric/warrior dichotomy in *Septimius Felton* will show, avoidance of the military mantle provides no guarantee of piety retained, and even if the clerical robes of the pious do not necessarily protect against the pollution of violence). Hawthorne does not divulge "into what pitfall, not more of vice than terrible calamity, he had precipitated himself"; he even professes a certain degree of ignorance on this point, but apprehends well enough that the man of sacred office has sunken to a "desecrated" state (5:28).[4]

With the stage directions and costumes thus settled, Hawthorne warms to his task: "The opportunity, I presume, does not often happen to a layman of administering moral and religious reproof to a Doctor of Divinity; but finding the occasion thrust upon me, and the hereditary Puritan waxing strong in my breast, I deemed it a matter of conscience not to let it pass entirely unimproved" (5:28). Hawthorne announces the arrival of a Puritan persona and completes that arrival with his diction; the last word expresses a characteristic Puritan desire to "improve the time," in this case, by reproving.

With energy and even pride, Hawthorne matches his own oratorical power against the preacher with the reputation for eloquence. In private correspondence, Hawthorne signals parenthetically that he had found himself especially motivated by the fact that his audience, if not an exact match for the Puritan waxing in his own heart, represented for him a tradition of hard-line piety. Hawthorne writes to Ticknor that "I wish you could have heard the lecture I gave him. . . . Not knowing whether I should ever have another opportunity of preaching to a Doctor of Divinity (an orthodox man, too) I laid it on without mercy" (May 27, 1855).[5]

Hawthorne writes that he was "unspeakably shocked," but not exactly with a shock of disillusionment: "Not, however, that I was then to learn that clergymen are made of the same flesh and blood as other people" (5:28). The nearer touchstone turns out to be not an imaginary Puritan, but the personal memory of an embodied representative of the faith: "But I remembered the innocent faith of my boyhood, and the good old, silver-headed clergyman, who seemed to me as much a Saint then on earth as he is now in Heaven, and partly for whose sake, through all these darkening years, I retain a devout, though not intact nor unwavering respect for the entire fraternity" (5:28) The remnants of respect for the brethren, animated on this occasion by the abdicating minister, also appear to drive some of the more pointed narratorial comments in *Septimius Felton,* whose title character turns his back on just such a venerable vessel of the faith as Hawthorne now fondly recalls.

In the warmth of this devout memory, Hawthorne feels an unprecedented license to preach: "So I spoke to the unhappy man as I never thought myself warranted in speaking to any other mortal, hitting him hard, doing my utmost to find out his vulnerable part and prick him into the depths of it" (5:29). He preaches, that is, as would a converting evangelist, one who believes, in the tradition of Thomas Hooker, that the heart must be broken.[6]

In the act of rebuke, Hawthorne assumes the absented role of the man whom he chastises. But he does not push the preacher aside to make room at the pulpit; the man of God falls, without any prior aggression on Hawthorne's part.[7] And on this occasion, Hawthorne performs the ministerial function without introducing an alien discourse; he wears the cloth without rending or even stretching the rhetorical seams. Which is not to say that he feels entirely comfortable in the collar.

He had preached to his "utmost" but with a conflicted sense of how the sermon was received: "And not without more effect than I had dreamed of, or desired!" (5:29). The hearer is broken and penitent, presenting a pitiful aspect to his rebuker. This audience reaction exceeds Hawthorne's fantasies of pulpit eloquence: that he affected the minister more than he "dreamed" may be a positive, if ambiguous, valuation; that he affected him more than he "desired" is surely grounds for regret.

Hawthorne ponders possible reasons for the unexpected impact of his sermon: "No doubt, the novelty of the Doctor's reversed position, thus standing up to receive such a fulmination as the clergy have heretofore arrogated the exclusive right of inflicting, might give additional weight and sting to the words which I found utterance for" (5:29). In the reversal of power, Hawthorne may appear to relish a kind of triumph. In choosing the words "arrogated," "exclusive," and "inflicting" (to describe the privilege typically enjoyed by the clergy), Hawthorne appears to reveal a frame of mind characteristic of a usurping, resentful "writing after the minister."

But, upon reflection, Hawthorne finds that the unexpected turning of the tables has not been the most significant condition for the wayward minister's shaken reception of his sermon. When the other reason for the audience's susceptibility dawns, the reader recognizes that Hawthorne's triumphalist rhetoric, with its tones of resentment, has been preparatory to an act of self-recrimination regarding the incident: "But there was another reason (which, had I in the least suspected it, would have closed my lips at once) for his feeling morbidly sensitive to the cruel rebuke that I administered. The unfortunate man had come to me, laboring under one of the consequences of his riotous outbreak in the shape of delirium tremens." Here Hawthorne's treatment turns both clinical and compassionate: "His emotions, as well as the external movement and expression of them by voice, countenance, and gesture, were terribly exaggerated by the tremendous vibration of nerves resulting from the disease. It was the deepest tragedy I ever witnessed" (5:29). He then repeats that key word in our contemporary understanding of alcoholism, "disease," if slightly mixing the diagnosis with another lexical register: "What had I to do with rebuking him? The disease, long latent in his heart, had shown itself in a frightful eruption on the surface of his life. That was all!" It is a "disease"; yet it abides in that most innately depraved if inscrutable of seats, the human "heart." A journal entry on the issue tends to side with the gentle clinician rather than the stern moralist: "In my opinion, he has incurred sin no further than as a madman may."[8]

The theological terms do not simply vanish from the equation, with Hawthorne suddenly swapping his imaginary collar for a caduceus. But as competing parallel roles, the doctor of medicine's insights do shake the doctor of divinity's confidence in his own righteous conduct. In the light of the real-life minister's disease, the minister-for-a-day finds himself on dangerous ground indeed: "He bore a hell within the compass of his own breast, all the torments of which blazed up with tenfold inveteracy when I thus took upon myself the devil's office of stirring up the red-hot embers" (5:29). Yet Hawthorne does not forswear the possibility of future sermons entirely, but rather promises to alter his tack: "For the future, if I ever have anything to do with sinners, I mean to operate upon them through sympathy, and not rebuke" (5:29). In this possible future, Hawthorne sees himself as the benevolent pastor, tending kindly to straying members of the flock.

And, leaving room for the mysteries of grace, Hawthorne imagines how the wayward minister may have returned to "his bereaved flock, who, very probably, were thereafter conscious of an increased unction in his soul-stirring eloquence, without suspecting the awful depths into which their pastor had dived in quest of it" (5:29). Here sounds the voice of Melville's Hawthorne, Hawthorne of the Melville who loved "all men who dive" and who loved in Hawthorne especially his deep-sea explorations into the true sight of sin. Hawthorne will not have been the first to construe such a vision as a means of salvation: "It has occurred to me that his dire calamity, as both he and I regarded it, might have been the only method by which precisely such a man as himself, and so situated, could be redeemed" (5:30). Having learned of the minister's death, Hawthorne closes the episode with pious euphemism and allusion to a final reckoning: As "his voice is now silent," the departed minister "has learned, ere now, how that matter [the question of his redemption] stood" (5:29, 30).

But Hawthorne cannot rest easy after his pulpit intervention, and the general tendency of his conclusions both to this episode and to "Consular

Experiences" as a whole is to restore the preacher to his proper role and to extricate the author from any appearance of clerical pretense. Hawthorne began the episode with a remark on the preacher's reputation for eloquence and concludes it with the hope that the "soul-stirring" quality of his sermons will only have increased. As for Hawthorne's own role, immediately after recounting the incident of his impromptu sermon, he reflects on not wanting to advise on "conduct" (5:30). He professes an anxiety of influencing: "I have always hated to give advice, especially when there is a prospect of its being taken" (5:30). Unlike "one-eyed" people who advise with confidence, Hawthorne counts himself as one who, with both eyes open, sees myriad reasonable possibilities and thus stands "likely to leave his friends to regulate their own conduct, and also to remain quiet as regards his especial affairs till necessity shall prick him onward." (This sort of reticence, this refusal to serve as a counselor in the conduct of life, finds a reflection in the character of Vine, whose distance frustrates the earnest, guideless title character in Melville's *Clarel.*)

Further on, Hawthorne repeats his claim to be uncomfortable with responsibility beyond authorial ambiguity: "I never in my life desired to be burdened with public influence" (5:37). This statement leads to a more general summing up of his chapter on "Consular Experiences," which experiences in "retrospect began to look unreal": "I could scarcely believe that it was I, that figure whom they called a Consul, but a sort of Double Ganger, who had been permitted to assume my aspect . . . while my real self had lain . . . in a state of suspended animation" (5:38). A general statement, but the first particular that recurs is the wayward preacher: "Is it not a dream altogether? The figure of that poor Doctor of Divinity looks wonderfully life-like. . . . But were they more than shadows? Surely, I think not" (5:38–39). The poor preacher had seemed to lose his identity altogether; in retrospect, it is Hawthorne who feels he had cast off his true identity in the exchange.

"The being a minister is of course out of the Question"

Apart from the brief service rendered to the displaced reverend, when the minister at Liverpool acted as a *minister,* Hawthorne presents the calling to preach almost exclusively as something chosen against, in favor of a literary vocation. Over the course of the career, however, the implied evaluations of this negative choice fluctuate. One purpose of this chapter on Hawthorne will be to offer a shape for these fluctuating perspectives, from his earliest life choices to his final *Elixir of Life* manuscripts (1861–64). In *Septimius Felton* (the most complete of the *Elixir* texts, published posthumously in 1872), I find an endpoint, if not perhaps the final word, in the narrator's reprimand of Septimius and endorsement of the ministerial calling.[9] As Septimius plunges onward in his Faustian quest, the narrator pauses to reflect on what might have been, had Septimius renounced his mad scientistic ambitions and pursued instead the call to the ministry that had once seemed his destined path: "How different would have been the life of Septimius;—a thoughtful preacher of God's word, taking severe, but conscientious views of man's state and relations, a heavy-browed walker and worker on earth, and finally the slumberer in an honored grave, with an epitaph bearing testimony to his great usefulness in his generation" (*CE* 13:53). The life that Hawthorne, that "heavy-browed walker," *did* pursue bears some resemblance to the "different" life he imagines for Septimius. Yet as an author rather than as the hypothetical preacher in this passage, the question of "usefulness in his generation" which the narrator puts to Septimius appears to have caused Hawthorne himself more than a little anxiety. He most famously expresses this concern in "The Custom-House" (1850), when he imagines his Puritan predecessors dismissing him as a mere "writer of story-books! What kind of business in life,—what mode of glorifying God, or being serviceable to mankind in his day and generation,—may that be?" (*Novels*, 127). Surely in his "thoughtful" work Hawthorne may be said to have taken "severe, but conscientious views of man's state and relations." But of course he expressed these views from no recognized pulpit and thus without the benefit of what Emerson would call (in 1847) a clearly "stated task."

The narrator of *Septimius Felton* posits a hypothetical life of the pulpit as a serious and rewarding alternative; the narrator's comments at this critical plot juncture in the life of Septimius open the question of whether Hawthorne's own views on clerical calling may have altered. The narrator's view could scarcely be at wider variance with that of the much younger Hawthorne. Given all that criticism has taught us about Hawthorne's intricate management of narrative voices, it would be dangerous to conclude from this *Septimius* passage alone that Hawthorne himself felt some deep specific regret over not entering the ministry. And "Feathertop" (1854) in particular may teach us to be wary of pronouncements about a "useful vocation," as the tale confers this praise upon the high calling of the cornfield scarecrow.[10] But that the elder author of *Septimius Felton* can even appear to imagine the ministry in a favorable light, as a missed opportunity for the young Septimius, might be sufficient to suggest a change of heart. Some forty years prior, Hawthorne claimed he could not even begin to entertain such an option for himself.

In a letter to his mother, March 13, 1821, the soon to be college-bound young man turns his mind to possible professions—and one impossible: "The being a minister is of course out of the Question. I should not think that even you could desire me to choose so dull a way of life. Oh, no, mother, I was not born to vegetate forever in one place, and to live and die as calm and tranquil as—a puddle of water" (Mellow, 25).

An unspoken constraint may contribute to the certainty in Hawthorne's "of course." Unlike Emerson, young Hawthorne entertained fewer hopes that he might someday triumph with "the strains of eloquence" and thus "thrive" in divinity. Hubert H. Hoeltje recounts an early experience leading to a relevant aversion: "Once, on some occasion in play hours, he went upon the schoolroom stage to declaim, when some larger boys ridiculed his efforts and pulled him down. Thereafter, as his college records show, he commonly refused to declaim, though his refusal entailed repeated punishments. It was only when he was a mature man, occupying the important post of U.S. Consul at Liverpool, that he brought himself to speak in public" (Hoeltje, 28–29). Hawthorne's service at the consulate is thus epochal by a second measure, one related to the episode discussed in the previous section: the delivery of his first "sermon" coincided with the time of his first public speaking. The consular years may have marked the first period of his adult life during which he could imagine the ministry as *not* out of the question, when considering the prospect of actual professional performance.

Yet to return to the text of his 1821 letter, Hawthorne nowhere voices serious doubts about his ability to perform a given role. He turns the options over in his mind in a manner suggesting the play of preference, grounded in an earnest consideration of consequences. The prospect of the occasional failure on the job does weigh significantly in this accounting, but appears under the rubric of unavoidable bad luck. The spoken questions do not concern his fitness to practice a given profession, but what might happen if he did. The screening of vocations begins with the ministry, in a series that builds teleologically toward quite another pole.

Among other professions, he feels that being a physician might be preferable to being a lawyer, "but yet I should not like to live by the diseases and infirmities of my fellow Creatures. And it would weigh very heavily on my conscience if, in the course of my practice, I should chance to send any unlucky patient 'ad inferum,' which is interpreted as 'to the realms below'" (Mellow, 25). Perhaps he even draws in his mind some connection between the doctor of medicine and the doctor of divinity. Though he portrays divinity as "dull," in that calling he would likewise be called upon to minister to certain "diseases and infirmities"; and this ministerial calling would also not be without its grave responsibilities and risks. Given a view of the universe that encompasses "realms below," any failure to heal an unfortunate religious charge entrusted to him could also "weigh very heavily" upon his conscience. The perception of any such unspoken affinities between the clerical and clinical professions would not mitigate his judgment on the former vocation, but would only strengthen his resolve against pursuing the pulpit. And the statement the teenage Hawthorne *does* give on his aversion to the ministry leaves little room for equivocation about his intentions: he prefers not to stagnate in the provincial puddle of New England divinity.

Having rejected a reasonable number of reputable paths, he turns at last to the proposal of what he most desires to become. Here Hawthorne addresses his mother directly for only the second time—the first time having been over the matter of "being a minister." The intervening list (lawyer, doctor), which he treats without recourse to the second person and with a somewhat more indifferent tone, serves as a buffer between the two items bearing the greatest potential for conflict. His dismissal of the ministerial option, so confident in its first note, shows signs of pressure, as assertion mixes with anxiety. He opens with a peremptory dismissal—his "of course" frames the matter as something that ought to go without saying—but he then moves on to an appeal for clemency: he cannot imagine that "even you could desire" such an unhappy fate for the supplicating son. He writes as if he fears, or perhaps even knows, that this is precisely what she does want; the "even you" suggests at the very least that she is just the sort of person who might be expected to harbor pious inclinations. After claiming his disbelief that she might possibly wish such a thing for him, he finds a further negation necessary: "Oh, no, mother"—not me. Compared to this charged territory, the lawyer and doctor options present a sort of neutral ground. And, having risked a cavalier attitude toward the ministry, the more religious tinge of his reflections on medical risk may seek to court approval and gather momentum toward a hoped-for outcome of consensus. His text thus decently defers bringing into direct opposition what he implies may be the wishes of the mother and what he will ultimately reveal to be his own.

Hawthorne raises the issue of his grandest aspirations playfully, tentatively, as if—Mellow observes—to "test his mother's sentiments" on a most serious matter: "What do you think of my becoming an author, and relying for support upon my pen? Indeed, I think the illegibility of my handwriting is very author-like. How proud you would feel to see my works praised by the reviewers, as equal to [the] proudest productions of the scribbling sons of John Bull. But authors are always poor devils, and therefore Satan may take them" (Mellow, 25–26). Hawthorne adds, in an anxious postscript, "Do not show this letter." Such earnest, troubled ambitions could scarcely walk about in the light of day, even under the protection of a whimsical tone.

In daring, however mockingly and provisionally, to imagine a vocation as a writer, Hawthorne draws two curiously inauspicious connections: between illegibility and authorship, and between authorship and the devil. In his letter, these connections appear as asides; they negatively frame his direct appeal to his mother—"How proud you would feel"—which he extends with the shining promise that his works might be "praised." He foresees a literary acclaim that would arise in the context of a rivalry with England, as embodied in the allegorical figure of John Bull and the real bodies of "his" sons.

Hawthorne voices this bold fantasy not long after Sydney Smith had thrown down that famous gauntlet of 1820, "Who reads an American book?"[11] The cofounder of the *Edinburgh Review* names a daunting prospect, that an American writer would not be read, even in America. Given the superiority of British culture and its ready availability, Smith cannot see why Americans would bother to produce or consume a literary culture of their own: "Why should the Americans write books, when a six weeks' passage brings them, in their own tongue, our sense, science and genius, in bales and hogsheads?"

Smith's image of English literature flooding the market by the bales and hogsheads suggests the status of print media as a raw commodity, cheaply gotten. And, as has been well documented, the low cost of bound matter featuring British authors was indeed the crueler, more material underside of Smith's smug declaration. Charvat and subsequent historians of the profession of authorship have pointed to a combination of economic and legal reasons why a would-be American author faced a stacked deck especially in the home country: in particular the lack of copyright protection on imported books meant that original British editions could be legally pirated for the American market with an ease and profitability against which any native original would have a hard time competing.[12]

Hawthorne may have heard rumors about the slender economic pickings available—authors, he knows, are "poor" devils. But economic worries would not seem to be foremost in his mind: the poverty of the author might involve the penury of an insufficient fortune but also ill fortune, the poverty of a wretched destiny, and a bad end. In the phrase "poor devils," the stronger emphasis in Hawthorne's imagination would appear to fall upon "devils": it is not the debt collector but "Satan" who "may take them." And in contrast to this dis-ease of the soul, the supposedly insurmountable superiority of British literature does not faze the young Hawthorne a bit. Moreover, he welcomes the challenge.

Hawthorne's middle point to his mother, of winning acclaim through transatlantic rivalry, holds for him one possible hope for evading the twin threats of unreadability and diabolism. To presume inspired literary authorship in New England is to risk writing a scripture whose reading is a priori interdicted by the proclaimed end of the age of revelation and to risk having that presumption read as the work of the devil. If Hawthorne could only shift the context of authorship to a transatlantic struggle, the problem of attaining authorship would become *merely* one of artistic belatedness, of having to overcome authors from Old England who had staked prior claims on the battlefield of cultural production, but who had already consecrated the calling of literary authorship. Thus might he navigate beyond the provincial Scylla and Charybdis delimiting the established "puddle" of theocratic tradition.

From the other side of the looking glass, Hawthorne revisits the drama of youthful calling in the story of Septimius Felton. In 1821, Hawthorne had tried to imagine the consequences of certain careers: his vision of what the future might hold for him as a minister left *that* out of the question; the perils related to attaining literary authorship presented themselves readily, but his desire propelled his hope beyond his fears. From the contest between ministry and authorship to his specific fears and his possible strategy to evade them, these same issues hang over the *Septimius Felton* passage cited above, in which the narrator laments Septimius's failure to choose the useful vocation of a "preacher of God's word" (*CE* 13:53).

The task to which Septimius has chosen to dedicate himself appears in the narrative as a direct displacement of the ministerial role: he seeks to decipher a difficult manuscript which he believes contains "the mode in which man might be restored to his originally undying state" (52)—a revelation in excess of God's word as received in the biblical tradition and a substitute for heaven as the ordinary reward. In Septimius's story, "writing after the minister" originates in "reading after the minister"; the narrative, with its emphasis on willful hermeneutics, brings the two acts together, presenting reading *as* writing. As James D. Wallace notes, the text Septimius constructs is the text he wishes into existence (26).

The origin of the manuscript upon which Septimius bases his own authorial project has its origin in England; that is, his acquisition of a claim to authorship replicates the gesture in Hawthorne's letter to his mother whereby the struggle for literary vocation is projected into a transatlantic context. Septimius has obtained the manuscript by triumphing in a violent rivalry: he takes it from a "haughty" (*CE* 13:26) British soldier he has killed, a proud son of John Bull—one of whose ancestors was the original proud scribbler of the hermetic writing.

Yet this victorious, confrontational origin at the site of English culture does not in fact dispel the two risks to American authorship that Hawthorne's 1821 letter identifies. More generally, the *Septimius* narrative repeatedly raises the specter of the shunned ministerial vocation. The ministry, with its waning yet still legitimate authority within the culture, holds the American claims to a popularly enduring if theoretically embattled textual authority. This exegetical power to circumscribe the readable may be said to underwrite the threats to the would-be literary author: of being misunderstood, ignored, or de facto censored (illegibility) and of being condemned (diabolism).

The shadow of Septimius's turning away from ministerial training precedes the passage in question. Septimius's feverish reading/writing has spilled over into his sleep; he awakens one morning "possessed by the idea that, in his dream, he had taken up this inscrutable document, and read it off as glibly as he would a page of a modern sermon" (*CE* 13:52). Of course modern sermons are precisely what Septimius, in abandoning his earlier study of divinity, has chosen *not* to read. That this plot point might not be forgotten, his aunt has just warned him that if he continues to pursue his mad scholarly quest, he will "never live to be a minister" (13:52).

Septimius brushes aside her warning and renews his authorial energies; but despite his dreams, the text he seeks to write remains unreadable. In the wake of his scorn for the ministry, the first corollary threat of the 1821 letter, "illegibility," seizes anew the hero's authorial presumptions:

> All was a blur, an inscrutableness, a scrawl of unintelligible characters, alike. . . . If, in that season, there had been a fire on the hearth, it is possible that easy realization of a destructive impulse might have caused him to fling the accursed scrawl into the hottest of the flames, and thus return it to the devil who, he suspected, was the original author of it. Had he done so, what strange and gloomy passages would I have been spared the pain of relating. How different would have been the life of Septimius;—a thoughtful preacher of God's word. (13:53)

The second corollary threat follows hot upon the heels of the first; in attempting to make legible the "accursed scrawl," Septimius has labored to complete the work of the devil, with whose presumed authorship the misguided protagonist would align his own.

The devil seems to lurk on the flip side of almost any endeavor: doctor, writer, even preacher (after remonstrating the wayward reverend in Liverpool, Hawthorne feared that he had been performing the "devil's office"). This probing of the possible evil consequences of any attempt to act positively would seem to reveal a Hawthornean habit of mind, a persistent moral skepticism. But the magnitude of possible regret seems greater in the fictional considerations of authorship than in the episode of Hawthorne's consular sermon. Weighing the latter incident for potential harm, Hawthorne resolved only that he would preach more sympathetically if presented with future opportunities. In the story of Septimius, the narrator presents the prospect of an entire life's being wasted, a life that ought to have been revised beginning with the moment of vocational decision.

In transgressing the textual bounds maintained by the clerical discipline, the poor devil who would forge a new textual vocation cannot even properly claim originality. However ingenious Septimius's construction of the text, the devil remains the "original author" behind all he would accomplish.[13]

At the juncture of invoking the devil's authorship, the narrator pauses to intrude his personal regrets. The upshot of the passage is that Septimius could have avoided much sorrow by abandoning his dangerous textual experiment and returning to the pastoral fold. But before drawing this conclusion, the narrator first insists upon the way such a wise decision would have bettered the teller's own fate: "Had he done so, what strange and gloomy passages would *I* have been spared the pain of relating." Septimius's choice of vocation is inextricable from the occupation of the tale's teller; the narrator laments both Septimius's life and his own authorial labor.[14]

Outside the Church: Hester's Emersonian Prophecy

Literary history has found Hawthorne's promise of a great work—to his mother and, later, to the public—of "a novel, that should evolve some deep lesson, and should possess physical substance enough to stand alone" ("The Old Manse," *Tales and Sketches,* 1124), to have been fulfilled in *The Scarlet Letter* (1850).[15] This signal text of the movement that came to be known as the "American Renaissance" is also Hawthorne's strongest positioning of his discourse as outside the church. The presentation of Dimmesdale's climactic sermon provides a key indication of this mapping. As Walter Benn Michaels wryly puts it, "Dimmesdale's election sermon at the end of *The Scarlet Letter* is heard by Hester Prynne from outside the church so she can't make out the actual words—a good thing, says Hawthorne."[16] Hawthorne's own words develop Hester's subjective spiritual experience as free from the minister's literal sermon:

> By this time the preliminary prayer had been offered in the meeting-house, and the accents of the Reverend Mr. Dimmesdale were heard commencing his discourse. An irresistible feeling kept Hester near the spot. As the sacred edifice was too much thronged to admit another auditor, she took up her position close beside the scaffold of the pillory. It was in sufficient proximity to bring the whole sermon to her ears, in the shape of an indistinct, but varied, murmur and flow of the minister's very peculiar voice.
>
> This vocal organ was in itself a rich endowment; insomuch that a listener, comprehending nothing of the language in which the preacher spoke, might still have been swayed to and fro by the mere tone and cadence. Like all other music, it breathed passion and pathos, and emotions high or tender, in a tongue native to the human heart, wherever educated.
>
> Muffled as the sound was by its passage through the church-walls, Hester Prynne listened with such intenseness, and sympathized so intimately, that the sermon had throughout a meaning for her, entirely apart from its indistinguishable words. These, perhaps, if more distinctly heard, might have been only a grosser medium, and have clogged the spiritual sense. (chap. 22, "The Procession," *Novels*, 327–28)

As the official procession had passed her by on its way into the church, "Hester Prynne, gazing steadfastly at the clergyman, felt a dreary influence come over her" (324): "He, moving proudly past, enveloped as it were, in the rich music, with the procession of majestic and venerable fathers; he, so unattainable in his worldly position, and still more so in that far vista of his unsympathizing thoughts, through which she now beheld him!" (325). As Dimmesdale passes her without even "one glance of recognition," Hester's "spirit sank with the idea that . . . there could be no real bond betwixt the clergyman and herself." Yet her spirit revives soon after this realization when, standing outside the church, she forgets the rich processional music of the "venerable fathers" and begins to hear a music of her own. Saddened that any "bond" to her beloved has been broken, his abandonment nevertheless leaves her free to apprehend a "spiritual sense" independent of the "dreary influence" of his official presence. Though the narration ultimately treats both Dimmesdale and Hester with a kind of tragic sympathy, her spiritual possibilities expand from this point onward, while the narrator censures the minister's decisions at this juncture and portrays his remaining spiritual possibilities as accordingly circumscribed.

Hawthorne's rebuke some years later of the wayward American minister in Liverpool, a certain Reverend Richards, is in some ways the opposite of *The Scarlet Letter*'s critique of Dimmesdale. In *The Scarlet Letter,* the narrator criticizes Dimmesdale precisely *in* the discharge of his assigned sermonic duty. Dimmesdale's waywardness with Hester is not the only or even the primary subject of the novel's disapproval and regret. More seriously, Dimmesdale's allegiance to his "official" capacities appears as a moral betrayal of his and Hester's spirit covenant. Hester had claimed that what she and Dimmesdale had shared "had a consecration of its own" (286). To the extent the novel allows her claim of "consecration" to stand, it establishes a decidedly extraclerical moral system.[17]

The Scarlet Letter discerns the emergence of Dimmesdale's most pitiable moral failing when he looks forward to his election-day sermon, even while he ostensibly participates in imagining a future with Hester. In discussing their plans to leave New England, Dimmesdale had asked Hester, "with no little interest," when their ship would leave. When she informs him that it would likely depart in four days, he says to himself, "That is most fortunate!" Dimmesdale's reasoning in this matter occasions the narrator's exploration of the reverend's weakness for seeking public and professional approval through his ministry:

> Now, why the Reverend Mr. Dimmesdale considered it so very fortunate, we hesitate to reveal. Nevertheless,—to hold nothing back from the reader,—it was because, on the third day from the present, he was to preach the Election Sermon, and, as such an occasion formed an honorable epoch in the life of a new England clergyman, he could not have chanced upon a more suitable mode

> and time of terminating his professional career. "At least, they shall say of me," thought this exemplary man, "that I leave no public duty unperformed, nor ill performed!"

The narrator's immediate commentary makes clear that the word "exemplary" cuts ironically: that Dimmesdale may be termed exemplary is a troubling fact for the community for which he is the moral model and for the office of which he is a representative example:

> Sad, indeed, that an introspection so profound and acute as this poor minister's could be so miserably deceived! We have had, and may have still, worse things to tell of him; but none, we apprehend, so pitiably weak; no evidence, at once so slight and irrefragable, of a subtle disease, that had long since begun to eat into the real substance of his character. No man, for any considerable period, can wear one face to himself, and another to the multitude, without finally getting bewildered as to which may be the true. (Chap. 20, "The Minister in a Maze," *Novels*, 304)

The novel tends to suggest that the true face is the one he had worn for Hester; or perhaps more justly, the novel tends to find truth in the face Hester shows to him, and to locate spiritual authority in her subjective and rather "antinomian" claims.

Though it is not within the aims of the present study to settle any long-standing critical debates about the novel, the crux of Hester's depiction needs to be addressed briefly. To see Hawthorne's writing as aligned with Hester's spirit, rather than with the letter of cultural discipline and punishment that would contain that spirit, depends upon reading *The Scarlet Letter* against Bercovitch's industrial-strength study of the novel's "office." Responses to Sacvan Bercovitch by Emily Miller Budick, Paul K. Johnston, Richard Millington, and others have taken up this daunting challenge ably.[18] Johnston concludes that "despite the fact that Hester lies in the grave by the novel's end, her spirit does not (though Dimmesdale's surely does). In her case, the scarlet letter does not do its office. Neither does the novel itself serve the office of the letter . . . but rather lays it bare, in the death of Dimmesdale, for the reader to recognize" (32).

Hester's much-debated "return" to the site of her punishment is not a capitulation, but a chance to inscribe her prophetic discourse upon the community after the minister's passing.[19] Though Hester rather humbly modifies her personal claim to be a "destined prophetess," she nevertheless insists upon heralding the advent of a "new truth" to be "revealed" (*Novels,* 344). Budick's discussion in particular brings this point home to an Emersonian reading of the novel:

> In Bercovitch's reading, as in Leland Person's, Hester's return is most notable for the silence that accompanies it, a silence packing ideological power. Might we instead understand this silence, not as signaling revenge (Person) or coercion (Bercovitch), but rather as a part of Hester's return to speaking? Might we take it, in an Emersonian, Cavellian mode, as the aversion of conformity, in which Hester, having turned away from society, returns to it once more, to assume the responsibilities of speaking and listening? . . . For Hester and the letter are hardly silent at the end of the book. The letter therefore figures neither Hester's subordination to Puritan speaking nor her withdrawal from society but rather her own free and uncircumscribed aversive speaking. (85–86)

Pointing out that Hawthorne "attributes the final words of the story to her," Budick connects the prophetic projects of author and character: "Having learned to speak for herself, Hester becomes the voice of the text itself" (86). The scene discussed above, in which Hester listens to the sound of Dimmesdale's sermon but hears her own, specifies the location for this liberating learning. As Hester, listening outside the church, constructs a parallel message "entirely apart" from the minister's words, she completes the project of the book itself: a meditation on the ministry that produces a prophetic discourse unconstrained by that tradition.

"The Problem" Revisited

In answer to a call to conduct possessing "a consecration of its own," Hester proposes that she and Arthur seek sanctuary "in our native land, whether in some remote village or in vast London,—or . . . in pleasant

Italy" (*Novels,* 286, 288). Hester and Dimmesdale determine that the "civilization and refinement" of the "old World" offers an "eligible shelter" for their new truths and prospective new life (303). *The Scarlet Letter* (1850) thus projects Europe as a place of relatively unfettered spiritual possibility, and it is there that the lawless Pearl makes her home. Beginning with his 1853 appointment as the American consul at Liverpool, Hawthorne gets an extended opportunity to visit this imagined space and to explore its spiritual resources and boundaries for himself.

In his peregrinations, the inveterate sermon dodger relapses, perhaps out of curiosity, and permits himself to once again darken the doors of a few churches. Adopting a persona that mingles aspects of both spiritual seeker and touristic observer, Hawthorne takes time to sample some of the varied forms of European religious expression. But these new experiences, however scandalous for a son of a Puritan (particularly in the sympathetic leeway he occasionally allows in his portrayals of Catholicism), may scarcely be said to have spurred him on to further antinomian experimentation in "new revelation." If anything, the view from Europe puts the American renegade in touch with his latent New England orthodox tendencies.

Strolling leisurely some Sundays through Greenwich Park, Hawthorne finds himself troubled amid a "festal" atmosphere contrary to proper Sabbath observance. The scene awakens a guilt anterior to any present sense of delinquency: "I am not ashamed to say, it a little disturbed whatever grimly ghost of Puritanic strictness might be lingering in the sombre depths of a New England heart, among severe and sunless remembrances of childhood, and pangs of ill-gotten lessons in the catechism, and for erratic fantasies or hardly suppressed laughter in the middle of long sermons" (*Our Old Home, CE* 5:225). Looking back thus at his personal history of Sunday sheepishness, in which fancy had interrupted the delivery of the sacred word, he labels the compunction felt as one "long-hoarded." In the English setting within which this repressed sense of repression returns, he does the best he can to lessen the "sting" by attending outdoor Methodist services (5:225).

One would overstate the case to characterize Hawthorne's pattern of Sunday observance in England as a "return to the fold" (and had he ever completely left, though absent?). But his return to churchgoing does mark a break from his adult habits, as he carefully investigates not only open-air evangelism but also England's venerable religious edifices and the possible edification of the worship services held therein. Yet amid all this exploration, the major significance of Hawthorne's return to church lies not in what he finds there, but rather in what he finds that he misses.

Of the Sundays he spent under "aged roofs of churches" or in "the Cathedrals" of the Church of England, Hawthorne complains that "the sermon is an exceedingly diminutive and unimportant part of the religious services—if, indeed, it be considered a part" (5:226). Thus the grand old trappings of contemporary worship in what Hawthorne terms "Our Old Home" ultimately seem a gaudy distraction in comparison to what the reformed tradition had set in place at the center of the New England service: "The magnificence of the setting quite dazzles out what we Puritans look upon as the chief jewel of the whole affair; for I presume it was our forefathers, the dissenters in England and America, who gave the sermon its present prominence in the Sabbath exercises" (5:227).

This lack of a proper sermon drives Hawthorne outside to find a closer approximation of real worship: "a Methodist preacher uplifts his voice and speedily gathers a congregation, his zeal for whose religious welfare impels the good man to such earnest vociferation and toilsome gesture" that Hawthorne fears the man may melt away, purchasing "every atom of spiritual increment to his hearers by loss of his own corporeal solidity" (5:226). Lest this comic hyperbole be taken for unkind mocking, Hawthorne notes that "if I smile at him, be it understood, it is not in scorn; he performs his sacred office more acceptably than many a prelate. These wayside services attract numbers who would not otherwise listen to prayer, sermon, or hymn, from one year's end to another, and who, for that very reason, are the auditors most likely to be moved by the preacher's eloquence" (5:226). Hawthorne, that "wayside" listener, counted himself among that number. Apart from the lending an ear to the occasional "eloquence" of the fervid Methodists, "I must frankly acknowledge that I never found it possible to give five minutes' attention to any other English preaching" (5:226).

The Methodists may outdo the Anglicans in their worship, but the real contrast is to the great New England divines of "we Puritans" (5:227). The glaring absence at the center of Hawthorne's European search for worship is the "long" New England sermon. Even if his actual memories of such include his own distracted tendencies to daydream and laugh, he hungers for an ideal sermon, no product of puny mind and voice, but one of intellectual and spiritual sustenance. Perhaps for one such as he might have been capable of producing.

One Sunday visiting Westminster Abbey, he finds the preaching so inadequate that he decides to turn his reverent attention to the building itself:

> But when it came to the sermon, the voice of preacher was puny, and so were his thoughts, and both seemed impertinent at such a time and place, when he and all of us were bodily included within a sublime act of religion. . . . The structure itself was the worship of the devout men of long ago, miraculously preserved. . . . I therefore came to the conclusion, that, in my particular case, it would be better and more reverent to let my eyes wander about the edifice, than to fasten them and my thoughts on the evidently uninspired mortal who was venturing—and felt it no venture at all—to speak here above his breath. (5:259–60)

If the English pulpit suffers from being "uninspired," the legacy of English architecture offers a wealth of examples suitable for pious contemplation. While researching the history of worship writ large in stone, Hawthorne does not limit himself to the churches per se, but some question of the Church tends to serve as his point of reference in these outside investigations. He adopts, with surprising sympathy, the perspective of the "churchman."

Making an architectural tour of London in 1855, Hawthorne reflects upon the nature of divine inspiration—or the artifice of its lack. Hawthorne finds the Houses of Parliament strangely unimpressive, given their immensity: "The reason must be, that the architect has not 'builded better than he knew'; there was no power higher and wiser than himself, making him its instrument;—he reckoned upon and contrived all his effects, with malice aforethought, and therefore missed the crowning effect—that being a happiness which God, out of his pure grace, mixes up with only the simple-hearted best efforts of men."[20] While editing Nathaniel's notebooks, Sophia recognized the quoted phrase above as a line from Emerson's poem "The Problem."[21] Nathaniel's application of a poem evidently so familiar in the Hawthorne home seems unlikely to have been careless. And his application is remarkable in the degree to which he uses the line to cut against the grain of the original poem.

The use Hawthorne makes of the phrase seems straightforward enough: that the architect has "not 'builded better than he knew'" describes an inferior result. Had he built better than he knew, he would have indeed built better. Sadly, in his contrivance, the English builder has missed out on grace. Building better than one knows is, in Hawthorne's analysis, a great blessing.

In Emerson's poem, this apparent blessing hardens into a kind of curse:

> The hand that rounded Peter's dome
> And groined the aisles of Christian Rome
> Wrought in a sad sincerity;
> Himself from God he could not free;
> He builded better than he knew,
> The conscious stone to beauty grew.
> (ll.19–24)

Building better than one knows is part of the problem Emerson laments in "The Problem." Here, "sincerity," an uncalculated obedience to "God," counts as "sad." Hawthorne reclaims as "happiness" such sincerity, "the simple-hearted best efforts." To Hawthorne's eye, the problem with the English architect is that he doesn't have the "problem" Emerson diagnoses. The sad fate of Emerson's Roman architect is that "himself from God he could not free"; the lack Hawthorne finds in the English architecture is that it is manifestly free of God's grace.[22]

Hawthorne and Emerson do not differ so greatly in their aesthetic evaluation of "inspired" architecture, as the last line of poetry quoted above shows. Emerson does not deny the powerful effect possible in art wrought by one not free from a commanding personal deity, even art wrought within the pious confines of the church. The "conscious stone"—a force of nature "Like the volcano's tongue of flame, / Up from the burning core below" (ll. 15–16)—grows to "beauty," apparently in spite of the sincere hand that labors to shape it.

Emerson's poem and Hawthorne's passage differ most markedly in representing the significance that dutiful labor holds for the "instrument" of grace "himself," the practitioner of a given craft who serves out an orthodox vocation. In "The Problem," that evaluation is ultimately negative. Thus Emerson speaks of "The burdens of the Bible old" (l. 14) as of an onerous obligation. No such rejection haunts Hawthorne's allusion to the "power higher and wiser than himself." Emerson likes the idea of access to such a power, but it had better not start to look like anything the Church would call "God." To repeat the crux of Emerson's "The Problem": "Yet not for all his faith can see / Would I that cowled churchman be."[23] If Hawthorne likewise shows little indication of wanting literally to *be* that churchman, neither does his response to "The Problem" indicate that he takes at face value Emerson's judgment of religious calling and cowling.[24]

"Instead of interpreting it truly": Septimius's Heresy

In the *Elixir of Life* manuscripts (begun in 1861 and worked on until Hawthorne's death in 1864), the scientistic rejection of a ministerial mentor figure—and hence a choice against ministerial calling—becomes The Problem for Hawthorne, and pursuing that problem gives energy to his last writing. According to what has become the traditional critical account, Hawthorne's problem regarding these final literary projects was of a much more general nature: the manuscripts have been taken to represent his late life failure as writer.[25] In a 2009 intervention, "Late Hawthorne: A Polemical Introduction," Magnus Ullén and David Greven rehearse this account and then go on to challenge it: "As most often told, the story of Hawthorne's last phase runs something like this: when Nathaniel Hawthorne returned to America from his seven years in Europe, his imaginative powers unaccountably but unquestionably expired" (1). Ullén and Greven offer another story that fits the facts at least as plausibly: Hawthorne returns to America with a "new artistic" sense of purpose (2). That purpose, I would argue, becomes increasingly retrospective and self-reflexive, and thus I underscore the way Ullén and Greven turn on its head one of the major premises of the failure narrative: "Unaccountably, critics have assumed, Hawthorne's sense of history failed him in his last years. We believe, on the contrary, that Hawthorne's historical sensibility in general, *and his historical understanding of his own cultural situation in particular,* did not fail him in his last years but intensified and grew deeper" (3; emphasis added). Neither lacking in imaginative and critical faculties nor losing contact with his world, Hawthorne persists as an effective writer, in spite of physical challenges that he faces: "He is increasingly plagued by ill-health, and for the last six months of his life virtually incapacitated for any kind of work. Yet through it all, until the illness (cancer, the biographers now speculate) wholly takes hold of him, he keeps on writing, producing a body of literary writings in three and a half years which in quantitative terms is on par with his famed outpouring in the years of the American Renaissance" (2). Among these late, ambitious projects, the *Septimius Felton* manuscript (the basis for the posthumous *Septimius Felton, or The Elixir of Life,* published under the direction of his daughter, Una Hawthorne, in 1872), is by all accounts the most complete (see, for example, the Centenary editors' singling it out as the only "completely plotted" of the versions, *CE* 13:565). *Septimius Felton, or The Elixir of Life,* thus arguably gives us the fullest reflection of Hawthorne's final sense of artistic purpose. And *Septimius Felton* makes explicit the antagonism between the elixir quest and the ministerial vocation. The text's resolution of this antagonism tends to go against the elixir quest; even while the plot pursues the earthly remedy and marginalizes the figure of the minister, the narration works to enlist Septimius's objection to mortality in the service of an orthodox faith. As I will argue, Hawthorne aligns Septimius's manner of pursuing immortality with a particular version of authorship, but in choosing against that model, the text does not abandon—or fail in—the vocation of writing, but rather pursues it in an altered mode of writing after the minister. Having just parted company with the kindly minister who sought to offer him guidance, Septimius experiences a "sense, which he had felt before, that he, at least, might never die." Drawing the reader aside for reassuring comment, the narrator confides that "the feeling was not peculiar to Septimius; it is an instinct, the meaning of which is mistaken. We have strongly within us the sense of an undying principle; and we transfer that true sense to this life, and to the body, instead of interpreting it truly as the promise of spiritual immortality" (*CE* 13:13). If the text may be said to possess a safe moral, this last sentence would encapsulate it quite well. In expressing it, the text itself takes on a modestly ministerial function.

And yet some of the most careful readers of Hawthorne's late manuscripts have insisted that in such a text, the pious narration may be at most an ascendant aspect of Hawthorne's authorial persona, gaining control over an impulse that may not be in all respects less authentic or noble. One journal entry from Hawthorne's *English Notebooks* has come, in particular, to be associated with *Septimius* as Hawthorne's strongest statement of the impulse towards immortality: "God himself cannot compensate us for being born, in any period short of eternity" (*CE* 21:153).[26] The extended passage merits a closer look, as it is typically cited only in this truncated form. Hawthorne's complete notebook entry for January 20, 1855, consists of three paragraphs, with rather abrupt transitions:

> Mr. Steele (an old gentleman of Rock Ferry) showed me, this morning, a pencil-case formerly belonging to Dr. Johnson. It is six or seven inches long, of large calibre, and very clumsily manufactured of iron, perhaps plated in its better days, but now quite bare;—indeed, it looks as rough as an article of kitchen furniture. . . . Mr. Steele says he has seen a cracked earthen tea-pot, of large size, in which Miss Williams used to make tea for Dr. Johnson.
>
> God himself cannot compensate us for being born, in any period short of eternity. All the misery we endure here constitutes a claim for another life;—and, still more, all the happiness, because all true happiness involves something more than the earth owns, and something more than mortal capacity for the enjoyment of it.
>
> After receiving an injury on the head, the person fancied, all the rest of his life, that he heard voices of people flouting, jeering, and upbraiding him. (CE 21:152–53)

James Wallace calls this passage Hawthorne's "cry of protest" (23), the cry taken up by Septimius. Other critics tend to agree; Hawthorne has lodged a complaint against God and the ordering of the universe, and he correspondingly endows Septimius with energies that Swann terms revolutionary and that Cagidemetrio identifies as utopian albeit deranged

(Swann, 241; Cagidemetrio, 96). Hawthorne's words do carry a great urgency: they may even contain a protest. But the passage as a whole does not warrant the interpretation that has too readily attached itself to the truncated version: "God himself cannot compensate us for being born, in any period short of eternity." Even this single sentence contains the unsaying of the alleged protest. The traditional reading of this sentence has placed too much emphasis on the first clause, has mismeasured the comma as a full stop, or has at least misconstrued the "eternity" named. Certainly the sentence does not read: "God himself cannot compensate us for being born." Though this phrase makes a sharp and scarcely pious start, the end of the sentence leaves open the possibility that eternity might suffice for such a compensation. And more to the point regarding the comparison to Septimius, Hawthorne's prospective eternity is not an earthly one. As the next sentence makes clear, if the accounts are ever to be set straight, the compensation must involve "something more than the earth owns, and something more than mortal capacity for the enjoyment of it." No doctrine of immanence will suffice; even given time, there simply is not world enough. And this world is all that one's mortal frame has the capacity to enjoy; not just more time and a new world, but a new body would be required to make good on the "claim for another life."

Hawthorne's private entry is no Sunday school text; the head-injury exhibit of the final paragraph offers a stark example of "all the misery" one might endure "here." But he offers the disturbing example, not exactly as a protest, to underscore the strength of his claim that "something more" is called for. Hawthorne's words register a protest against the universe only to the extent that he fears that nothing more may be forthcoming in an afterlife. But the passage labors with the negative above all to exorcise this fear: to make the thought of annihilation so truly, cosmically, monstrous as to render the possibility unthinkable.

One protest that the journal passage does lodge strikes against Dr. Johnson's "awful dread of death" (*CE* 5:122). This much may be surmised from the train of associations. Hawthorne has been describing, with the pathos of flat description, Johnson's earthly effects; then suddenly he leaps into his argument for the doctrine of immortality. But there is another presence in the room when Hawthorne records this passage. Hawthorne's precise wording implies an unnamed party. "God cannot compensate us" would have been a one-party assertion. But the additional word *himself* suggests that a comparison is being made to a third person, that a retort has been issued in a philosophical conversation. The debate is about compensation; the interlocutor is Emerson.

"God himself cannot compensate us for being born, in any period short of eternity": if the Supreme Being can't manage this trick, then what can Emerson, with his famous notion of "compensation," do? Emerson's 1841 essay expressing that doctrine, "Compensation," makes a fundamental assault on the Christian notion of heavenly reward, with a critique that originated for Emerson in his early dissent from the clergy. So long has the idea of compensation occupied him that it may even be the origin of his antagonism to clerical tradition: "It seemed to me when very young, that on this subject life was ahead of theology, and the people knew more than the preachers taught"; and "I was lately confirmed in these desires by hearing a sermon at church" delivered by a "preacher, a man esteemed for his orthodoxy" (*CW* 2:55). Against the doctrine of the Last Judgment, Emerson asserts the adequacy of nature to govern action and reaction, to enforce immediate and strict moral accountability.

Emerson's law of compensation, his faith that justice is done in this world rather than in the next, is easily caricatured and misrepresented. My point here is not to suggest that Hawthorne's journal entry cheaply mocks this doctrine of Emerson's; in fact, Emerson's emphasis in "Compensation" on "the present action of the Soul in this world" (*CW* 2:55) pervades Hawthorne's writing until the very end. I have in mind at this textual juncture a more specific dialogue between Hawthorne's words and an Emersonian example that does not actually appear in the essay "Compensation": the Hawthorne journal entry comes very close to being a direct response to one Emersonian form of compensation as given in the essay on "Shakspeare" from *Representative Men.* Here Emerson explains the earthly means by which the genius readily achieves greatness: "Every master has found his materials collected, and his power lay in his sympathy with his people, and in his love of the materials he wrought in. What an economy of power! and what a compensation for the shortness of life! All is done to his hand. The world has brought him thus far on his way" (*CW* 2:348). When Hawthorne writes that "God himself cannot compensate us for being born, in any period short of eternity," he may be heard to respond to the phrase, "what a compensation for the shortness of life!"

One reason for Hawthorne's objection may have to do with differing approaches to composition. Hawthorne might never have found any of Emerson's or Shakespeare's blessed "economy of power!" while crafting his meticulously researched plots and revising his pitch-perfect prose. As Hawthorne famously lamented to the editor James T. Fields in 1864, his rather limited literary output had eventuated from "a life of much smoulder, but scanty fire" (*CE* 18:641). In discussing what she refers to as Hawthorne's "actually quite small" output, Brenda Wineapple juxtaposes this 1864 quotation with Hawthorne's 1851 complaint to Horatio Bridge, "How slowly I make my way in life!"[27] In "Hawthorne, Melville, and the Fiction of Prophecy," Richard Brodhead notes that in both productivity and proclivity to exert influence, Hawthorne was "unlike the magnificent egotists who typically call traditions into being" and, pointedly, "[u]nlike his neighbor Emerson" (14). In discussing Hawthorne's career summary, "much smoulder, but scanty fire," Brodhead outlines the gaps between productive periods, gaps to which any number of psychodynamic theories may attach themselves, but which also seem to correspond to a scholarly model of writing, with periods of research and preparation between publications.

Thus a certain sympathy with Samuel Johnson may play into this response to Emerson's Shakespearean compensation: the pencil case serving as a token reminder of the years Johnson spent laboring over—or neglecting—his (long-promised and long-delayed) edition of Shakespeare.[28] All was not done "to" or for his hand, all was done *by* his hand. All his materials were not "collected" for him—he had to dig up every last scrap, and kick himself every step of the way just to keep moving. And if Hawthorne here disagrees with Emerson's notion that the way the world brings one along compensates for the shortness of life, his portrayal of Septimius only increases the divergence of opinion. Like the Emersonian "master" in *Representative Men* who would draw "power" from "a sympathy with his people" and avail himself of all the world's "materials collected" (*CW* 2:348), Septimius fancies that he will "try the life of power," commencing by traveling "over all this world of mine," to make inventory "as a man newly coming into possession of an estate goes over it," gaining acquaintance with all of its elements and with the people "to whom it is my mission to be their benefactor" (*CE* 13:170). Through Septimius and his grand schemes, Hawthorne will hint that such limitless advantages would not compensate even a lengthened earthly life.

Selling the Secrets of Septimius

Regarding Septimius Felton's ambition to acquire "the art of living long" (*CE* 13:75), the afterlife of Hawthorne's manuscript as a printed artifact itself casts light on some of the desires to which the text might answer. The posthumous marketing of the English edition, *Septimius; A Romance*, replays one potential split between pious and promethean receptions of the text.[29] Bound at the back is a May 1872 advertisement for titles of related interest from the publisher's catalog. *Septimius* heads the list, introduced as a sort of biographical curiosity: "A peculiar interest attaches to this work. It was the last thing the author ever wrote, and he may be said to have died as he wrote it." Here the defining fact that conditions consumption of the text is mortality; the publisher presents the author's own inescapable death as the tragic-comic key for reading the futility of the Romantic quest. Along with this memento mori from the "author of 'The Scarlet Letter,' 'Transformation' [the English title for *The Marble Faun*], & c," the catalog prominently features a number of collected sermons. Placing *Septimius* in this column of pulpit exhortations, the publisher aligns the elixir tale with a clerically endorsed program of spiritual edification.

But the publisher also keeps an eye on those who would seek to extend their earthly portion of years. A bit further down the list, past the new "International Science Series," the catalog heralds the forthcoming promise of *The Secret of Long Life*. A blurb placed in the catalog, taken from a *Public Opinion* review, gives the gist of this anonymous work: "Some shrewd observations illustrated with references to a number of remarkable instances of long life." The promising secret attaches to an authorship that cannot be claimed publicly, but which is no less shrewd for that shrouding, and no less attuned to public appetite.

Leo Spitzer, in his groundbreaking essay "American Advertising as Popular Art," makes a pertinent observation on the incipient American advertising scene contemporary with Hawthorne's art: "It may be noted that the first advertisements to appear in American newspapers (in the middle of the nineteenth century) were those of patent medicines, with their claims of miraculous efficacy. It is highly significant that the industry of advertising had its inception in an appeal to the age-old craving to be saved by magic from the ills and shortcomings of the flesh" (355). Hawthorne was not perhaps entirely immune to such "a craving," but that he would have written, in *Septimius*, a text to flatter or endorse this desire seems unlikely; the presentation of *The Secret of Long Life* on the list of books that the publisher hoped his readers might also like should not be taken to imply a close analogy between the purposes of Hawthorne's project and those of the shrewd trafficker in the science of longevity. The prevalence of the commercial discourse Spitzer identifies seems more plausibly to provide a context within which the elixir impulse might be presented as compelling yet debased. Though the purport of the posthumous artifact may have been up for grabs in the popular book markets of the 1870s, the artisan appears to have left a few discernible marks of his struggle to impose his own meaning on the text. And some of these marks belong to the kind a critical edition makes accessible to an academic market, an audience with its own peculiar appetite for secrets of life.

As presented through the painstaking efforts of the Centenary editors, the Septimius Felton text as unfinished manuscript offers a few unusual glimpses of the author at work and in his work. I quote one passage at length, to convey the sense of crisis in the making of the text and to give the impact of the occasional striking transition the manuscript contains. Here the passage builds to an odd lapse in the narration that at some more formative level may not be a lapse at all. After many months of uninterrupted study, Septimius sets out upon a walk and stumbles onto a moment of clarity, as

> with every step that he took, it seemed as if he were coming out of a mist; out of an enchanted land, where things had seemed to him not as they really were; where impossibilities looked like things of everyday occurrence. . . . Then a great depression fell upon him; he had flung himself so earnestly and entirely upon his strange purpose, that when it seemed about to be removed from him, he felt that he must wander vaguely, stagger, go no whither, and finally sit down by the wayside, and remain there, staring at the wayfarers who *had* a purpose, until he died. I know well what his feeling was! I have had it oftentimes myself, when long brooding

> and busying myself on some idle tale, and keeping my faith in it by estrangement from all intercourse besides, I have chanced to be drawn out of the precincts enchanted by my poor magic; and the look back upon what I have thought, how faded, how monstrous, how apart from all truth it looks, being now seen apart from its own atmosphere, which is entirely essential to its effect. (*CE* 13:129–30)

At the end of this outpouring, Hawthorne apparently notices that he has slipped from exposition into confession. He adds this note to the foregoing: "(Put the above in the third person)."

Hawthorne's distance from his fiction has collapsed at the point where Septimius's illusion falters. All along the narrator has been insisting that Septimius has sadly misspent his efforts. When Septimius's thoughts begin to merge with the narrator's perspective, Hawthorne begins to speak in his own voice. Hawthorne's sympathy is with Septimius and the pain of his disillusionment; the force of that disenchantment reveals Hawthorne's more considered opinion as aligned with that of the narrator.

Pondering "The Field of Dead Bodies," the epithet for Samuel Johnson's birthplace, Lichfield, Hawthorne recoils at "how much mischief has been wrought upon us by this invariable gloom of the Gothic imagination, flinging itself like a death-scented pall over our conceptions of the future state, smothering our hopes, hiding our sky, and inducing dismal efforts to raise the harvest of immortality out of what is most opposite to it—the grave!" (*CE* 5:128). No less a harvest will Septimius attempt; and "dismal efforts" will the narrator deem his labors to be. In the light of this passage on "the harvest of immortality," Hawthorne's *Elixir* manuscripts may be read as a rejection of "the Gothic imagination." One critical essay on the late manuscripts treats them as "the failure of a gothic theme."[30] A better word than "failure" might be "repudiation."

The prospect of an earthly immortality recurs repeatedly within the tales and sketches. The reveries of "The Haunted Mind" (1835) include the wish that Father Time might slumber and permit mortals to live on forever. More frequently, the theme receives a more ironic or ambivalent treatment. In "Dr. Heidegger's Experiment" (1837) water from the Fountain of Youth primarily facilitates the exposure of the vanity of human wishes. A fountain said to have the qualities of the Fountain of Youth likewise occupies the center of "The Hall of Fantasy" (1843). In this tale, an outcry rises up against the end of days, as the reformers demand thousands of years for the testing of their cherished theories (Septimius's ambitious plans will similarly replay this mixture of altruism and selfish curiosity).

The tales that name an "elixir" as such tend toward a darker ambivalence. While touring "A Virtuoso's Collection" (1842), the narrator is invited to quaff of the "Elixir Vitæ" but explains that he has no desire for earthly immortality, believing that the true effect would be death, merely the enduring shadow of life. Even so, the Septimius impulse does not fall entirely silent in the face of this prudent rebuff, as the guide responds that earthly life is the only good. Throughout the tales, the recurring elixir impulse is always carefully set aside: well-preserved, though never allowed to occupy the central action. In the more properly laboratory setting of "The Birth-Mark" (1843) the "Elixir Vitæ" remains on the shelf as a curse and a poison, a dangerous substance from which even the deadly scientist Aylmer refrains. The elixir topos also turns up in *The Scarlet Letter* (1850), with Chillingworth lending his sinister tinge to its appearance in the chapters on "The Leech" and "The Leech and His Patient" (chaps. 9 and 10). But again, Hawthorne's treatment of the topic remains tangential, and in fact merely hypothetical: Chillingworth "soon manifested his familiarity with the ponderous and imposing machinery of antique physic; in which every remedy contained a multitude of far-fetched and heterogeneous ingredients, as elaborately compounded as if the proposed result had been the Elixir of Life."

One later textual moment in *The Marble Faun* seems particularly to point toward the presentation in *Elixir* of Septimius's immortality quest as earnest but misguided. The narrator alludes to the myth of the Sibyl, who obtained "the grievous boon of immortality" from Apollo without due regard to the possible consequences of that wish: "Still, when people insist on building indestructible houses, they incur, or their children do, a misfortune analogous to that of the Sibyl, when she obtained the grievous boon of immortality. So, we may build almost immortal habitations, it is true; but we cannot keep them from growing old, musty, unwholesome, dreary, full of death-scents, ghosts, and murder-stains" (*Novels,* 1103). Echoing this harsh Sibylline lesson, in *Elixir* it falls to a character named "Sybil" to disillusion Septimius of his folly.

It is a folly whose appeal Hawthorne taps into as early as 1828, as his first (anonymous) publication finds the seminarian Fanshawe holed up in his study, surrounded by books "like those fabled volumes of Magic, from which the reader could not turn away his eye. . . . He called up in review the years, that, even at his early age, he had spent in solitary study" (*Novels,* 18). Fanshawe's reflections give rise to a frustrated protest: "He had climbed but a few steps of a ladder that reached to infinity—he had thrown away his life discovering, that, after a thousand such lives, he should still know comparatively nothing" (18). Despite the glimmerings of Ecclesiastical wisdom in these sentiments, Fanshawe ultimately does not renounce his "insane eagerness for knowledge" and studies himself into an early grave (113). Septimius will, of course, rethink the value of Fanshawe's hypothetical "thousand such lives" and hatch his own rebellious project accordingly. As one of Paul Auster's author figures states the case in *The Locked Room,* with words that could belong to Hawthorne, "It seems to me now that Fanshawe was always there. He is the place where everything begins for me, and without him I would hardly know who I am."[31]

In his article on "Immortality in *Septimius Felton,*" James Wallace contends that "in light of his lifelong struggle to resolve his own conflicts regarding the inevitability of death, it would be illogical to conclude, as Crews has, that Hawthorne disapproves of Septimius Felton or his thanatophobia; his attitude toward his protagonist is much more complex" (23). Wallace's essay explores that complexity credibly, but Frederick Crews does have a point as well. Nothing necessarily "illogical" inheres in the position that Hawthorne shares important traits with Septimius and simultaneously disapproves of him: such a case merely would require Hawthorne to be writing in a mode of self-criticism. In the character of Septimius, Hawthorne does see his former authorial self and part of his present authorial self, but this recognition now has the power to dismay him.

Crews thus asserts that in presenting the quests of the last romances as wholly mad, Hawthorne issues a stern retrospective judgment on his earlier subversive impulses:

> Hawthorne can express his old feeling for hidden truth only when he plainly calls it error—as when, to take one example, Septimius Felton is roundly rebuked both by his minister adviser and by Hawthorne himself for making this radical speech: "'It has seemed to me,' observed Septimius, 'that it is not the prevailing mood, the

> most common one, that is to be trusted. This is habit, formality, the shallow covering which we close over what is real, and seldom suffer to be blown aside. But it is the snakelike doubt that thrusts out its head, which gives us a glimpse of reality. Surely, such moments are a hundred times as real as the dull, quiet moments of faith or what you call such'" (XI, 237). Hawthorne's career as a serious writer is based on this premise, but now it scandalizes him. (Crews, 246)

Having made this point, Crews seems to lose it en route to his conclusion that "in the late works Hawthorne has conspicuously failed to add the stucco of ideas and moralizations to his structure of obsession. No 'meaning' in a rational sense attaches to these fragments" (256–57).

But Crews already *has* supplied a rational meaning: *Septimius* casts a conflicted but unmistakably disapproving eye on the boldest productions of Hawthorne's earlier career—so much so that to have completed the Septimius narratives could have meant giving formal expression to the end of Hawthorne's career as an author. Brenda Wineapple stands out in her rich appreciation of the Septimius texts: "Unlike the crude claimant manuscripts, the unfinished 'Septimius' manuscript is supple, sharp, and, though incomplete, still complex . . . and it contains the ripest, most coruscating of his satires, including—significant from a biographical point of view—his most searing self-portrait to date."[32] Crews ultimately opts for a more clinical, Freudian diagnosis in his major conclusions (a tendency Crews subsequently and famously submitted to tough self-criticism), making Oedipal strife the root condition of which the text manifests symptoms: symptoms to which he claims no stucco of moralizations has been added. Yet perhaps in this case, moralization should not be considered as a facade to be *added* to the text. What if, instead, a self-scrutinizing morality proved to be the text's constitutive principle, and its shaky foundation a distrust of the author's own earlier flashes of Emersonian confidence?

Septimius as "The American Scholar"

The issue of compensation, discussed above, is but one of several echoes of Emerson to be found in Hawthorne's portrayal of Septimius, who may be read as a figure of the younger and rebellious Emersonian Hawthorne.

Throughout the 1840s—"his Emerson-inspired 1840s," as Michael Colacurcio has seen fit to call them (*Selected,* xxvi)—the hitherto largely antiquarian Hawthorne turned his focus from Puritan to Transcendental problems of faith and spirit. After the encounter with Emerson's powerful emanations—after, in fact, Hawthorne has mused in the very room of the Old Manse where Emerson penned *Nature* (1836)[33]—Hawthorne's writing is transfigured. In "The Old Manse" (1846), Hawthorne refers to "circumstances around me, which made it difficult to view the world precisely as it exists" (*CE* 10:30); one name for this transformative mediation of perception would be "Idealism," the vision of Emerson's *Nature.* From the vantage of "The Custom-House" (1850), Hawthorne looks back upon the Old Manse period as "living for three years within the subtile influence of an intellect like Emerson's" (*CE* 1:25); when he finds his fancy numbed, he bestirs himself "to seek that invigorating charm of Nature, which used to give me such freshness and activity of thought, the moment that I stepped across the threshold of the Old Manse" (1:35). The word "across" is ambiguous, as may be "Nature": whether Hawthorne speaks of the echoes of *Nature* inside the Manse, or Nature without as viewed through *Nature,* the Emersonian "charm" would work when traversing the threshold in either direction. Colacurcio has highlighted a number of *Manse* tales that bear the Emersonian stamp (*Selected,* xxix–xxxii). Even when Hawthorne is most intensely critical of Emerson in his transcendentalist phase, many of his tales draw their fire from Emerson's apocalyptic idealism.[34]

In the illumination of the great "beacon" of Concord—whose "light revealed objects unseen before . . . glimpses of a creation" (*CE* 10:31)—the Hawthornean literary project joins a call for a displacement of orthodox scripture. In his 1842 journal he would proclaim, "We certainly do need a new revelation—a new system—for there seems to be no life in the old one" (*CE* 8:352). To demand a new revelation—this is to answer the call to Emersonian prophecy. In 1838, Emerson had found it his duty to report to the Harvard Divinity School that "the need was never greater of new revelation than now." In the 1840s, Hawthorne found himself affirming that controversial impulse. Beginning with the Old Manse phase, Hawthorne would redefine, if often against Emerson, the shape of that new revelation. Through Septimius, Hawthorne reconsiders such a project of heterodox scripturism. As Colacurcio cautions, "It might turn out to be too much to insist that Emerson is somehow the master key to the rich intellectual treasures of Hawthorne's Old Manse period" (*Province of Piety,* 30), and a similar caveat may be applied to the hypothesis here offered, that Hawthorne's ongoing concern with the spiritual issues raised by Emerson play out in the struggles of (and with) Septimius. But, in what follows, including a constellation of Emersonian touchstones measuring Hawthorne's final efforts, an attempt is made to follow up on the Colacurcian assertion of cultural engagement: "This much at least seems obvious and necessary: from 1842 on, the intellectual and moral dilemmas of mid-nineteenth-century America would never be far from the thematic center of Hawthorne's adult 'histories'" (31). Larry J. Reynolds notes that "Hawthorne places his protagonist in 'Septimius' within the heart of transcendentalism, the town of Concord, and shows him struggling unsuccessfully to make his way out of that bewitched land."[35] If the 1840s saw Hawthorne "take up the project of writing—in his own Romantic-allegoric way—the History of His Own Times," *Septimius* finds an author wrestling reflexively with the same dilemmas and with some of the later Emersonian reassessments still casting their spell over Concord (30).

The Emersonian echoes begin with Septimius's name itself, although the connection is not immediately obvious. The clearest contemporary flesh-and-blood source for the name "Septimius Felton" would be Cornelius Felton (1807–62). A professor of Greek at Harvard University and later its president in the final two years of his life, Cornelius Felton was an American scholar not lacking in his own associations with Hawthorne and the *Septimius* manuscripts: a gift from Professor Felton, an illustrated edition of Homer's *Iliad,* served as the conversation piece on Hawthorne's first visit to the family of his future wife. From 1857 on, Felton was a member of the Saturday Club, which Hawthorne attended in his last years, following his 1860 return from Europe. Felton translated Menzel's history of German literature, noteworthy for its assault on the Faustian Goethe; he was a man of science and regent of the Smithsonian Institute.[36]

Nevertheless, one intends no slight to the memory of Cornelius Felton in saying that his greatest contribution to American literature was that he invited Emerson to deliver the Phi Beta Kappa address to Harvard's class of 1837.[37] And this address, known as "The American Scholar," may illuminate much about Septimius's creative strivings.

Septimius's project begins with a cry of defiance: "Let him that is strong enough, live!" Soon "after the flash of this heroic mood, the fire subsided," and Septimius returns to pore over the books in his study. These now seem to him "dead and moldy" (*CE* 13:13): "Then he suspected that the way truly to live and answer the purposes of life was not to gather up thoughts into books, where they grow so dry, but to live" (*CE* 13:14). Septimius's rebellion against orthodoxy spurs his dissatisfaction with a mere dead-end bookishness. Emerson opens "The American Scholar" with a similar note of dissatisfaction: "Instead of Man Thinking, we have the bookworm" (*CW* 1:56). And Emerson likewise contrasts bookish pursuits with moments of immediate inspiration: "Books are for the scholar's idle times. When he can read God directly, the hour is too precious to be wasted in other men's transcripts of their readings" (*CW* 1:57). But, like Septimius's fleeting moods of fire, such moments pass, and the scholar must periodically turn to books to fuel the furnace. Even while studying, the scholar must never entirely be drawn out of the active world into a passive and contemplative "orbit" of the text: "a great soul will be *strong to live,* as well as strong to think" (*CW* 1:61; emphasis added). Septimius, committed to his own scholarly program, insists upon strong thinking (and strong reading) for strong living.

Septimius applies himself with earnest diligence to read a "mysterious manuscript," wherefrom he hopes to derive the secret of living long. Though at first the document appears to contain only "misty and undefined germs of thought," when Septimius concentrates his mind upon them, these hitherto vague writings take more distinct shape (*CE* 13:101). He thus begins to derive "rules of life" from the manuscript (*CE* 13:102). Hawthorne emphasizes the creative activity of Septimius's hermeneutics: "Not that all this was in the document itself; but by studying it so earnestly, and as it were creating its meaning anew for himself" (*CE* 13:103), Septimius constructs a reading that serves his own intentions. Septimius's creative rendering of reality gets to the heart of Emerson's advice in "The American Scholar": "One must be an inventor to read well" (*CW* 1:58).

Though Emerson's remarks may be applied to a general project of reading, his address places the emphasis on "American" as well as on "Scholar." "The American Scholar" addresses the particular case of how an American writer should make use of the literary past without remaining secondary to the tradition of the transatlantic precursors. In Oliver Wendell Holmes's famous tagline, "The American Scholar" is "our intellectual Declaration of Independence."[38] The historical setting and circumstances of Septimius's project resonate with this culture-founding impulse of Emerson's address. Working against the backdrop of the American Revolution, Septimius follows Emerson's advice in achieving originality through appropriation: Septimius rewrites an English manuscript that he takes from a British soldier whom he has killed on American soil. In forging his own new meaning for the document, Septimius declares his independence as an American Scholar. The declaration is, of course, oddly dependent: far from claiming authorship through an act of ex nihilo creation, this assertion of American letters depends upon violent appropriation of a British legacy. In stark contrast to the literary origin myth of an American Adam, Hawthorne here gives us an American Cain.[39]

In crafting such an identity, achieving independence from British letters presents but one scale of challenge; siblings on both sides of the Atlantic must be supplanted. To claim originality, the American scholar must assert independence from local and sometimes family tradition as well. Septimius must evade the expectation that "you'll be a mighty man in the pulpit yet, and worthy to keep up the name of your great grandfather" (*CE* 13:15). To this end, he has for some time been subjecting his own religious heritage to an Emersonian program of strong reading.[40] Septimius has seized upon the books of "good and earnest divines, whose wisdom he had happened, by help of the devil, to turn to mischief; reading them by the light of hell-fire." Indeed, Septimius is no mere novice in his assault on orthodoxy; "it seemed to him as if he had never been other than a doubter and a questioner, even in his boyhood" (*CE* 13:13). The disposition, a thoroughgoing skepticism, is often shared by Hawthorne. To call Septimius's project Emersonian is not to mistake Septimius for Emerson. Rather, it is to recognize in Septimius, not merely through verbal echoes, but above all in the boldness of the design, the fever pitch of Hawthorne at his most inspired. And to recognize in the writing of *Septimius Felton* a Hawthorne who, as Larry Reynolds felicitously puts it, viewed Emerson as an "angelic friend" but one whose influence could be "Satanic in its effects" (*CE* 13:12). Septimius writes in the light of "hell-fire" and out of a dangerous Emersonian willfulness. The text does not so much scoff at Emerson as make stern observations and a rueful lament about an author who has imbibed his spirit.

Septimius's Form of Infidelity

The language with which Hawthorne frames Septimius's transgressive ambition locates the protagonist in the midst of the Transcendentalist controversy and what Andrews Norton in 1839 had termed "The Latest Form of Infidelity" (11). The minister speaks to Septimius in terms that recall Norton's reply to Emerson's Divinity School Address: "'Well, Septimius,' said the minister, sadly—yet not as one shocked by what he had never seen before—'I must leave you to struggle through this *form of unbelief* as best you may'" (*CE* 13:12; emphasis added). The old clergyman knows all too well the venerable history of human desires to sample the fruit of the tree of life and become like God; Septimius's infidelity is merely the "latest form." Though the *Septimius Felton* manuscript gives this minister no name, the later *Septimius Norton* draft refers to him as the Rev. Mr. Norton (*CE* 13:197, 198). Further into the manuscript, the name Norton attaches itself to Septimius. Transferred from theological mentor to his failed charge, this naming evokes the family history of the Nortons, from "Unitarian Pope" Andrews to his son Charles Eliot, agnostic apostle of liberal education.[41]

The form of infidelity itself remains more Emersonian than (Charles Eliot) Nortonian. Turning from the description of how Septimius had long been reading sermons "by the light of hell-fire," the narrator presents the fruit of that willful apprenticeship: "And now this new, strange thought of the sufficiency of the world for man, if man were only sufficient for that, kept recurring to him; and with it came a certain sense . . . that he, at least, might never die" (*CE* 13:13). Emerson's essay on "History" (1841) offers but one instance of this key Emersonian doctrine of the "sufficiency of the world *for* man": "The world exists for the education of each man. . . . He should see that he can live all history in his own person" (*CW* 2:5-6).

Here Emerson's idea that one person might "live all history" does not refer to a literal prolongation of life, but rather to a compression of experience: "Every thing tends in a wonderful manner to abbreviate itself and yield its own virtue to him" (*CW* 2:6). This effective abbreviation of history may be recognized as one of the advantages enjoyed by the great author in "Shakspeare": the "economy of power" that offers a "compensation for the shortness of life" (*CW* 2:348). Nevertheless, later in the essay on "History," Emerson offers an *apologia* for the immortality impulse and its cohort as "the obscure efforts of the mind in the right direction": "Magic, and all that is ascribed to it, is a deep presentiment of the powers of science. . . . The preternatural prowess of the hero, the gift of perpetual youth, and the like, are alike the endeavour of the human spirit 'to bend the shows of things to the desires of the mind'" (2:253).

In Hawthorne's rendering, this "deep presentiment of the powers of science" holds the more misguided of the story's characters in its thrall. With all the time in the world before them, Septimius and Sybil Dacy speculate about the future, budgeting major projects at a century apiece. They plan hundreds of years of learning, playing, philosophy building and philosophy smashing, and history making and history writing. Septimius calculates that, after several such centuries, "I shall have pretty well prepared myself for what I have been contemplating from the first. I will become a religious teacher, and promulgate a faith, and prove it by prophecies and miracles; for my long experience will enable me to do the first, and the acquaintance which I will have formed with the mysteries of science will put the latter at my fingers' ends" (*CE* 13:173–74). He will exploit his technical mastery to compel the masses to put all their hopes in "my doctrine"; wielding his scientific power, he will "make" everyone "good, holy, happy" (*CE* 13:174).

At some level anticipating the emptiness of such a charade, Septimius suspects that the life of "Saint and Prophet" may grow tiresome. If the revelation of Septimius's "religious" ambition, the grand scheme he has been plotting "from the first," were not enough to cast a moral pall over the elixir project, his proposed sequel to his dalliance in prophecy goes even further to confirm his decadence: "So—in the next hundred years, Sybil—in that one little century—methinks I would fain be what men call wicked. . . . Imagination is only a dream; I can imagine myself a murderer, and all other modes of crime; but it leaves no real impression upon the heart. I must live these things. The rampant unrestraint, which is the joy of wickedness" (*CE* 13:174). The offhand manner of these remarks seems calculated to shock, as an indication that Septimius has strayed too far indeed.

In discussing similar topics, Emerson too knows something about casual rhetoric calculated to shock, as he self-consciously walks the thin line between repelling his readers and prodding them with what he intends as salutary "provocation." Within the context of the *Elixir* narration, Hawthorne crosses that line and makes Septimius's thoughts deliberately repellent. Emerson, in one of his more outrageous-sounding provocations, supposes that "good and bad are but names very readily transferable to that or this" (*CW* 2:30). When Septimius muses that he "would fain be what men *call* wicked," he invokes a similarly sophistic distinction about the arbitrary conventions of naming. Imagining himself in the role of prophet and then declaring himself free to act from a position beyond good and evil—that is, starting from an ambition to authorize his own religion and proceeding to a possible logical next step, that of dispensing with any concern for existing moral standards—Septimius takes this quasi-Nietzschean principle and uses it as a speculative pretext for murder.

Hawthorne presents this decadence as a by-product of the elixir quest. The great initial aim, albeit one Septimius foresees carelessly tossing aside, is the new faith proven by science. What Septimius proposes as a charlatan, Emerson pursues as an earnest quest. Laura Dassow Walls writes that "Emerson sought to integrate poetry, culture, religion, society, and science into one grand and coherent whole, and in so doing he offered to America a new faith: science" ("Anatomy of Truth," 425).[42] Walls's interpretation, shared by Lee Rust Brown and others, is no stretch. In "Worship," from *The Conduct of Life,* Emerson states this position in so many words: "The scientific mind must have a faith which is science" (*CW* 6:128).

Emerson in no way proposes the kind of deliberate mystification that Septimius plots, which seems to amount to a self-consciously false prophecy. An important difference lies in point of view and access to knowledge—Septimius shares Emerson's faith in science, but Septimius's would-be converts would merely place their faith in him: "We will smile superior, to see what a facile thing it is, to make a people happy . . . and when this is effected, we will vanish from our loving people, and be seen no more, but be reverenced as gods—we, meanwhile, serene, overlooked, and smiling to ourselves, amid the very crowd that is looking for us" (*CE* 13:173). Septimius represents, in the extreme, the amoral student of Emersonian power.

Septimius Reads The Conduct of Life

The specific content of Septimius's curriculum in power, his reconstruction of the elixir manuscripts, reflects an imbalanced version of Emerson's *Conduct of Life.* Albert von Frank, discussing the literary context for 1860, notes that "Hawthorne's *Marble Faun,* published this year, was certainly a puzzle to Emerson, while Emerson's *Conduct of Life,* published this year, was very likely a puzzle to Hawthorne" (*Chronology,* 348). One might add that the elixir of life project, begun shortly after the publication of the *Conduct of Life,* bears the marks of that probable puzzling. Alide Cagidemetrio even ventures in passing that some of Hawthorne's *Septimius Felton* reads like a satire on "Fate" from the *Conduct* series (97).

A focus on this one dimension of *Conduct* to the exclusion of others is not uncommon in the criticism, but in this case, a closer look at Hawthorne's text may point toward something strategic in the imbalance. Septimius's fullest overview of the deciphered manuscript readily evokes Emerson's *Conduct of Life* both in its general impression and in its verbal theme and variation. The repetitive stream of phrases all but names the title of Emerson's book:

> Amid a great deal of misty stuff, he found the document to consist chiefly . . . of certain *rules of life;* he would have taken it, at a casual inspection, for an essay of counsel, addressed by some great and sagacious man, to a youth in whom he felt an interest; such excellent maxims there were, so sound and good a *doctrine of life* propounded, such wisdom in all matter that came within the writer's purview. It was as much like a digested synopsis of some old philosopher's wise *rules of conduct,* as anything else (*CE* 13:102; emphasis added).

This sketch might plausibly be imagined to conjure the words of the old "Concord Sage." *The Conduct of Life* purports to be Emerson's summa, proposing at its outset the "method of taking up in turn each of the leading topics which belong to our scheme of human life" (*CW* 6:2); it would thus cover, as Septimius initially discerns in the text he reads, "all matter that came within the writer's purview." Septimius's description does not end here. Something about this "conduct" book strikes Septimius as peculiar: "But, on closer inspection, Septimius . . . was not so well satisfied. True; everything that was said seemed not discordant with the rules of sound morality; not unwise; it was shrewd, sagacious, it did not appear to infringe upon the rights of mankind; but there was something left out, something unsatisfactory—what was it?" (*CE* 13:102). Elsewhere in the romance, Hawthorne drops some clearer clues about the mysterious essence of the "something left out." During another laborious session with the text, Septimius gathers a similar sense of the overall purpose of the author: "Judging by what he could pick out, he would have thought the whole essay was upon the moral conduct" or "rule of life" (*CE* 13:66). In this reading, Septimius more clearly identifies the "something unsatisfactory" as a paradox; the text appears to be an essay on "moral" conduct in some broad sense, "although without any discoverable reference to religious or moral motives" (13:66). This impression of a categorical absence accords with some of the specific rules that Septimius later deciphers, for example the "shrewd" maxim, "Say thy prayers at bedtime, if thou deemest it will give thee the quieter sleep; yet let it not trouble thee if thou forgettest them" (13:107).

As he begins to work his way through the text, Septimius notes that religion has been omitted. Emerson says as much about his own text. He foregrounds the early exclusion of religious considerations as a calculated feature of *The Conduct of Life:* in the second chapter, on "Power," Emerson notes that "there are sources on which I have not drawn. I know what I abstain from. I adjourn what I have to say on this topic to the chapters on Culture and Worship" (*CW* 6:42). Septimius's initial encounters with the manuscript seem to register this deferral. Thus far, that is, Hawthorne's text does not offer a criticism of Emerson's *Conduct* so much as an attentive unfolding of its rhetorical progress.

When Emerson finally gets around to "Worship" four chapters later, he begins with the report that "some of my friends have complained, when the preceding papers were read, that we discussed Fate, Power, and Wealth, on too low a platform" (*CW* 6:107). Against such concern, Emerson avers that he has no "fear that a skeptical bias can be given by leaning hard on the sides of fate, of practical power, or of trade, which the doctrine of Faith cannot down-weigh" (*CW* 6:107).

Hawthorne's narrative, and Septimius's understanding of the elixir of life project, takes a similar path of deferral. After the descriptions cited above, in which Septimius repeatedly construes the manuscript as a book of counsel with something missing, Hawthorne makes the following note to himself in his own manuscript: "<bring in religion finally>" (*CE* 13:127). The clearest entry of religion as a topic arrives when Septimius explains his long-term plan to "promulgate" his a new "faith" by drawing upon his intimate acquaintance with "the mysteries of science" (*CE* 13:173–74). This scheme bears some resemblance to the doctrine of faith Emerson ultimately espouses in "Worship": "a faith which is science" (*CW* 6:128). But en route to this doctrine, Hawthorne has Septimius leave out a key ingredient. The resulting doctrine is the purely scientific side of "Worship," one that omits the relational dynamic found elsewhere in Emerson's essay.

In his finally triumphant construction of the manuscript, Septimius exults, "I see, I see, it requires a strong spirit, capable of much lonely endurance, able to be sufficient unto itself, loving not too much, dependent on no sweet ties of affection, to be capable of the mighty trial which now devolves on me" (*CE* 13:163–64). "Loving not too much": here sits a coldly reductive formulation of Emerson's familiar injunction against the idolatry of persons—but without any counterbalancing word in defense of human fellowship. This formula does not represent the Emerson of "Worship" who would willingly embrace a friend who would "help in counsel or conduct" (*CW* 6:113), and who, once assured of that friend's earnestness, would "set no limit" to the expectations of guidance by the "moral sentiment" of another (*CW* 6:115). In words that might serve as a tonic to Septimius's fantastical dreams of murder, Emerson prescribes that "the remedy for all blunders, the cure of blindness, the cure of crime, is love" (*CW* 6:115).

Though sadly mistaken, Septimius takes on an impersonal approach to *Conduct,* which is not entirely unfounded: even in "Worship," Emerson does require one to be "capable of much lonely endurance," the course that Septimius chooses. But Emerson's text does not consistently *prefer* the course that Septimius embraces. Although the "new church founded on moral science" will indeed make one know "that much of the time he must have himself to [be] his [only] friend," Emerson does not celebrate the bitter truth of this imparted knowledge (*CW* 6:128). One "must" make do with oneself, because at times, if all friends have departed, one will have no choice; but one does not do so out of a refusal to love, the deliberate avoidance of sweet ties, religious and relational, that Septimius equates with a strong spirit and reads as the prescription of the *Elixir* text.

The Septimian reading of *The Conduct of Life* implies a caution about the Emersonian—and Hawthornean—tendency to slip willingly out of fellowship and into solitude. In response to the suggestion that *he* might take the lead in gathering what would become "The Saturday Club," Emerson fears that he is "the worst person that could be named, except Hawthorne, to attempt it" (Edward Emerson, 8). But he did join that circle of friends, as did Hawthorne, even if the latter, in choosing seats at the table, often limited his dinnertime-conversation duties by putting himself under Emerson's "protection" (Edward Emerson, 208). *The Conduct of Life,* too, does get around to affirming a social dimension to "Worship," but this term can seem all too prone to falling out of the Emersonian equation.[43] As Septimius's elixir of life project dramatizes, *The Conduct of Life* can make for dangerous reading if it falls into the wrong "strong" hands. Through Septimius Felton, Hawthorne shows us *The Conduct of Life* as read by the American Scholar.

CHAPTER 4

Melville's Benediction

Clarel's Recollection of Calling: Melville and Emerson

Annotating his copy of *The Conduct of Life* (1860), Melville notices that Emerson "jumps into the pulpit, from off the tripod here."[1] As noted at the beginning of the chapter on Emerson, Melville's marginal comment sheds light on a general movement of Emerson's career around the time that he was composing the lectures that became *Conduct,* as Emerson returned to a more ministerial role in his speaking and writing. The tripod belongs to the position of the seer; to leap from thence into the pulpit entails a shift from prophecy to preaching.

Melville compresses his commentary through a shorthand of imagery not merely rich in connotation but also precisely indexed to an earlier Emerson essay of great personal significance to Melville. To note Emerson's vocational jump, Melville alludes to "Shakspeare; or, the Poet," from *Representative Men* (1850).

Emerson describes the hermetic, oracular quality of Shakespeare's writing, the wisdom that can touch only "the Shakspeare in us" (*CW* 4:119). For the genius to condescend and explain would be fruitless: "He cannot step *from off his tripod,* and give us anecdotes of his inspirations" (4:119; emphasis added). The oracle cannot stoop to reach his audience; he will not preach to the nonelect.

Emerson uses this hermetic quality as one criterion to judge the authenticity of Shakespearean authorship (as, indeed, the author of *The Prophetic Melville* uses this criterion to trace what he sees as Melville's decline: from the prophetic visionary of *Moby-Dick* who presents mystery and "wonder" to a later Melville who supplies "commentary" in an increasingly "didactic" manner that betrays "the tragic denouement of the writer-prophet's sense of himself").[2] Emerson has acquainted himself with contemporary scholarship that traces the "indebtedness" of the bard and that suggests that substantial portions of certain plays "were written by some author preceding Shakspeare" (*CW* 4:112). Reading *Henry VIII* in the light of this hypothesis, Emerson believes he can "see plainly the cropping out of the original rock on which his own finer stratum was laid" (4:112). Unlike the verse of Shakespeare himself, rhythmically true only to its own meaning rather than reliant upon conventional forms, "here the lines are constructed on a given tune, and the verse has even a trace of *pulpit* eloquence" (4:112; emphasis added). The "pulpit" belongs to Shakespeare's precursor; the genius has outgrown this constraint; the "tripod" of inspiration is Shakespeare's own. To complete the expansion of Melville's commentary: to jump "into the pulpit, from off the tripod" is to return to the position of the precursor and the mode of writing the author has overthrown.

Shakespeare, the figure Melville calls to mind to mark Emerson's turn from inspiration to exhortation, bears a special emblematic significance to the author of *Moby-Dick*. Shakespeare played a formative role in his own development as an author and served as the touchstone for measuring the American literary achievements of his own day. In 1849, Melville reads both Emerson and Shakespeare for the first time. In these authors, he sees the possibility of a new "literary genius and messianic spiritual power," as Richard Brodhead underscores in "Hawthorne, Melville, and the Fiction of Prophecy."[3] In a letter to Evert Duyckinck on March 3, 1849, Melville verbally slaps his forehead with the force of an epiphany: "Dolt & ass that I am have lived more than 29 years, & until a few days ago, never made close acquaintance with the divine William. Ah, he's full of sermons-on-the-mount, and gentle, aye, almost as Jesus. I fancy that this moment Shakspeare in heaven ranks with Gabriel Raphael and Michael. And if another Messiah ever comes twill be in Shakesper's person."[4] Of course the most famous Second Coming Melville heralded was the advent of Shakespeare in the person of Nathaniel Hawthorne, as he exulted in the 1850 "Hawthorne and His Mosses." From this turning point onward, Emerson, Hawthorne, and Shakespeare are linked to prophetic authorship for Melville. If F. O. Matthiessen could have presented the term "American Renaissance" to the foremost authors alleged to have defined the period and asked them to ascribe a meaning to the phrase, one possible response might have lain in this comparison drawn by Melville. In his generation, he had believed, America was enjoying the advent of literary genius on par with the best the English Renaissance had produced.[5] Among *Representative Men,* Emerson's contribution during Matthiessen's blockbuster years (1850–55), "Shakspeare" was more representative than most for Melville.

Reading *The Conduct of Life,* he observes that the rhetoric of New England literature has changed again. Melville responds in the margins, but also, less directly, in his subsequent writing. In *Melville's Bibles*, Ilana Pardes traces an "exegetical" preoccupation throughout the career but grants unique status to "*Moby-Dick* because it is undoubtedly the climactic moment of this project. It is the one book in Melville's oeuvre that aspired to be a grand Bible and has become one"(11).[6] *Clarel,* on the other hand, no longer seeking to *be* original scripture, "depicts every step in the Holy Land as a step into numerous biblical texts" (11). Merton Sealts, Jr., in his invaluable study of *Melville's Reading,* notes that 1870 is the year Melville begins to buy books about the Holy Land, presumably to assist him in the preparation of *Clarel: A Poem and Pilgrimage in the Holy Land* (1876), then underway. "In this same year," Sealts observes, "Melville also acquired other books not directly related to the poem"; among these was Emerson's *The Conduct of Life*—not directly related perhaps, but not unrelated either.[7] A theme of Melville's marginalia on *Conduct* also proves to be an overriding concern for *Clarel:* the question of religious vocation.

The curiously named title character of *Clarel* is a young divinity student undergoing a crisis of faith; he hopes that a pilgrimage to the Holy Land will settle his doubts. Stan Goldman, in his persuasive study of *Melville's Protest Theism*, suggests that "Clar-el" signifies the search for God, or the Hebrew "El" (3). The content of the poem is surely consistent with this suggestion, and Goldman's argument scarcely rests upon this single conjecture. That said, I would like to propose another meaning for "Clarel," based upon a word that is juxtaposed with the character's name on several occasions, often closely, as in the phrase, "Clarel.—'I recall'" (115) and, by way of simple functional definition of what the poem does, "Clarel recalls" (88).[8] That word, "recall," also happens to be an anagram of "Clarel." Its various related significances resonate throughout the poem: in the recurring memories that haunt Clarel during his pilgrimage, "recall" means to remember; also, to call *again,* to re-call, perhaps to recall and be called once more to one's calling; or to call *back,* back to a point of origin, especially to repair or to remake. When Emerson jumps into the pulpit again, he issues a recall. In the metaphysical encyclopedia that is *Clarel,* Melville records his own total recall of his calling to prophecy and gives a new form of expression to his lifelong spiritual restlessness.

Responsive Readings: Emerson and Hawthorne and Melville

In 1872, another book indirectly related to *Clarel* makes its way into Melville's library, as a gift from his wife, Elizabeth: *Septimius Felton; or, The Elixir of Life.*[9] Hawthorne's narrative resonates at several junctures with *Clarel,* particularly in anticipating the latter work's preoccupation with death and what may lie beyond. Septimius objects that life is pointless because it is "so soon stilled, before your activity has come to any definite end. . . . I doubt, if it had been left to my choice, whether I should have taken existence on such terms; so much trouble of preparation to live, and then no life at all; a ponderous beginning, and nothing more."[10] His neighbor, the wholesome and pious Rose, replies to Septimius's quarrel with "Providence": "But I think it was worth while to be born, if only for the sake of one such pleasant spring morning as this; and God gives us many, and better things when these are past." Septimius may become the dupe of outlandish ambitions, but Hawthorne also permits him the simple poignancy of earnest doubts. His reply to Rose's assurances captures this more human tone: "We hope so," said Septimius, who was again looking on the ground. "But who knows?" (*CE* 13:7).

Melville's and Hawthorne's troubled young divinity students share this nagging doubt. One line in *Clarel* stands out, literally, in voicing this uncertainty. The vast majority of the poem's eighteen thousand lines scan as tetrameter. But in the midst of this long four-beat march, one alexandrine obtrusively drags its six slow feet across the reader's field of vision. The line is spoken by Rolfe, the pilgrim critics most frequently identify as a version of the mature Melville (Rolfe and Clarel share together in the experience of pilgrimage, an experience beset by struggles with doubt; I would offer that Rolfe presents a plausible image of Melville in the Holy Land in 1856–57, but I would make a distinction between the pilgrim of 1856 and the poet of 1876, whose persona comes to us through the most understudied character in *Clarel:* that of the narrator).[11] Soon after the (Arnoldian) mention of life as a "darkling" stream, perhaps a dream, Rolfe utters the following reverie: "Yea, much as man might hope, and more than heaven may mean?" (373).[12] The extra (post-tetrameter) syllables, with their desolate echo, all fall after the word "more": what "heaven may mean" lies beyond the boundaries of formal expression allotted to the body of the poem.

In his doubts, Clarel finds himself chilled above all by what he calls the "naturalistic knell" of modern science (*NN* 12:4). Here too, he picks up on a concern of his kindred seeker in *Elixir:* "May it not be possible," asked Septimius, "to have too profound a sense of the marvellous contrivance and adaptation of this material world, to require or believe in anything spiritual?" (*CE* 13:11) Here lies the materialist threat of Emerson's projection of "a faith which is science": a faith which is not.

As outlined in "Worship," Emerson's new church "founded on moral science" would have "science for symbol and illustration" (*CW* 6:128). In Clarel's ears, science is a clanging symbol, its doleful knell speaking neither in the tongues of men nor of angels. Emerson gives fair warning that the illustration of science may present a lonely picture: "Was never stoicism so stern and exigent as this shall be. It shall send man home to his central solitude" (*CW* 6:128). But as was noted in the previous chapter, even Emerson seems not quite content for this solitude to remain absolute. Elsewhere in the essay on "Worship," he clearly makes room for a religious sentiment that may bind two together in spiritual friendship (*CW* 6:115-16). For Hawthorne's and Melville's late questers, such companionship becomes the object of intense experimentation. Emerson's prediction that the new worshipper "shall expect no coöperation, he shall walk with no companion" (*CW* 6:128) often seems all too sadly real for each protagonist, although *Clarel* offers more glimpses of communion. Having rejected his ministerial mentor and devoted himself to self-reliant scientific inquiry, Septimius finds himself "at the point of despair, for want of a guide" (*CE* 13:68), and "astray, seeking everywhere" for counsel (13:73). Clarel, too, cut off from the resources of a traditional faith, seeks a guide out of a sense of desperation. By conventional account, Clarel's experiments with spiritual companionship all terminate in failure, and, for Clarel the young pilgrim, that account rings true, notably with the reticent Vine (commonly supposed to have been modeled on Hawthorne).

Clarel ultimately describes a circle, in the cartography of Clarel's journey and in the spiritual odyssey of his doubting Cartesian self. On the circuit of his pilgrimage, Clarel fails to secure the spiritual certainty, guidance, or even friendship he seeks. The poem opens and closes in Jerusalem, with Clarel in his room, alone with his doubts. Leaving Clarel with the same problem with which he began, the poem's narrator gestures once more toward the prospect of hope: "Even death may prove unreal at the last. . . . Then keep thy heart, though yet but ill-resigned— . . . Emerge thou mayst from the last whelming sea" (*NN* 12:499). However one takes the tone of these final lines—whether genuine hope or cruel mockery—the prime fact of their expression is their subjunctive mood. As long as such possibilities *may* apply, however "ill-resigned" Clarel's heart, the motive for cyclical questing remains. As has been suggested by Slavoj Žižek, such a circular, Sisyphean, movement corresponds to an intense and unquenchable desire.[13]

Nathaniel Hawthorne's much-quoted description of his friend's earnest restlessness still captures this spirit best:

> Melville, as he always does, began to reason of Providence and futurity, and of everything that lies beyond human ken, and informed me that he had "pretty much made up his mind to be annihilated"; but still he does not seem to rest in that anticipation; and, I think, will never rest until he gets hold of a definite belief. It is strange how he persists—and has persisted ever since I knew him, and probably long before—in wandering to-and-fro over these deserts, as dismal and monotonous as the sand hills amid which we were sitting. He can neither believe, nor be comfortable in his unbelief; and he is too honest and courageous not to try to do one or the other. If he were a religious man, he would be one of the most truly religious and reverential; he has a very high and noble nature, and better worth immortality than most of us.

Hawthorne entered these thoughts in his notebook on November 20, 1856, after Melville had visited him at the Liverpool Consulate, en route to the Mediterranean—and from thence, to wander the deserts that would provide the setting for *Clarel.*

During the long gestation of *Clarel,* between Melville's own pilgrimage to the Holy Land and the publication of the poem in 1876, Melville singled out for especial approval a chapter from Hawthorne's *Marble Faun* (1860). Hawthorne's discourse on "The Emptiness of Picture Galleries" Melville judged to be "admirable, and, doubtless, too true."[14] In this passage, Hilda, daughter of the Puritans, has turned, "in her present need and hunger for a spiritual revelation," to the contemplation of art. But she finds mostly the "Emptiness" named in the chapter's title. The narrator observes that "if Art had not strayed away from its legitimate paths and aims, it ought to soften and sweeten the lives of its worshippers. . . . But, of its own potency, it has no such effect; and it fails, likewise, in that other test of its moral value. . . . It cannot comfort the heart in affliction; it grows dim when the shadow is upon us (*Novels,* 1135). But there remains the rare example of a spiritual art that has not "strayed" or "lost its consecration": a fresco of Christ bound to a pillar shows what "art, devoutly exercised, might effect in behalf of religious truth; involving, as it does, deeper mysteries of Revelation, and bringing them closer to man's heart, and making him tenderer to be impressed by them, than the most eloquent words of preacher or prophet" (1134–35). The narrator does not limit his treatise to pictorial art; the writerly artist may be held to no less lofty a standard: "Is a painter more sacred than a poet?" (1135). In this account, the author's efficacy may be compared to that of the prophet, but only in remaining true to a calling of making accessible the prophet's truth, not in claiming an original voice. Literature becomes a supplement, extending scriptural truth to the worshipper.

Whether or not we see Melville's *Clarel* as the spiritual supplement *The Marble Faun* proposes—and I will argue that it offers more to "comfort the heart in affliction" than critics have typically allowed—it surely represents an altered mode of writing after the minister, one driven by the "emptiness" that Hawthorne describes and that Melville recognizes. No longer presuming to write the new spirit-filled "gospel in this century," Melville designs his late poem as a spiritual quest, one undertaken to bring closer to the heart the mysteries of revelation. In the wake of his readings of later Emerson and Hawthorne, Melville forges a new role for the writer. He discovers that there yet remains something he can do as persistently and reverentially as any "preacher or prophet": to write in pursuit of spiritual desire.

Poem and Pilgrimage

Melville does so as a poet, even as the "sacred" poet for whom Hawthorne calls from those empty galleries. And he does so in a vein that might well be compared to the Emersonian path, especially if we take seriously David Robinson's corrective view of Emerson and how he experienced the "close identity between poetry and the spiritual life, a closeness that at times transformed 'poetry' into a kind of synonym for religious insight."[15] But not, when viewed closely over some four decades of Emerson's career, an insight marked by blithe prophetic confidence: "Despite his ostensible identity as both a visionary and an optimist, the history of Emerson's religious experience is one of crisis, inner struggle, and a personal attempt to find a new grounding and stable assurance for his religious outlook. In that effort the poet and his methods were a crucial point of reference" (95). *Clarel* records such a crisis, through a poetics forged to enact an earnest spiritual striving in the aftermath of certainty (whether previously seized in romantic presumption or assumed through a short-circuiting of orthodox faith). In its syntactical difficulty and its argumentative flux, it achieves an Emersonian ideal of poetry: "By setting the mind's energy in motion, poetry causes all settled things to be reconsidered.[16] Poetry drives us out of complacency; its 'supreme value' is 'to educate us to a height beyond itself'" (108). Undertaking what Emerson terms the "lonely faith" of poetry (109), *Clarel,* as *Poem and Pilgrimage,* marks the slow and painful process toward that self-transcending education.

Discovering how Melville's poetic method might contribute to that journey has been a long-standing challenge. As one 1876 reviewer usefully framed the problem (only to dismiss it), "We confess that we are puzzled by the title of Mr. Herman Melville's last volume—'Clarel: A Poem and Pilgrimage in the Holy Land.' How a book can be a poem in the Holy Land, or a pilgrimage in the Holy Land, or a pilgrimage at all, or how it can be both a poem and a pilgrimage, we cannot really discover. The fact of the matter, set forth in simple English, is, that 'Clarel' is a poem which narrates and comments upon a pilgrimage in the Holy Land" (*The*

Galaxy, 22.2 [August 1876], 286).[17] But of course the poem itself is not set forth in this reviewer's version of simple English, and, especially as *Clarel* explicitly arrays its poetic resources against the clarifying reductions of "prosing Science" (113) and its accounting for matters of fact, we might do well to recall that Melville here offers something other than prose narrative.[18]

A dominant critical assessment of the later Melville applauds him for a tough-minded, clear-eyed empiricism. "The sentence we need," Denis Donoghue tells us, "is, 'Rejecting all solutions, he but acknowledged facts.'"[19] This plain-spoken assertion is taken as "Melville's ideal human image. We find it in the character of Rolfe, Melville's spokesman in *Clarel,* whose mind, Clarel tells us in Part IV of the poem, is 'poised at self-center and mature'" (Donoghue, 93; *Clarel, NN* 12:398). Donoghue characterizes this humanist self-sufficiency in "facts" as "essentially the comic poise," the final "stability" resulting from "Melville's famous 'quarrel with God'": "Melville imitates God primarily in his comic indifference. Instead of suffering from alienation, he will make alienation the very idiom of his life, and the initiative, this time, will be his own" (Donoghue, 93). But such a perspective, a self-satisfaction at isolation, can ultimately find very little to say about the poem and pilgrimage that is *Clarel:* "In *Clarel* there is nothing as fine as the description of corrupt Jerusalem; the rest of it is a gift for the man who has everything" (94). On the contrary, *Clarel* offers an account of how little the self possesses and a record of the consequent desire for spiritual communion.[20] No mere prosing description of barren facts in the Holy Land, *Clarel* offers a poetry that seeks something through and beyond the limits of the material scene, and "quite behind" conventional accounts of it (*Clarel, NN* 12:96). And Rolfe leads the way:

> To Jewry Rolfe had made return;
> To Jewry's inexhausted shore
> Of barrenness, where evermore
> Some lurking something he hoped to gain—
> (96)

Rolfe quests, recursively, for an elusive object of metaphysical desire. Even the moment of "mature" poise that Donoghue cites does not represent a final attainment of stability. An Ahabian dictum that Dennis Berthold has aptly chosen as an epigraph for his discussion of *Clarel* gives the contours of the poem's flux: "There is no steady unretracing progress in this life; we do not advance through fixed gradations, and at the last one pause:—through infancy's unconscious spell, boyhood's thoughtless faith, adolescence's doubt (the common doom), then skepticism, then disbelief, resting at last in manhood's pondering repose of If. But once gone through, we trace the round again; and are infants, boys, and men, and Ifs eternally."[21] The Melvillean soul may indeed trace the round repeatedly. And yet the last-named "Ifs"—on this account, and, I would argue, especially in *Clarel*—claim a somewhat privileged status. For the consciousness that can achieve such a synoptic perspective on these fluxional states, knowing that neither belief nor disbelief can settle the question, and eternal If emerges, not as a mature state of repose, but as both a recurrence and flickering average of a dynamic oscillation. I concur with the justness of Berthold's structural account of the poem, but not with his sense of its tone or effects: "The narrative's circular structure—it begins and ends in the same place, Jerusalem—implies an endless questing in a wearisome cycle of seeking, finding, and losing. . . . Love and death, sin and redemption, isolation and community all revolve in endless cycles of discovery and loss that stunt human spiritual growth" (230). The cycles of isolation and community, though arduous, need not be viewed as "wearisome," and the cycles of discovery and loss need not "stunt" human spiritual growth, but may rather inform it. The eternal "If" motivates the "may" and "mayst" of the poem's conclusion: "Even death may prove unreal at the last . . . Emerge though mayst from the last whelming sea" (*NN* 12:499). Here, what "heaven may mean" (*NN* 12:373) points toward a possibility that would add significance to the cycles of love and death, a hope despite returns to the same lonely place.

In this unsettled perspective on spiritual life and its intermittent recurrence to isolation, we may discern increasing resonance between later Melville and what David Robinson characterizes as Emerson's "philosophical reorientation" after "Experience": "'Life is a series of surprises, and would not be worth taking or keeping, if it were not. God delights to isolate us every day, and hide us from the past and the future' (*CW* 3:34). Cut off from past and future, isolated in the particular moment, we cannot retain the illusion of balance, temperate accomplishment, and control that Emerson had previously sketched. . . . Emerson names this manifestation of isolation 'surprise,' and it is essentially an affirmation that experience remains open and unpredictable, and that, as a result, life can always provide something new. But as Emerson surely knew as he wrote 'Experience,' life holds many kinds of surprises, some of them tragic. The open door to the new that he describes also casts a shadow, reminding us of the fragility and dependence at the basis of human life."[22] The problem of "grief" at the emotional core of Emerson's "Experience" is the problem of "Ruth" in *Clarel.* Again, as Berthold concisely sums it, "In the major plot line, the poem's eponymous hero, Clarel, finds love in the Holy Land, leaves his beloved so she can properly mourn her father's death, and returns to find her dead" (230). *Clarel* indeed tells a cyclical story of discovery and loss, connection and isolation, insisting upon the potentially tragic influx of Emerson's "surprise"—as does "Experience," in recounting the death of Emerson's son. *Clarel's* Ruth plot embodies and allegorizes the dynamic of loss. That is, Clarel loses Ruth, his beloved, but also, in keeping with the plaint of "Experience," will find himself subject to the loss of what her biblical name represents, "sorrow." Loss through death delivers us unto grief, but even that state of sorrow shall pass away, abandoning us without the comfort of resolution or repose. Clarel finds isolation in the loss, but further alienation in the attempt to grieve: "But Ruth—ah, how estranged in face! / He knew her by no earthly grace: / Nor might he reach to her in place" (*NN* 12:494). Clarel cannot grasp even his sorrow. For both Emerson and Melville, the "ungraspable phantom" (to borrow Ishmael's phrasing in *Moby-Dick*) represents both a general problem and one keyed particularly to grief. Emerson takes this "evanescence and lubricity of all objects, which lets them slip through our fingers then when we clutch hardest, to be the most unhandsome part of our condition" ("Experience," *CW* 3:29). Of the loss of his son, Emerson laments that "I cannot get it nearer to me" and "it does not touch me" (3:29). Yet precisely the inaccessibility of "objects" points the soul toward spirit. What Emerson calls this quality of "scene painting," this play "about the surface," drives—as for Rolfe in his desire for some lurking thing "behind"—a transcendental theory: "Grief too will make us idealists" (3:29).

As Robinson has thoroughly demonstrated, Emerson subsequently develops from this problem a pragmatic and ethical calling, and one, as I have specified in the present study, that includes a return to the duty of Sunday speaking after a hiatus during the 1840s. If young Clarel, the character, gives us the problem of "Experience" (1844), a problem of unresolved grief concomitant to a problem of ministerial vocation, the poem *Clarel* and its narrator take us through the harsh realism of "Fate" and ultimately unto an undiminished call to "Worship" (1847–60). *Clarel,* I am suggesting, follows a development parallel to the later Emerson that emerges from the "calamity" of "Experience" and its concluding hope for practical "victory." In a later series explicitly historicist in its framing, Mind and Manners of the Nineteenth Century (1848–50), Emerson delivers a lecture explicitly vocational in its address, "The Tendencies and Duties of Men of Thought." Here, as Robinson emphasizes, Emerson pursues the problem of "Experience" to a reorientation that moves away from what Anderson famously termed the Imperial Self: "The only comfort I can lay to my own sorrow, is, that we have a higher than a personal interest, which, in the ruin of the personal, is secured" (Robinson, "Reorientation," 402; *LL* 1:182). This perspective, requiring us to "command by obeying" that which the "Intellect" cannot control by "volition," entails a kind of priestly calling: "by faithful serving, we shall complete our novitiate to this subtle art" (*LL* 1:182). In "Melville the Poet," William Spengemann discovers in the later verse just such an art that arises from "the ruin of the personal." Making a case for Melville as a proto-modernist "who approaches Eliot's idea of poetry as an escape from personality" (600), Spengemann hypothesizes that a failure to grant what Emerson terms "a higher than a personal interest" has contributed to critical impatience with the verse: "Searching the poems for the person who wrote—or rather, is written by—the fiction, Melvilleans have tended to disparage the verse for withholding that subject, instead of chastising themselves for seeking the very thing that the poems were written to escape, the illusory self whose disappearance the poems acknowledge and struggle to overcome" (605).[23]

In *Clarel,* the ruin of the personal eventuates not in impersonal repose (also a potential misunderstanding of late Emerson) but in interpersonal desire and the mutual spiritual instruction that transpires through that attraction, an engine driving through cycles of communion and isolation. One could argue that the poem repeatedly dramatizes, through the interactions of the characters, the dynamic which Spengemann argues that the poetry as a whole performs: the withholding of the subject by characters who appear to the seeker Clarel provisionally, modeling commitment to Spengemann's "fictiveness of the speaking subject" (605) by truthfully falling into silence. *Clarel* certainly does give us scenarios for the new Emersonian "Worship": "Was never Stoicism so stern and exigent as this shall be," a stoicism that may seek guidance but that braces for isolation. Emerson includes this warning passage on stoicism both in the lecture on "Duties" and in "Worship": "It shall send man home to his central solitude" and "make him know that, much of the time, he must have himself to his friend" (*LL* 1:189). And yet, as Robinson detects, "There is a deeper sense of what we may call a giving up in Emerson's new stoicism, not a final surrender to defeat, but an ever-present humility, an ongoing acknowledgment that 'nature never spares the individual'" (*LL,* 1:187; Robinson "Reorientation," 403). A kindred humility finds expression even in "the form of *Clarel,*" as William Ellery Sedgwick suggests, "in the very fact that it was antithetical to Melville's most characteristic prose," its metricality thus corresponding "to his new state of consciousness, in which his spontaneous ego or self-consciousness no longer played an all-commanding role."[24] In terms of the entire career, Sedgwick finds that the reorientation of *Clarel* marks a decisive shift: "It is not the perspective of a romantic ideal of the individual, such as he had portrayed in Taji, Captain Ahab and Pierre" (215). For Emerson, this stoicism regarding the individual renews its strength in commitment to a larger "duty" or "labor," and the conclusion that "Work is victory. Wherever work is done, victory is obtained" (Robinson, "Reorientation," 403, 405; *LL* 1:188). The prospect of victory at the end of *Clarel* is the prospect of victory for the Emersonian stoic, both the result of intellectual labor and yet an experiential surprise on the other side of a life shadowed by doubts:

> But through such strange illusions have they passed
> Who in life's pilgrimage have baffled striven—
> Even death may prove unreal at the last
> And stoics be astounded into heaven.
> (498–99)

The narrator offers this prospect to Clarel, while urging upon him the mental frame of an incipient vocational duty: "Then keep thy heart, though yet but ill-resigned— / Clarel, thy heart, the issues there but mind" (499). By minding spiritual matters in his heart, Clarel shall live in neither certain assurance nor despair, but, learning the duties of a man of thought, with purpose:

> That like the crocus budding through the snow—
> That like a swimmer rising from the deep—
> That like a burning secret which doth go
> Even from the bosom that would hoard and keep;
> Emerge though mayst from the last whelming sea
> And prove that death but routs life into victory.
> (499)

In a lecture on religion composed in 1861, Emerson articulates the ongoing ethical victory of a life thus lived under the aspect of eternal victory's uncertain possibility: "It is not my duty to prove the immortality of the soul. That secret is hidden very cunningly: perhaps the archangels cannot find the secret of their existence, as the eye cannot see itself; but it is my duty, ending or endless, to live while I live. I can see that there are evidences and probabilities, and they are noble, wholesome, and moral" (*LL* 2:182–83).

Further intimations from Emerson's later lectures, in resonance with Clarel's quest for vocation, move further toward a recovery of a ministerial role. The 1848 lecture on the "Duties of Men of Thought," though it implies a leadership role in "the religion which is to guide and satisfy the present and coming ages," leaves the possibility for interpersonal ministry relatively muted (*LL* 1:189). Emerson does acknowledge the "singular credulity which no experience will cure us of, that another man has seen or may see somewhat more than we" (*LL* 1:176). Pejoratively framed as something in need of a cure, this "credulity" in another's vision would seem at cross purposes to Emerson's insistence, in this lecture, upon "Instinct," the "source of truth" to which each individual has access and to which "reliance" is due (*LL* 1:175–76). And yet, the very ineradicableness of that faith in another grants it a status that begins to look rather like Instinct itself: "All true wisdom of thought comes in deference to this instinct, patience with its delays. We are to know that we are never without a pilot. When we know how to steer, and dare not hoist a sail, we can drift: The current knows the way, though we do not" (*LL* 1:176). If we forever drift toward faith in another's guidance, why should not we trust our Instinct thus far?

Emerson does not directly address that interpersonal possibility within the "Duties" lecture, but, when incorporating the stoic conclusions of "Duties" into "Worship" (1860), he indeed affirms such an inference. The backhanded admission of a belief "that another man has seen or may see somewhat more than we" becomes, in "Worship," a crucial basis for seeking the guidance of a ministerial figure, a role fulfilled by those who "can help in counsel or conduct . . . who were appointed by God Almighty" (*CW* 6:113). As we have seen, Emerson quite self-reflexively confesses that "we very slowly admit in another man a higher degree of moral sentiment than our own" (*CW* 6:115). The movement from "Duties" to "Worship" and beyond, to even later lectures on spiritual guidance, charts the course of that slow admission. We see a version of this reluctance in Clarel's interaction with Rolfe. The moment that Donoghue cites—with Rolfe presented as "poised at self-center and mature" (*NN* 12:398)—as exemplifying the self-sufficient stability that acknowledges facts and embraces alienation does not give us some privileged insight into Rolfe's allegedly confident subjectivity, but rather provides only the confused and inexperienced Clarel's impression of the older man. Wondering that the world "can baffle so," Clarel sees himself looking to Rolfe for answers, and he doesn't like what he sees: "Green and unsure, / And in attendance on a mind / Poised at self-center and mature / Do I but lacquey it behind?" (12:398). Though perplexed and casting about for direction, Clarel yet finds himself reluctant to follow Rolfe as a model "in frame of thought and word" (12:398). The word "lacquey" conveys the distaste of one raised, perhaps, on the orientations of "The Divinity School Address" (1838)—"The imitator dooms himself to hopeless mediocrity. . . . Cast behind you all conformity" (*CW* 1:90)—and "Self-Reliance" (1841)—in praise of "him who has cast off the common motives of humanity, and has ventured to trust himself" (*CW* 2:43)—or even *Nature* (1836), which mocks the current generation for masquerading in a "faded wardrobe" (*CW* 1:7).

Yet even in such moments of reluctance, as in Clarel's having second thoughts about looking to Rolfe as a guide, Melville's poem forever testifies to that "singular credulity which no experience will cure us of, that another man has seen or may see more than we" (*LL* 1:176). With an extended simile on follow-the-leader that files down the page across a triple rhyme, the canto entitled "Rolfe" describes that figure's influence upon Clarel:

> As horsemen, camels, footmen all,
> Soldier and merchant, free and thrall,
> Pour by in tide processional;
> So to the novice streamed along
> Rolfe's filing thoughts, a wildering throng.
> Their sway he owned.
> (103)

Moreover, Rolfe's thoughts that here sway Clarel are themselves about the ineradicable tendency toward faith *and* the endurance of the priest's influence despite the apparent advent of a secular age. Clarel, his own "vocation fled" at this juncture, finds the bit about the priest especially surprising, so Rolfe repeats it:

> The priest, I said. Though some be hurled
> From anchor, nor a haven find;
> Not less religion's ancient port,
> Till the crack of doom, shall be resort
> In stress of weather for mankind.
> Yea, long as children feel affright
> In darkness, men shall fear a God;
> And long as daisies yield delight
> Shall see His footprints in the sod.
> Is't ignorance? This ignorant state
> Science doth but elucidate—
> Deepen, enlarge. But though 'twere made
> Demonstrable that God is not—
> What then? it would not change this lot:
> The ghost would haunt, nor could be laid.
> (100–101)[25]

Rolfe's influence upon Clarel is to recall and predict the survival of religion—call it ignorance, call it credulity, or call it faith—and a clergy to tend its earthly course, "so long as spins / This star of tragedies, this orb of sins" (100).

Emerson, in a lecture on "Natural Religion" delivered throughout the 1860s, presents a position similar to Rolfe's, attesting to the endurance of the clerical vocation, despite the best or worst that scientific materialism can do: "I know there are transition periods, when the old forms rattle, and the new delay to appear,—when material and industrial activity has absorbed the mind, and the mind, haughty with its sciences, disdains the religious forms as childish. Neither is the office of the preacher to be dispensed with" (*LL* 2:182). The abrupt "Neither" may strike us as odd; it is as if Emerson has skipped a step. What he leaves unspoken, to be inferred by the listener, is the *But* that would set up the "Neither," and that the concessional "I know" anticipates. "I know" that in the face of haughty sciences, things look bad for faith, *But* some form of faith will endure; "Neither is the office of the preacher to be dispensed with." Emerson may skip the intermediate, general step because it has become so familiar in his discourse on religion. In the earlier "Duties" lecture that partially informed "Worship," we find this affirmation that follows after a similar invocation of a "transition period": "There is a religion which survives immutably all persons and fashions" (*LL* 1:189). Such a statement could have done serviceable duty as a bridge sentence to the "Neither." But Emerson evidently deemed it unnecessary, something understood. What *is* new in "Natural Religion" is the forthright sentence on "the preacher," rendered in higher relief against the unspoken affirmation of faith. The conclusion that the office of the preacher shall remain necessary may be seen as a logical development of "Duties," but only the later lecture gives the full articulation. In "Duties," we may read a primary self-reliance that begins to be modulated: "You want but one verdict. If you have your own, you are secure of the rest. And yet, if witnesses were wanted, witnesses are near. I cannot see, without awe, that no man thinks alone, and no man acts alone; but the divine assessors, who came up with him into life, now under one disguise, now another . . . walk with him step by step through all the kingdom of time" (*LL* 1:188). "Natural Religion" and Rolfe's speech that so surprises Clarel go so far as to suppose that this service of witness to divinity may even be performed in the unexpected disguise of . . . a cleric. What remains masked or reluctantly granted in "Duties" comes to fuller acceptance and expression in "Worship" and "Natural Religion." The grudging acknowledgment of "a singular credulity" in the vision of another (*LL* 1:176), wryly noted as that which "we very slowly admit in another man" (*CW* 6:115), becomes, in the 1860s, a pedagogical admonition to experience the joy in another's guidance: "Learn the joy felt in others' superiority. . . . So that I know the truth, what matters it whether I or another saw it first?" (*LL* 2:190). Brushing aside any anxiety, like Clarel's, of being a "lacquey," the later Emerson here delivers an exhortation to open up a receptivity to preaching. This shift on interpersonal spiritual instruction plays out dramatically in the role Emerson himself performs in his own choices of occasion and venue. Emerson delivers "Duties of Men of Thought" on June 10, 1848, January 24, 1849, March 9, 1849, April 25, 1849, April 2, 1850, and he mined it on at least four other occasions within other lectures (*LL* 1:173–74). This range of dates covers almost every day of the week: Emerson spoke of these duties on Monday, Tuesday, Wednesday, Thursday, Friday, and Saturday, but never on Sunday. In this lecture and its pattern of delivery, we find Emerson still exhibiting the vestiges of his "silent years" on religious topics, albeit voicing intimations that will very shortly emerge in "Worship," perhaps begun in 1847 and first delivered with frequency, and on Sundays, in 1850–51. Starting in 1861, Emerson delivers "Natural Religion"—congruently to "Worship" and conversely to "Duties"—on February 3, 1861, possibly in conjunction with "Immortality" on April 12, 1863, and again on October 22, 1865 and April 4, 1869: always on Sunday (*LL* 2:177–78). In these later performances, we find an Emerson with a reclaimed sense of ministerial vocation, willing to extol the interpersonal possibility and occupy the space and time of that unique "work" of the Sabbath. "Neither is the office of the preacher to be dispensed with" (*LL* 2:182).

In *Clarel,* Rolfe—though himself very much a co-participant with Clarel in the doubt-faith dialectic—provisionally voices the position on religious survival and the priest's enduring role.[26] *Clarel*'s final canto recapitulates Rolfe's position on faith and science in a powerful opening couplet:

> If Luther's day expand to Darwin's year,
> Shall that exclude the hope—foreclose the fear?
> (498)

Rolfe's point about the priestly function receives no explicit mention; rather, the ministerial role has been subsumed to the narrative voice itself. Emerson has re-opened the possibility of ministerial guidance to be performed by those who "can help in counsel or conduct" (*CW* 6:113) and has occupied that role in the voice that says, "Learn" (*LL* 2:190). In *Clarel,* that voice of guidance ultimately belongs to the narrator:

> Then keep thy heart, though yet but ill-resigned—
> Clarel, thy heart, the issues there but mind.
> (499)

As Ronald Mason long ago noted in *The Spirit above the Dust* (1951), "This is, in the main, the lesson of *Clarel.* It records, and recommends, an act of faith rather than any panacea for general doubt" (242). Though the plotline leaves the character in a state of general doubt, the Epilogue, in Mason's account, belongs to the more seasoned perspective of wisdom that speaks from the heart, to the heart, from beyond such a moment of intellectual perplexity: "The Epilogue, a sudden and inspiring fanfare of trumpets, proclaims a triumph that the inconclusive debate and minor tragedies of the superficial narrative do not seem to warrant. The triumph is in fact not Clarel's but Melville's" (242). Addressing advice to Clarel in a kindly tone of pastoral care, "the Epilogue is as much a recapitulation of Melville's emotional history as the whole long poem of *Clarel* is of intellectual progress. In his own despairing period he had scrawled his own bitter pasquinades across the brow of the statuesque riddle of life—*Moby-Dick, Pierre, The Encantadas, Bartleby, The Confidence-Man.* In his turn he was to experience, as *Clarel* suggests, a resurgence of faith; and faith alone could give him restoration" (242). In this achieved emotional perspective, Mason sees Melville in "abrogation of the scolding intellect in favour of the receptive imagination," having traversed "the deserts of intellectual speculation," and now, in *Clarel,* "repudiating just that image of his earlier years" (243). The narrator seeks to impart this resurgence of faith to Clarel in a relay of ministerial calling. Completing this liturgically oriented poem, the action of which culminates in "The Passion Week" (canto 4.32) and "Easter" (canto 4.33), the poem's final cantos give us first Clarel's melancholy meditations along the "Via Crucis" (4.34) and, finally, in the "Epilogue" (4.35), an inspiriting sermon for "Whitsuntide" (*NN* 12:497).[27] A sermon, that is, for the feast of the Pentecost, in commemoration of the founding of the church in the wake of Christ's ascension, and of the origins of preaching in the aftermath of prophecy.

The turn to this message of spiritual counsel in *Clarel*'s "Epilogue" arises from a dialectic, as does the turn to those who can help with counsel in *The Conduct of Life*. As Richard Lee Francis observes, the structure of Emerson's *Conduct* is dialectical; the first two essays establish the contest between "Fate" and "Power," a dialectic which Emerson synthesizes in "Worship": "And so I think that the last lesson of life, the choral song which rises from all elements and all angels, is a voluntary obedience, a necessitated freedom" (*CW* 6:127–28). Larry Wegener similarly traces the dialectic of freedom and fate in *Clarel*, one that eventuates in what Wegener terms a "rational necessity"—that is, as for Emerson, a cognitive perspective through which necessity is embraced by the will.[28] Or, as the narrator advises Clarel—regarding the "running battle" of elements and angels, of "star and clod" (*NN* 12: 498): "The issues there but mind" (499). Throughout *Clarel*, this dialectic finds a recurrent form in an Armenian burial chant, one that haunts Clarel as a corollary of the poem's structural process of discovery and loss but that yet models, in its every appearance, the voluntary perseverance of faithful observance even in the face of mortality's inescapable fate:

> But, hark: responsive marching choirs,
> Robed men and boys, in rhythmic law
> A contest undetermined keep:
> Ay, as the bass in dolings deep
> The serious, solemn thought inspires—
> In unconcern of rallying sort
> The urchin-treble shrills report.
> (130–31)

The "rhythmic law" itself bespeaks an aesthetic of necessity, an expression that adheres to metrical rule. The line announcing that regularity, "Robed **men** and **boys**, || in **rhyth**mic **law**," does so in perfectly symmetrical tetrameter, with two iambic feet on either side of a mid-line caesura. That multi-scaled symmetry (the line given in two halves of two feet each, each foot of two contrastive syllables) suggests the responsive back and forth of the chant and mirrors the two lines each afforded to the bass dirge of the elders and the rallying treble of the young boys. When, back in Jerusalem at journey's end, Clarel hears the "cheerful choral strain" (492) of another Armenian processional, this one in celebration of Palm Sunday, his thoughts recur to the antiphonal dirge:

> In treble shrill and bass how deep
> The men and boys he heard again
> The undetermined contest keep.
> (493)

The dialectic has doubled, the men and boys within the dirge remembered against the blest anthem he hears; in *Clarel,* it seems, it's dialectics all the way down. Or, all the way up, in accordance with the Epilogue's recommendation to keep the "undetermined contest" in mind, but to do so in an act of faith modeled upon the religious communities that sing such chants, to keep open a hope for the upside of uncertainty.

What the Armenian burial chant reminds Clarel of is the loss of Ruth. But what the antiphonal train could yet show him, from the perspective that the narrator would like to impart to him, is the "poetry" of "setting the mind's energy in motion"—as David M. Robinson characterizes this Emerson activity—a practice of faith in dynamic flux that unsettles the stasis of despair, or what Donoghue terms the "stability" of "comic poise" achieved by supreme "indifference" (97).[29] Writing on "The Suspense of Faith" in 1859, Herman and Elizabeth Melville's pastor, Henry Whitney Bellows, identifies "two motions of the human spirit in relation to God . . . a centrifugal and a centripetal motion—the motion that sends man away from God, to learn his freedom, to develope [*sic*] his personal powers . . . and the motion that draws him back to God, to receive the inspiration, nurture, and endowment, which he has become strong enough to hold."[30] Though the plot begins and ends with Clarel alone in Jerusalem, the poem does not settle for acknowledging this mournful fact, nor does it infer that the motion away from God is a one-way ticket with a firm destination. "Transition" was the heading that Emerson gave to a journal entry of 1847, and it forms a key concept in Robinson's account of Emerson's working out of the problem of "Experience"—the problem replayed in Clarel's loss of Ruth—and particularly the problem of isolation: "Detachment, and isolation, may be facts, but they are not finalities" (Robinson, "Reorientation," 399).

Clarel's closing, opening to a spiritual prospect that unsettles any sense of finality in "facts," arrives not, as has too often been claimed, as an abrupt non sequitur, but rather as a contingent vista for which the poem as pilgrimage has prepared.[31] In a poem whose final word is "victory," Melville's favored word for the progress of the pilgrimage is the verb "to win." While the pilgrims frequently encounter death and loss—and while most critics have attended primarily to these discouraging thematics—the narrator's language figures their actions as a series of small victories, won every step of the way.[32]

Most frequently, the verb corresponds to an act of incremental ascent: "They fare / And win the designated stair, / And climb" (438); they "Climbed, and an upper chamber won" (71).[33] These images of stepwise victory correspond to an even distribution of "win" or "won" at every stage of the poem, with the verb occurring almost once per canto.[34] The poem records the persistent effort of those steps, in the Emersonian spirit from *The Conduct of Life* that "Work is victory." The labor of pilgrimage is the victory of "Worship." As the pilgrims win by steps, they gain perspective, and a series of views at elevation: "The pilgrims muster; and they win / A common terrace of the inn, / Which, lifted on Mount Acra's cope, / Looks off" (131); "Another brink they win, and view" (291); "In ascent / They win the port's high battlement, / And thence in sweep they view at will" (83). And what do they see? Frequently, either the urban corruption or the natural desolation that have so impressed critics. And yet, the encouraging voice of the narrator follows upon such descriptions, in words that point to victory of mind and soul: "But shows there naught / To win here a redeeming thought? / Yes" (83).

In this question, as in the example of Rolfe, victory is not an achieved certainty, but rather the prospect pursued, an object of spiritual desire that lies beyond the horizon of human knowledge. Attempting to find words adequate for eulogy of the faithful pilgrim Nehemiah, Rolfe wins a provisional victory in a language of anticipation: "Rolfe in his reaching heart did win / Prelude remote" (258). Registering this emotional effort, this seeking of a distant prospect, the prelusive language that Rolfe finds takes the form of a question: "His poor thin life: the end? no more?" (259). As Hawthorne might say, "All the misery we endure here constitutes a claim for another life" (*CE* 21:153). The question and the claim remain unresolved, and perhaps *Clarel*'s most characteristic use of "to win" tinges that verb, and the pilgrims' progress, with thoughtful uncertainty: "they pensive win" (153). Ascending, yet burdened by the work of the mind—as "pensive," like "ponder," derives from a sense of weight, and suggests unease or sadness—the pilgrims contemplate a view that might integrate the dialectic of "star and clod" (498):

> In silence now they pensive win
> A slope of upland over hill
> Eastward, where heaven and earth be twin
> In quiet, and earth seems heaven's sill.
> (153)

Melville here also contemplates the conditions for the perception of the heavenly. As the prepositional bookends of the above passage suggest, "In silence" and "In quiet," such insight will tend to emerge—may even depend upon—the cessations of discourse.

This "sill" marks another characteristic interest of the poem. Having set in motion its various related dialectics, *Clarel* seeks to identify lines of contact, where vectors emanating from opposing sides might converge, and where erstwhile representatives from those sides might become "twin." In a version of the heaven-and-earth horizon, the encounter between the divinity student Clarel and the skeptic Celio presents an instructive early instance of the poem's capacity to twin faith and doubt:

> Mutual in approach may glide
> Minds which from poles adverse have come,
> Belief and unbelief? may doom
> Of doubt make such to coincide—
> Upon one frontier . . . ?
> (48–49)

We may note that the phrase "doom of doubt" preserves an association between terms from Ahab's cycle of faith: "adolescence's doubt (the common doom)." Celio and Clarel may thus be seen as passing through a common stage, though Clarel, lacking the narrator's perspective, fails to seize this moment of commonality and moreover fails to imagine this stage as other than a dead end. But in particular, this stage stands out from the remainder of Ahab's diagram: unlike infancy, boyhood, or manhood, *adolescence* names not just an epoch but a process—one adolesces, and adolescent corresponds to the Latin present participle of *adolescere,* to grow up. Celio and Clarel meet as souls set in motion—participants in what Emerson calls "the active soul"—each having let go of a fixity. The two face each other, moved by doubt, a besetting uncertainty: Clarel loses his grip on belief, and Celio relinquishes his determined disbelief. The identification of "Belief and unbelief" as static "poles" implies an important distinction within *Clarel.* When the "Earnest" Clarel, troubled by doubt, announces, "Tis the uprooting of content!" (6), this newly dislodged state might be better understood as the unsettling of complacent belief: not the certain death of faith, but potential occasion for its growth. In the process of adolescence we may discern a twin engine for Ahab's cycle, as the doom of doubt drives the dynamism of faith. Robert Milder, in his eloquent discussion of "Unworldly Yearners," makes an apt comparison to the theology of Paul Tillich to illuminate the convergence of Clarel and Celio from positions of belief and unbelief: "The situation of doubt, even of doubt about God, need not separate us from God. There is faith in every serious doubt, namely, the faith in truth as such, even if the only truth we can express is our lack of truth. But if this is expressed in its depth and as an ultimate concern [as it certainly is for "Earnest" Clarel] the divine is present."[35] Milder thus helps us to understand how the "'faith' that *Clarel* testifies to is not in God or immortality (though the poem retains a hope of both) but in the sanctifying power of living in a state of intellectual and spiritual aspiration" (194).

In a moving account of "Melville's Traveling God," Jenny Franchot finds this life of aspiration in *Clarel*'s very form: "The poem's concluding juxtaposition of the ballooning discourse of despair with faith's cramped script echoes its formal structure—an immense length unfolding in cramped sequences of metrically difficult versification. On the one hand, the exacting trial of Melville's chosen verse form mimics the labor and tribulation of Clarel's religious inquiry. But on the other, the readerly trial imposed by the verse form, as it impedes and renders painful the telling of Clarel's despair, as it mimics and requires perseverance, is also the very trace of faith."[36] Of this redemptive trace of the difficulties of despair, one may further note that while Clarel's encounter with Celio demonstrates a way that doubt and faith may twin, "Celio" already intimates such twinning. Bezanson emphasizes that Melville compares Celio to both Savanarola and Leopardi, martyrs, respectively of "zeal devout" and "Doubt," and notes that "Celio" is an anagram for "Cielo." That Italian word is itself ambiguous, pointing toward "heaven" or the more neutrally natural "sky." Bezanson gives the definition as "heaven," but notes the association may be read as both "ironic" and as an "accolade" of spiritual status (618). Berthold astutely notes a further tension in the name: in Italian, *celio* would also be the first person singular of the *celiare,* "to jest" (240), perhaps a jesting of skeptical spiritual protest. Yet as Milder's perspective would allow us to construe such a gesture of doubt, Celio possesses the capacity to act both as earthly skeptic and bearer of celestial impulse.

In discussing "*Clarel* and the Search for the Divine Body," Clark Davis finds a related integration of poles in Rolfe: "Despite his own difficulty with absolute faith, he nevertheless continues to investigate the potential benefits of such belief without sacrificing his considerable mental abilities. Rolfe thus unites . . . the opposing poles of the book's dialectic by avoiding the dogmatism of overcommitment."[37] Rolfe, characterized in terms often invoked to compare him to Melville, "supplemented Plato's theme / With daedal life in boats and tents, / A messmate of the elements" (*NN* 12:96). This philosophical and practical synthesis of the ideal with the material bears upon a spiritual theory of art: "Rolfe joins religious desire with aesthetic and sensuous appreciation and so strengthens the former through a connection that places belief beyond the reach of scientific logic or 'proof'" (Davis, *After the Whale,* 144–45). For Davis, tracking the development of Melville *After the Whale,* "the experience of writing and living *Clarel*" in this spirit enables the concluding hope of the poem, one that "reveals the modification of Melville's own metaphysical doubt to include fulfillment despite the apparent failure of the search. In short, the transcendence of spirit over body appears here for the first time in the Melville oeuvre" (150).[38]

Insofar as *Clarel* records what Davis terms "the search for the divine body," one of its greatest poetic—and perhaps sermonic—precursors would be *The Divine Comedy,* which James Russell Lowell referred to as "a sermon and song in one, a sermon which sings and a song which preaches."[39] Berthold's study of "*Mardi*'s Dantean Intertext" has newly illuminated the significance of the *Commedia* to Melville's career; Berthold observes, for example, that Melville marked his copy of the Cary translation "even more thoroughly than his set of Shakespeare" (*Risorgimento,* 68; and Shakespeare is surely the authorial association most closely tied to the Melville revival, from Olson's *Call Me Ishmael* to Matthiessen's *American Renaissance*). In scrutinizing the role of the *Commedia* in *Mardi,* Berthold stipulates that "Melville could not accompany Dante into Paradise" (92). But if Davis is correct about the decisive turn in the Melville corpus, *Clarel* may be precisely where Melville does so. Indeed, as Berthold reports, Melville in 1860 travelled with a copy of the *Commedia* along with Hawthorne's just-published *The Marble Faun,* and Berthold notes that Melville's "copious marking, particularly in the heavily sidelined third book 'Paradise,' parallel his late interest in theology, and may have been made while he was writing *Clarel*" (70).

Paradiso stands apart from the previous *cantiche,* by virtue of its ineffable subject matter, as a poem about its own impossibility. As John Freccero has shown, the problem of expressing the pilgrim's vision "demands straining the representational value of poetry to the ultimate, approaching silence as its limit. Insofar as the *Paradiso* exists at all, therefore, it is an accommodation, a compromise short of silence, as Dante suggests in the first canto" (*Poetics of Conversion*, 211): "To represent transhumanise in words / Impossible were" (Longfellow translation); "Words may not tell of that transhuman change" (Cary translation). Figuring the vision of Paradise as a voyage over uncharted waters—"The sea I sail has never yet been passed" (*Paradiso* II.7, Cary)—Dante yet accommodates those spiritual waters to earthly sensory detail with a commitment that earns his status as both *Poet of the Desert* (as per Giuseppe Mazzotta) and *Poet of the Secular World* (as per Erich Auerbach; Edward Said notes that "the crucial word *irdischen,* or 'earthly,' was only partly rendered by the considerably less concrete 'secular'"—nor does "earthly" automatically deconsecrate Dante's handling of the mundane elements.)[40] For Melville, attempting to write toward what Hawthorne termed "everything that lies beyond human ken," the uncharted sea of *Paradiso*'s opening becomes, in the secularizing nineteenth century, the "whelming sea" of *Clarel*'s Epilogue (499), in which the poet struggles to keep afloat a final hope. As it does for Dante, the metaphor of the ocean pervades Melville's poem of the desert, as Lawrence Buell notes: "Melville was hardly the first literary traveler to image the desert as sea; but *Clarel* must surely be the ne plus ultra of that tradition, so exhaustively doe it pursue that sustained analogy from the first canto to the last."[41] Scrutinizing the later poetry, Spengemann finds in Melville's shuttling between earthly metaphors and visions of the sea a linguistic accommodation parallel to the one Freccero discerns in *Paradiso:* "Terrene metaphors seek to bridge the epistemological gulf between 'man's strain' and the sea's silence" (594).[42]

Approaching that ultimate silence in *Paradiso*'s final canto, Dante turns to a more abstract metaphor to meditate upon the difficulty of giving expression to the heavenly body. In a geometrical figure that Melville describes as "three spheres insphered" on the endpaper to his personal copy, Dante addresses the mystery of the Trinity and (the Incarnation thus begotten), identified as such in a note by Cary that is bracketed in Melville's copy (527n1); the notes in Melville's hand on the endpaper supply the gloss that "3 expresses a unity but involves a plurality" (rear free endpaper).[43] Gazing into an "abyss / Of radiance" at what seem "Three orbs of triple hue," Dante confesses the failure of his poetic power:

> As one
> Who vers'd in geometric lore, would fain
> Measure the circle; and though pondering long
> And deeply, that beginning, which he needs,
> Finds not; e'en such was I, intent to scan
> The novel wonder, and trace out the form,
> How to the circle fitted.
> (*Paradiso XXXIII* 133–39, Cary translation; entire
> passage bracketed in pencil in Melville's copy)

This figure of squaring the circle—i.e., the intractable problem of constructing a square with area exactly equal to that of a circle, using a straight edge and a compass—surfaces in *Moby-Dick* (1851; we may note that Melville acquired the Cary translation of Dante in 1848; Berthold, *Risorgimento,* 65).[44] Implicitly tackling the problem of inferring "mind from matter"—the "true brain" from the "false bow" that the Leviathan wears—Ishmael posits that "if the Sperm Whale be physiognomically a Sphinx, to the phrenologist his brain seems that geometrical circle which it is impossible to square" (*Moby-Dick*, chap. 80; *LCRE* 313).[45] The humble square can never match the mystical circle, whose area depends upon the ratio π, a number both irrational and, as was proven in the nineteenth century, transcendental—one that cannot be expressed by a finite number of algebraic operations.[46]

Clarel revisits a version of Dante's geometry problem of straining to give full measure by rectilinear means: "Life is not by square and line" (298).[47] Nor, certainly, is the afterlife. If Dante's final problem in the *Paradiso* is to square the circle—to find an earthly accommodation for approximating a vouchsafed vision of the divine—Melville's challenge in *Clarel* may be to circle the square—to find inferential hope for supposing a transcendental circle while living squarely within the bounds of mundanity. As Franchot suggests, the poem's struggle with the "cramped" verse form may itself be the very "trace of faith" that perseveres within those limits (182). Before proceeding to a closer examination of Melville's use of verse form, I would like to offer a speculation about *Clarel*'s form writ large. Even viewed from a distance, *Clarel*'s size and shape announce an ambition to divine proportions of a Dantean cast, as in the designation of the poetic units as cantos. Dante famously arranges his hundred cantos into three canticles, of thirty-three cantos each (plus a prologue), and he builds the entire poem, line by line, on a scheme of *terza rima*. But whereas Dante constructs the *Commedia* on a principle of threes, Melville may be said to pursue his poem and pilgrimage with a modulus of four: *Clarel* divides its hundred and fifty cantos into four parts (the first containing forty-four cantos) and establishes its rhythms with a dominant four-beat line. Whereas Dante's perfect threes bespeak a mystical achievement of vision, Melville's four-square *Clarel* records a persevering desire for transcendence that continually acknowledges its own finitude. Whereas the *Commedia* culminates in trinitarian completion of three circles, each reflected from each other "As rainbow is from rainbow" (*Paradiso XXXIII* 118, Cary), *Clarel*'s only comparable vision appears at the poem's midpoint (the end of part 2), and as but a partial intimation of a transcendent figure that touches the limits of earthly markings:

They turn; and, in that silence sealed,
What works there from behind the veil?
A counter object is revealed—
A thing of heaven, and yet how frail:
Up in thin mist above the sea
Humid is formed, and noiselessly,
The fog-bow: segment of an oval
Set in a colorless removal
Against a vertical shaft, or slight
Slim pencil
(261)

This fragmentary and imperfect glimpse of a circle for the square flashes and vanishes before the pilgrims move on: "Suspended there, the segment hung / . . . It showed half spent— / Hovered and trembled, paled away, and—went" (261). And yet, as the pilgrims do go on in this half-spent poem, *Clarel*'s fours may also correspond to something super-added, by the human work that is victory, to the closed-loop circularity of the physical journey the poem recounts.

By way of topological analogy, one might think of another late nineteenth-century text of pilgrimage modeled upon Dante, Edwin A. Abbott's *Flatland: A Romance of Many Dimensions, With Illustrations by the Author, A SQUARE.* Upon ascending into the third dimension and becoming capable of distinguishing between a circle and a sphere, the author from Flatland reports that he had reached "the Climax, the Paradise, of my strange eventful history" (86–87). Having achieved his *Paradiso,* the Author finds himself speculating upon a possible fourth dimension and thence encouraged to receive a summation of all in a "Vision" (92). In the preface to the second revised edition, 1884, the editor includes a conversation with the author to further elucidate the difficulty in conceiving of dimensions unavailable to the immediate senses:

> It is true that we have really in Flatland a Third unrecognized Dimension called 'height,' just as it is true that you have really in Spaceland a Fourth unrecognized Dimension, called by no name at present, but which I will call 'extra-height.' But we can no more

> take cognizance of our 'height' than you can of your 'extra-height.' Even I—who have been in Spaceland, and have had the privilege of understanding for twenty-four hours the meaning of 'height'—even I cannot now comprehend it, nor realize it by sense of sight or by any process of reason; I can but apprehend it by faith.

Within the space of *Clarel,* we find repeated attainments of height, as we have seen, but little immediate cognizance by Clarel of any "extra-height." Yet, each time, for instance, a "tower they win" (113), the narrator registers a vector toward a victory. All these winnings accumulate in a fourth dimension: time, the extension of duration, supplies the "extra-height" that makes possible the narrator's perspective. Toward prospectives for hope at the end of "Experience," Emerson enjoins faith in this same dimension: "Far be from me the despair which prejudges the law by a paltry empiricism,—since there never was a right endeavor, but it succeeded. Patience and patience, we shall win at the last" (*CW* 3:48-49). Clarel needs such patience, and *Clarel* demands it. Clarel, stuck in a moment of despair, cannot see, beyond his apparent empirical certainties, that eternal Ifs await, as he shall trace the rounds again. But time, and its scribe, memory, informs the counsel of the Epilogue. Clarel cannot yet see what *Clarel* ultimately recalls.

Clarel's *Poetics of Silence*

Clarel's poetics nevertheless tend to convey Clarel's limited perspective, the real-time confines of pilgrim experience most often taking immediate precedence over authorial retrospective. As, from the frame of the narrated action, the possibility of hope exists mostly undetected at the far end of an as-yet-untraced timeline, *Clarel*'s language frequently takes its shape from states of deferral and silence.[48] Melville the poet makes use of several formal features that suspend utterance: an inverted syntax that delays signals on the semantic channel and a flexible use of enjambment and caesura to give prosodic emphasis to a thematics of silence.

The poem's first stanza establishes a steady baseline:

> In chamber low and scored by time,
> Masonry old, late washed with lime—

Much like a tomb new-cut in stone;
Elbow on knee, and brow sustained
All motionless on sidelong hand,
A student sits, and broods alone.
(3)

The lines give us, first and foremost, the situation of the poem: IN the Holy Land, IN a closed space. The human and grammatical subject appears at the bottom of the stack, as the poetry delivers primarily the weight of stone, and entirely omits anything resembling a lyric Romantic "I," or even a personable-if-alienated "Call me Ishmael." The action, such as it is, similarly appears only in the sixth line, after over thirty words that condition and constrain it. As the student sits and broods, his very thoughts seem bounded by the oppressive masonry and its funereal associations. Following the contours of this chamber scored by time, the prosody remains, thus far, a highly symmetrical tetrameter. The only prosodic variation, already showing the poet's firm hand, provides but an additional pattern of one-two regularity: every other line contains a hard caesura (||) punctuated precisely at its metrical midpoint—and even this strong pause only subtly distinguishes these lines from the odd ones, in which the mid-line measure tends to divide the line's eight syllables between discernible verbal units, with the possibility of a soft pause, as in the first line (|):

In chamber low | and scored by time,
Masonry old, || late washed with lime—
Much like a tomb | new-cut in stone;
Elbow on knee, || and brow sustained
All motionless | on sidelong hand,
A student sits, || and broods alone.

Likewise, the lineation for this tomb-like scene is heavily end-stopped, with the sole enjambment serving to further emphasize the absence of activity within this setting: "brow sustained / All motionless" (3). The word "sustained" hangs at the end of the line, maintaining the brooding brow in a frozen frame through the turn, as line succeeds line yet all remains "motionless." Yet as thoroughly as the entire passage conveys silence and inactivity, it deliberately withholds the precise *who* subject to that constrained circumstance. Taking a form typical of *Clarel*'s syntactic method, the sentence parcels out pieces that cohere into a complete picture and grammatical statement only within the final line of the stanza (Here, an opening stanza that is literally—as Dante insists we recall what the word means—a closed *stanza,* the Italian for "room.")

Studying how Melville defined himself as a poet in the 1860s, Hershel Parker points to a likely model for such a syntactical style, one found in "The Life Poetic" by Henry Taylor (Parker, *Poet,* 156–57). Melville, as his underlining indicates, found in Henry Taylor a guide to a seventeenth-century metaphysical style (exemplified, coincidentally, in the writings of clergyman Jeremy Taylor) that requires patience from the reader—with long deferrals of grammatical completion—but that rewards that patience with balanced cadences that facilitate final assembly: "if we look at the long-suspended sentences of those days, with all their convolutions and intertextures—<u>the many parts waiting for the ultimate wholeness</u>—we shall perceive that without distinctive movement and <u>rhythmical significance of a very high order,</u> it would be impossible that they could be sustained in any sort of clearness" (quoted in Parker, *Poet,* 160; underlining by Melville).

If *Clarel*'s opening stanza exemplifies the suspended sentence sustained unto clearness with the aid of rhythmical significance, later portions of the poem more intensely develop the convolutions of which Taylor writes. Still in Jerusalem, the poem describes the intertextures of natural growth that have managed to survive in the interstices of the grim masonry:

> Thin grasses, such as sprout in sand,
> Clarel observes in crannies old
> Along the cornice. Not his hand
> The mower fills with such, nor arms
> Of him that binds the sheaf, enfold.
> (118)

The first sentence of this passage exhibits a relatively mild, albeit characteristic syntactical inversion, with subject and verb ("Clarel observes") placed after "Thin grasses," the object—and *Clarel* certainly projects a landscape in which objective matter threatens to overwhelm the human subject. But the degree of syntactical convolution in the second sentence, albeit roughly based upon the same inversion that defers subject and action, pushes its grammar toward the status of a puzzle. Parker expounds Taylor's theory about such a technique: "Taylor celebrated a style difficult enough that a reader would be forced to suspend in mind complex thought" (*Poet,* 160), delivered, as with this description of the grass, in bits of grammar that must be held and slotted until a complete statement becomes comprehensible. This particular passage in many ways echoes the scenario of Longfellow's 1873 poem "Aftermath," which likewise states its relation to mowing grass by way of negation:

> Not the sweet, new grass with flowers
> Is this harvesting of ours;
> Not the upland clover bloom;
> But the rowen mixed with weeds,
> Tangled tufts from marsh and meads,
> Where the poppy drops its seeds,
> In the silence and the gloom.

Clarel and "Aftermath" both present the prospect of a difficult harvest—for Clarel an all but inaccessible one. Melville's verse more particularly creates for the reader the experience of such difficulty.

For both Longfellow and Melville, the lines on difficult harvest may be taken as reflections upon a late-career literary aftermath. In the case of the "Thin grasses, such as sprout in sand," the immediately preceding context points to what may have been washed ashore and survived in the wake of the Whale. Addressing Clarel about the "prior life" of the pilgrim Nehemiah, Rolfe has offered a "sketch" of "a mariner like him" that "I recall": "Hardy he was, sanguine and bold, / The master of a ship" and one evincing a certain phase of Emersonian confidence: "Man-like he stood by man's free will / And power to effect each thing he would, / Did reason but pronounce it good" (116). The captain commits himself to the Ahabian ambition drawn from Emerson's *Nature* (1836): "Nature is not fixed but fluid. Spirit alters, moulds, makes it. . . . Build therefore your own world" (*CW* 1:44-45). But: "No; a whale / Of purpose aiming, stove the bow: They foundered" (*NN* 12:117). In this wreck of the individual's philosophically idealist ambition, Ahab becomes Nehemiah, rebellious idolater shifting into faithful alignment with the prophet of old, and with a "Worship" that celebrates the Beautiful Necessity: "He ate what came, though but a crust; / In Calvin's creed his put his trust; / Praised heaven, and said that God was good" (118). And journeyed to the land of thin and sandy grasses, to gather in his final blessings.

For Melville's *Clarel,* as for Emerson's *The Conduct of Life* and Hawthorne's *Elixir of Life* project, this sense of literary aftermath as modest and work-intensive harvest corresponds to a later phase of writing after the minister—that is, as a writing willing to consider the value of a ministerial model—to weigh what a returning preacher might glean after the bold young prophet has swept the field—and to write after it. Hershel Parker's linkage of Henry Taylor's (1800–1886) poetic coaching to the exemplar of Jeremy Taylor (1613–67) proves especially apt in this regard (Parker, *Poet,* 160). For in matters of substance and style, the clergyman Jeremy Taylor has an added role in the structure of *Clarel.* According to Parker, Melville most likely began composing *Clarel* in 1870, a hypothesis consistent with Agnes Dicken Cannon's belief that Matthew Arnold's *Essays in Criticism,* an 1869 acquisition, inspired Melville to "devise a meter for *Clarel*" (Sealts, *Reading,* 118). I would place, alongside this source of metrical guidance, another 1869 acquisition highlighted by Merton M. Sealts: Jeremy Taylor's *Rule and Exercise of Holy Dying* (Sealts, 118, 218). Melville here turns to a work on pastoral care, in which the roles of minister and stylist converge. Henry Taylor, the writer concerned with the most edifying way to bring home complex poetic insight meets Jeremy Taylor, the pastor concerned with finding spiritual dignity through the art of Holy Dying. These questions concern manner—for "God loveth adverbs" (C. Taylor, *Sources,* 224)—and, for both poet and pastor, pertain most especially to the making of a good end. And *Clarel,* from start to finish, concerns itself with a poetics of dying.

Jeremy Taylor conveys the essence of Holy Dying through suggested "Offices to be said by the minister": "Thou, O Lord, knowest all the necessities and all the infirmities of thy servant; fortify his spirit with spiritual joys and perfect resignation . . . and enlarge his heart with desires of being with thee" (*Holy Dying,* chap. 8). The life of Mortmain supplies a useful test case for *Clarel*'s art of Holy Dying in a period of aftermath, as Bezanson's note identifies Mortmain as the "dominant dark figure of the two middle Parts of the poem" (*NN* 12:626), and an unlikely candidate for, at least, fortification with spiritual joys. This onetime "Psalmanazer" and revolutionary "prophet" has found himself deeply disappointed in his "warm desires and schemes for man" (*NN* 12:147), as he learns that "Prose overtakes" (148) even apparent political victory, as human evil inevitably compromises the putting of Revolution's "dream" into practice: "Experience with her sharper touch / Stung Mortmain: Why, if men prove such, / Dote I? love theory overmuch?" (147). As Bezanson summarizes in the notes, Mortmain's bitterness has "flowered into political, philosophical, and religious despair" (NN 12:626). Though his despair drives him toward death, and "though he sees little hope of immortality, at the end he turns to the Palm of Mar Saba and invokes the Holy Spirit (3.28), perhaps 'in assent' (3.30.132)" (627). That invocation looks toward the moment of his death,

> When the last light shall fade from me,
> If, groping round, no hand I meet;
> Thee I'll recall—invoke thee, Palm:
> Comfort me then, thou Paraclete!
> The lull late mine beneath thy lee,
> Then, then renew, and seal the calm.
> (371)

The pilgrims find his body, his face "Upturned toward the Palm in thought," and "Fixed seemed it in assent indeed / Which indexed all?" (377). Bezanson's "perhaps," noting the final question, indicates a characteristic Melvillean difference from certainty of affirmation, yet the words and picture given, of Mortmain seeking a final "calm," and possibly attaining it in a spirit of "assent," would seem to partake of that "perfect resignation" enjoined by Taylor.[49] Taylor's ministry, that is, attends this death in a spirit of what one might tentatively term a contingent Christian stoicism, and, in that spirit, Mortmain's trajectory looks forward to the prospect of *Clarel*'s Epilogue: Mortmain rests with the "stoics" who may "be astounded into heaven" (499).[50] We may note that Taylor's formula for the suspension and delivery of ultimate meaning fits such an outcome and thus works at several scales, from sentence level to character arc to the culmination of the poem as a whole. Parker notes that Taylor quotes the poetry of George Herbert as exemplary, and these structures of long-deferred resolution may call to mind a certain Herbertian trajectory. One may think, for example, of "The Collar," a poem with which Emerson's Divinity School Address notably converses in working out its sense of vocation—and which appears in *The Temple* (1633), which Melville commented upon in 1859 (Sealts, *Melville's Reading*, 185).[51] In a poem of thirty-six lines, Herbert's speaker devotes the first thirty-two lines to a record of spiritual protest and rebellion, only to experience, in closing, the grace that allows for a final moment—in the poem's last two syllables—of assent:

> But as I raved and grew more fierce and wilde
>   At every word,
> Me thoughts I heard one calling, *Childe!*
>   And I reply'd, *My Lord.*

Mortmain, looking back upon his life in the moments before his appeal to the Paraclete, suggests the possibility of a similar proportion, with long-standing spiritual rebellion and despair reversed by a sudden late influx of desire for atonement:

>   . . . all came back,
> The years outlived, with all their black;
> While bright he saw the angel-tree
> Across the gulf alluring sway:
> Come over! be—forever be.
> (371)

The narrator, in the Epilogue, calls out to Clarel with a similar prospective appeal and one even more closely attuned to "The Collar," as Clarel's ability to "keep his heart" might enable a renewal of priestly vocation, the specific issue for Herbert's speaker.[52] But the vocational angle crucially informs the Mortmain narrative as well.

The Palm through which Mortmain seeks intercession of the Paraclete exists at the Santa Saba monastery. Tended by generations of priests faithful to their callings—to the duties of the collar—the Palm stands as a material expression of their ministry, maintained in the continuity of a faith community. Thus Mortmain may, in a mood objective if also mystical, address the Palm as a ministerial messenger: "Envoy, whose looks the pang assuage, / Disclose thy heavenly embassage!" (370). The Palm that has found nourishment in a human world whose evil has tempted Mortmain to turn "misanthrope" (369) can thus "seal the calm" (371) of his final assent: "Toward *me* can such a symbol sway!" (370; emphasis Mortmain's, in wonderment that even he may be a candidate for grace in his dying moments).[53]

Two instances of unique wording place Melville's Santa Saba architecture, and the witnessing it inspires, within the realm of Jeremy Taylor, and Emerson's vocational wrestling with his legacy. We receive a first subtle hint of this context as the pilgrims arrive at the monastery: they "win the tall / Towers of Saba, and huge wall / Builded along the steep" (296). As Lawrence Buell observes in the most technically precise and insightful study of *Clarel*'s poetics, "Melville the Poet" often achieves metrical (and visual) underscoring "by one of the signature devices of Melville's prosody: enjambment of selected lines so as to accentuate key initial stresses" (143–44). The passage introducing Santa Saba contains two such emphatic enjambments: "**tall / Tow**ers" and "**wall / Build**ed"—with the latter further emphasized by the archaic diction, Builded. The word here, from Melville's pen and in connection with a religious edifice, evokes Emerson's "The Problem":

> The hand that rounded Peter's dome
> And groined the aisles of Christian Rome
> Wrought in a sad sincerity;
> Himself from God he could not free;
> He builded better than he knew;—[54]

Melville, like Hawthorne, knew this poem well, and had previously keyed in upon the beauty "builded" by the unconscious aesthetic wisdom accorded to faithful vision. Parker reports that Melville received a copy of Emerson's *Poems* in 1859 and notes that "chances are that he sampled some Emerson poems" earlier (*Poet,* 108). Indeed, by internal evidence, we can date Melville's familiarity with "The Problem" to at least as early as "The Piazza," in which the narrator praises the original builder of his house for having oriented the structure with a view of Mount Greylock: "Whoever built the house, he builded better than he knew" (*NN* 9:1). Hawthorne, as we have seen, likewise utilized this line as a touchstone, remarking in 1855 of the Houses of Parliament that their "architect has not 'builded better than he knew'; there was no power higher and wiser than himself, making him its instrument" (*English Notebooks,* CE 21:376). For Melville, the monks of Santa Saba *have* "builded" thus, as faithful instruments of a higher purpose, and hence, the fruits of their care manage to convey, even to the embittered Mortmain, what Hawthorne terms that "happiness which God, out of his pure grace, mixes up with only the simple-hearted best efforts of men" (376). Both Bezanson in his notes to *Clarel* and William Shurr in *The Mystery of Iniquity* observe that "mortmain" is a legal term "indicating perpetual ownership, as by ecclesiastics" (*NN* 12:628), whose possessions would remain "inalienable as long as the organization existed" (Shurr, 88). The faith community at Santa Saba has maintained its plant, and the inalienable soul of Mortmain may come to rest within their priestly care, in their well-built sanctuary.

Vine's own response to the Palm of Santa Saba provides an even clearer echo of "The Problem," and one that illuminates Melville's view of Hawthorne in the aftermath of Emersonian prophecy. Preparing to address the Palm, Vine says he'll "try an invocation free— / Invoke it in a style sublime, / Yet sad as sad sincerity" (*NN* 12:362). This "sad sincerity" marks the mode of beauty that Emerson acknowledges but ultimately refuses, most particularly in the clerical example which closes the poem:

> Taylor, the Shakspeare of divines.
> His words are music in my ear,
> I see his cowlèd portrait dear;
> And yet, for all his faith could see,
> I would not the good bishop be.

Melville, through Vine's sincere testimony to the Palm that "Intimates a Paradise" (362), here imagines a Hawthorne who *would* align himself with Jeremy Taylor, "the Shakspeare of Divines." The Hawthorne projected by

Melville's "Mosses," one feels, would not have settled for the vocational delimiter, nor for the pious affirmation of faith Vine here delivers. No, the thunderous Hawthorne of "Mosses," bold prophet probing at the hitherto unspoken axis of reality, partook of the blackness that makes Shakespeare Shakespeare. In Melville's earlier account, the Hawthorne of "Young Goodman Brown" is no Shakespeare of traditionary divines, but a fresh Shakespeare for America. But Melville's later Hawthorne, refracted through Vine, chooses the role of the faithful servant, the instrument of spirit and not the self-authorized bard. Even so, Vine, by *choosing* this mode of sincerity, both is and is not the "good churchman" of Emerson's poem, nor is he unequivocally the artisan who "himself from God he could not free." Vine declares his invocation "free—" and "Yet" bound by faithful sincerity. Highlighting Vine's embrace of a conscious "voluntary obedience," Melville here gives us a Hawthorne coincident with the one who excoriates Septimius's rebellion—not the scholar mad for Emersonian Power, but an adherent to the Beautiful Necessity of Emersonian Worship.

Facilitating the prospective "assent" of Mortmain and the "sincerity" of Vine, the experience of Santa Saba also models another mode of ministry crucial to *Clarel* as a whole. Approaching the "builded" wall for the first time, the pilgrims seek entry:

> Weary now the train
> At eve halt by the gate and knock.
> No answer. Belex shouts amain:
> As well invoke the Pico Rock.
> "Bide," breathes the Druze, and dropping rein,
> He points.
> (296)

This silent reception indicates not a lack of hospitality, but, as the Druze knows, follows from monastic practice. "Admission shall that arch afford / To any," but no answer will it give. Its prospect of refuge may be only patiently indicated, awaited with the certainty that a portal will open and the uncertainty of what may lie on the other side: "'Bide,' breathes the Druze," as, simply, "He points." Santa Saba thus models *Clarel*'s discourse on death and heaven, above all through the silence that pervades Melville's poetics.

In this passage, the heavy use of punctuated full stops emphasizes the absence of audible replies to the pilgrims' knock and shout. The terse report of "No answer," falling between two periods, produces a dramatic dead spot: the letters occupying little space but creating a pause of long duration. "No answer"—just three stark syllables that pull the line up short with a caesura before its midpoint. Such shifting of the caesura was at the time associated with Arthur Hugh Clough—whose work Melville likely encountered at least in *Living Authors of England* (Parker, *Poet,* 88)—who in turn, in a letter to Emerson, credited Longfellow's *Evangeline* for inspiring his metrical experimentation in *Bothie of Toper-na-Fuosich* (Phelan, 176). As Joseph Patrick Phelan observes in his study of "Radical Metre" in Clough's *Bothie,* Longfellow in *Evangeline* "highlights the tremendous mimetic effects that can be achieved by skilful manipulation of the position of the caesura" (177). Melville employs such mimetic effects quite directly throughout *Clarel* to unite a poetics and thematics of silence.[55] The more sympathetic of *Clarel*'s early reviewers credited Melville with an intentional experimentation reminiscent of Clough's techniques: "A rugged inattention to niceties of rhyme and metre here and there seems rather deliberate than careless. In this, in the musical verse where the writer chooses to be musical, in the subtle blending of old and new thought, in the unexpected turns of argument, and in the hidden connection between things outwardly separate, Mr. Melville reminds us of A. H. Clough" (*London Academy* 10 [August 19, 1876] 185).[56] More curiously, Clough, Longfellow, and Melville had appeared together in an 1849 New Bedford *Mercury* review of, respectively, *The Bothie, Kavanagh,* and *Mardi.* Parker highlights the reviewer's remarkable comment that "we are not sure but that we ought to have entitled this notice—Three new *poems*" (Parker, *Poet,* 17). Mardi did, certainly, approach the question of the poetics of silence, pondering the paradoxically beautiful "fullness" of "the Ineffable Silence" (*NN* 230), and also, as Parker emphasizes, theorizing that "Great Love is sad; and heaven is Love. Sadness makes the silence throughout all the realms of space" (Parker, 91; *Mardi,* chap. 188, *NN* 636).[57]

In Melville's Holy Land, the reception of "No answer" forms both a stumbling block to certain belief and yet, to the ears of faith and of doubt mutually approaching the same phenomenon, the true voice of heaven.

The initially alienating scene of unanswered petition indelibly informed Melville's Holy Land experience of 1856:

> Armenian funerals winding through the streets. Coffin covered with flowers and borne on a bier. . . . Boys and men chanting alternately. Striking effect, winding through the narrow lanes.—Saw a burial. Armenian . . . —Nearby, saw a woman over a new grave—no grass on it yet. Such abandonment of misery! Called to the dead, put her head down as close to it as possible; as if calling down a hatchway or cellar; besought—'Why dont [*sic*] you speak to me? My God!—It is I!—Ah, speak—but one word!—All deaf.—So much for consolation.—This woman & her cries haunt me horribly.— (Sunday, December 14, 1856; *Journals, NN* 15:67)

The word "deaf" here implies perhaps a sharpness of despair beyond a less-committal report of "No answer." Yet Melville's careful observation supplied the elements that will permit a somewhat different consideration of the entire scene, one that Melville replays along the length of *Clarel.*

For one thing, as with the silence of Santa Saba, an absence of cultural literacy may initially impede the understanding of the inexperienced pilgrim. Bezanson provides context for Melville's observation by quoting Emilia Hornby's 1858 account of Armenian funeral processions, events typically accompanied by women making "loud lamentations, after the fashion of the East" (*NN* 15:402). Recognizing the cultural convention of "abandonment" to grief does not deny the real and personal sadness of the event, but rather situates it within a time-and-faith-honored process of intense mourning.[58] The co-presence of the procession, what Melville calls "the incantations of the priest—making signs & c.—" (*NN* 15:62), hints at a traditional, ritualized context for the entire scene, even the lamentation without reply. Though the wailing may have hit an intonation unsettling to the untrained American ear, by *Clarel* Melville gives us a narrator capable of provincializing that sort of touristic shock:

> Might it be
> That Clarel, who recoil did here,
> Shared but that shock of novelty

> Which makes some Protestants unglad . . . ?[59]
> (*NN* 12:19)

Even Clarel wonders if he may be over-reacting to a culturally specific instance of a universal human experience: "Biers need be borne; why such a shock / When passes this Armenian one?" (131). Here, Clarel's tone of self-address smacks somewhat of whistling in the graveyard, and indeed he fails to dismiss the specter of "that recurrent haunting bier" (487), "the bier—the bier Armenian" (493); he tries to turn his thoughts to Ruth, "While in perverse recurrence ran / Dreams of the bier Armenian" (234).[60]

Clarel not only hints at a cultural context for the bier and lament that haunted Melville, but relates the form of the procession to the expression of grief, making musical sense of the funeral elements that the 1856 journal passage merely closely juxtaposed. In *Clarel,* "the boys and men chanting alternately," whose "striking effect" remains unglossed in the journal, enact what the narrator construes as a ritually contested dialectic of interpretation, of "treble" cheer and "dolings deep," hope and despair, or faith and doubt (130). Moreover, this "contest undetermined" forms a second-order dialectic, one commenting upon the primary dialectic that so disturbed the pilgrim of 1856, the one-sided dialogue between the cry of grief and silent death. The chanted dialectic of interpretation winds "through the narrow lanes" of *Clarel*'s poetics, and at its heart lies the primary dialectic of mournful petition met by no answer.

The word "answer" appears thirteen times in *Clarel,* and predominantly under negation: "Answer none" (53), "No answer gets.—" (119), "No answer made he" (355). The negations appear in wry indirection, "Let the horse answer" (413), or flatly, "No answer" (296). But also modulated into modest affirmation: "No answer knew I, save this way: / 'Faith bideth'—" (190). An extended metaphor—with extended syntax terminating in abrupt caesura—locates this pattern of petition-without-reply not merely within orthodox liturgy, but, more fundamentally, as Goldman has demonstrated, within Hebrew scriptural tradition. The passage begins and ends with silence:

> Now mid the quiet which becharms
> That mural wilderness remote,
> Querulous came the little note

Of bird familiar—one of them
So numerous in Jerusalem,
. . . .

The sparrow. But this single one
Plaining upon a terrace nigh,
Was like the Psalmist's making moan
For loss of mate—forsaken quite,
Which on the house-top doth alight
And watches, and her lonely cry
No answer gets.—
(118–19)

The mourning woman in the Armenian cemetery here gains the context of the Psalms, witnessing to a grief no less than faithful in its expression for going unrequited.[61] Later in the same canto, Rolfe observes that "to moderns death is drear" as "No rite we seek, no rite decline" (122).[62] Attempting to address this lack, Rolfe's own brief eulogy for Nehemiah, questioning heaven in the face of death, meets the same silent response as had the mourning sparrow:

"His poor thin life: the end? no more?
The end here by the Dead Sea shore?"
He turned him, as awaiting nod
Or answer from earth, air, or skies;
But be it ether or the clod,
The elements yield no replies.
(259)

In a poem filled with emphatic pauses, the interactions of the characters sometimes instructively model the dialogue between earthly petition and heavenly silence. As Goldman has suggested, "The key to Melville's theological reflection in *Clarel* is the reciprocal relationship between two hidden, divine subjects: human beings and God" (40). With a name recalling the "Vine evangelic" (223) invoked within the poem, *Clarel*'s figure of Hawthorne acts as analogue and supporting witness to the solicitous potential of God's silent presence:

> The informal salutation done,
> Vine into his dumb castle went—
> Not as all parley he would shun,
> But looking down from battlement,
> Ready, if need be, to accord
> Reception to the other's word,—
> Nay, far from wishing to decline,
> And neutral not without design,
> May be.—
> (97)

Vine's silence, far from the "deaf" nonresponse Melville perceived at graveside, promises receptivity as the other side of one-way dialogue. Rolfe the pilgrim, though Clarel intuits Vine and Rolfe as likely "peers" when considering "each clear or latent sign / Expressive in [Rolfe's] the stranger's air" (96), has not yet learned to abide in such silence. That "May be.—" hangs, breaking the line, and Rolfe speaks first "to fill trying pause alone":

> May be.—
> "Look . . ."
> Cried Rolfe.
> (97)

Similarly, at another lapse of discourse emphasized by enjambment, caesura, and broken line, Rolfe jumps in to stem the silence:

> —And fell delay
> Of talk; they mused.—
> "To Cicero,"
> Rolfe sudden said . . .
> (102–3)

What Rolfe goes on to say does compel Clarel to an extent. Meditating on Rolfe's "lesson" that "Time, God, are inexhaustible," Clarel owns the "sway" of these "filing thoughts" (102). But after a mid-line caesura, Clarel's focus shifts to the even more compelling model for his quest:

And yet how Vine—
Who breathed few words, or gave dumb sign—
Him more allured, suggestive more
Of choicer treasure, rarer store
Reserved, like Kidd's doubloons long sought.
(103)[63]

If one wished to boost the readership for this poem, lamented by Melville as "eminently adapted for unpopularity," one could do worse than to suggest that its rhymes contain encoded directions to pirate gold. But the map here intimated remains elusively metaphysical, albeit one the pilgrims seek to follow. For the poem and pilgrimage proceed, in its struggling yet more hopeful moments, under the sign of Vine's silence:

The ball of thought
And chain yet dragging, on the strained
Oblique along the upland—slow
And mute, until a point they gained
Where devotees will pause, and know
A tenderness, may be.
(103)

Sustaining itself through such "slow / And mute" enjambments, the poem, as does Rolfe, turns its course to the example of Vine:

So inly Rolfe; and did incline
In briefer question there to Vine,
Who could but answer him with eyes
Opulent in withheld replies.
(401)

In keeping with the valued "opulence" and "treasure" of Vine's silence, Charles Olson's *Call Me Ishmael* suggests that "it all finally has to do with the throat, SPEECH. Jesus unstrung him. The creator of *Moby-Dick* comes to value the secretive and silent."[64] Olson points to Melville's reading and marginalia from 1869, in the aftermath of prophetic Renaissance: "The American Elizabethan ends by agreeing with a Maurice de Guérin:

'There is more power and beauty in the well-kept secret of one's self and one's thoughts than in the display of a whole heaven that one may have inside one.' Melville's comment, 1869: 'This is the finest verbal statement of a truth which everyone who thinks in these days must have felt'" (Olson, 105).[65] Melville's qualification of the statement as "verbal" is not gratuitous, but rather necessary to avoid contradicting it. The *finest* statement, absolute, is Hawthorne's silence. From *Moby-Dick* to *Clarel*, we move from the direct address of second-person intimacy, "Call me Ishmael," to the halting invocation of a third-person mediator: "Name him—Vine" (91). Though "Vine's manner shy / A clog, a hindrance might imply," he yet best conveys, within the sustained silence of enjambment, "grace / Which is in substance deep" (91).[66] The God of Melville's Holy Land is silent, and Hawthorne is his minister.

Of Elizabeth Melville's Fist and the Spirit above the Dust

In the years after his visit to the Holy Land, Melville tried a brief stint of public speaking. Listeners experienced in his 1858 lecture on "Statues in Rome" a style similar to the one that Melville himself would attribute to the great long poem that would follow. In Milder's words, newspapers found Melville's manner "ill-adapted for a popular audience" (165). The style of delivery bore shades of Hawthorne and Vine, and even Rolfe in moments of restraint: "Melville seems almost to have been courting rejection, not so much from defiance or a perverse will to failure as from a desire to exemplify, for himself and others, a standard of intellectual seriousness and an undemonstrative dignity" (*Milder*, 165). At least one reporter found something to admire in this reserved demeanor, bearing an effect "not devoid of impressiveness, which sometimes approached the ministerially solemn" (166).

Yet a solemn, quiet ministry opulent in withheld replies does not quite account for the entirety of *Clarel*'s delivery. There is here, too, a voice of encouragement, one that seeks to engage an audience and to inspire. Evaluating the lyric of the Epilogue, Mason deems it "splendidly invigorating," albeit built upon the "commonplace" and flavored by a "revivalist emotion" that Mason implicitly deems distasteful (243). Mason's identification of a kind of ordinary homiletics does not mislead, but we might do well to note first that Melville fits its revivalism to an architectonics of an entirely different order than the poetics that have preceded throughout the body of the poem.

In this final shift, Melville hits upon a daring solution to the formal problem of how to end a poem. The end of the poem, as Giorgio Agamben has observed, places the verse, by definition, in a "state of poetic emergency" (*End,* 113). This crisis follows directly from a general definition of poetry entirely appropriate to the case of *Clarel:* a discourse in which it is possible to oppose "a metrical limit to a syntactical limit, . . . a prosodic pause to a semantic pause" (109, also 34). According to this definition, "the possibility of enjambment constitutes the only criterion for distinguishing poetry from prose" (109). Agamben, building from the tension between "sound and sense" (34), establishes enjambment as a general category to which *Clarel's* other signature devices also belong: "Enjambment thus thematically marks the 'rupture' between metrical pause and syntactical pause that (as George Lote's analyses of *pauza suspensiva* and *pauza plana* demonstrate) also characterizes caesura and rhyme" (34). "Verse is a being that dwells in this schism; it is a being made of *murs et paliz,*" to use the words of Brunetto Latini, Dante's teacher—"walls and palisades" (110). *Clarel* preeminently breathes within this continual tension of lines constrained by walls and cliffs; *Clarel's* verse defines a realm

> Where silence and seclusion rule,
> Hemmed in by walls of nature's sort,
> Base to stone structures seeming one
> E'en with the steeps they stand upon.
> (7)

Melville's poetry of enjambment plays against and across these *murs et paliz:* "Out through the vaulted gate we slipped / Beyond the walls" (4).

But this poetic richness gives rise to a final difficulty: "What happens at the point at which the poem ends? Clearly, here can be no opposition between a metrical limit and a semantic limit. . . . If poetry is defined precisely by the possibility of enjambment, it follows that the last verse of a poem is not a verse" (Agamben, *End,* 112). Melville, in a unique solution to this quandary, shifts gears for the entirety of the final canto. *Clarel* has wound its way through thousands of lines marked by enjambment, caesura, and syntactical suspense, and has done so within a tetrameter whose short measure heightens the relative impact of each of these techniques.[67] Melville's final canto bursts forth in unfettered pentameter, its individual lines accommodating full statements, sometimes flowing to eleven or twelve syllables: "Even death may prove unreal at the last, / And stoics be astounded into heaven" (499). The lines, almost entirely unencumbered by enjambment or caesura, themselves convey a palpable sense of relief in moving right past the metrical barrier that has thus far defined the experience of *Clarel.* And the full-phrased lines speak of just such a movement, in the prospect of hope that the narrator extends to Clarel: "That like the crocus budding through the snow— / That like a swimmer rising from the deep—/"—that like these verses slipping past the walls, "Emerge thou mayst from the last whelming sea" (499). Technically, these lines dispense with enjambment, yet they maintain themselves as poetry according to that definition of a tension between semantic and prosodic limits, with each semantic completion exceeding the long-engrained prosodic palisades of the entire poem. And, viewed philosophically, these final verses may be said to shift the enjambment to another plane. The hope they express, as we have noted, exists purely in the conditional tense. The pentameter lends itself to full, clear utterance, but these lines can declare only what *may* be the case, in expectation of all that lies beyond human ken. Melville gives us lines of grammatical completion, but ontological suspense, a metaphysical anticipation that turns our thoughts beyond what the final line can see.[68]

"Faith" herself, embodying the evidence of things unseen, becomes the author of a crucial line at the center of this final canto. Turning away from the "bitter pasquinade" scrawled by "Despair," Faith, though "wounded," inscribes on her own "shards"—and thus across a rare last-canto caesura—a message of hope: "The sign o' the cross—*the spirit above the dust!*" (498; italics in original). What I believe has not been remarked, even in the important study that takes this phrase as its title, is that the italicized words form a quotation, and one that partakes directly in ministerial tradition. This gap in the scholarship is understandable, for, as Sealts reminds us, "whatever strictly religious and theological works Melville may have had at hand while he was writing *Clarel* is simply not known. It should be remembered, however, that his library reportedly included many 'theological' works that were scrapped after his death

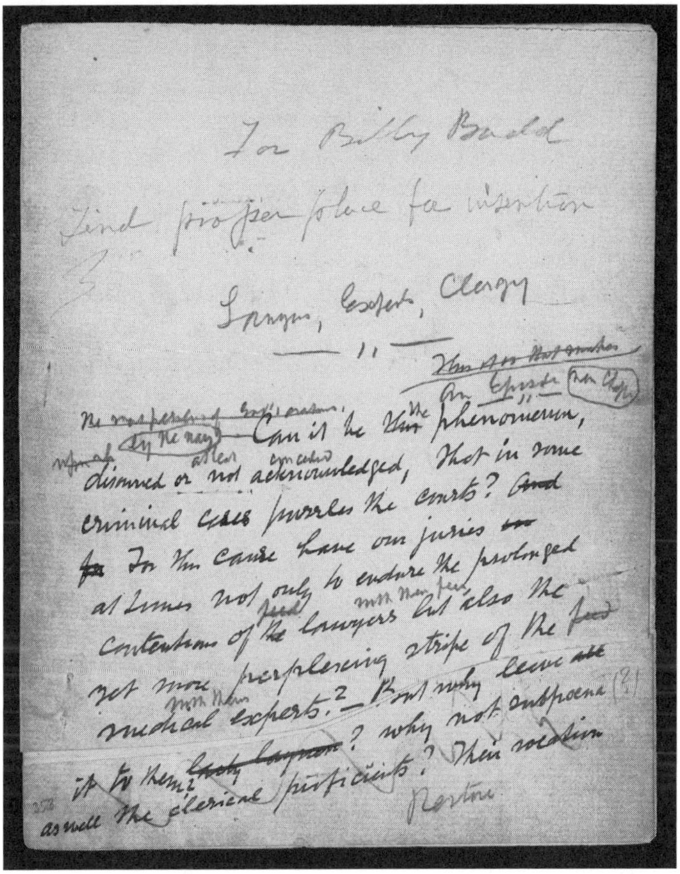
For Billy Budd

Find proper place for insertion

Lawyers, Experts, Clergy

FIGURE 4: *Billy Budd* manuscript passage, "Lawyers, Experts, Clergy." (MS Am 188 (363) [leaf 353], by permission of the Houghton Library, Harvard University)

as unsuitable for resale" (*Reading*, 122; see also Shurr, 8). But on the basis of the Epilogue's affirmation of "*the spirit above the dust*," we may consider at least two more books for shelf space next to Taylor's *Rule and Exercise of Holy Dying*. The phrase appears in *The Manse of Mastland*, an 1860 translation of the life of a Dutch village pastor, Cornelis Elisa van Koetsveld. In a chapter treating pastoral care at "The Death-Bed," the Rev. van Koetsveld affirms this motto for the living and well as the dying: "'*To raise the spirit above the dust, and to secure its strength and its repose through a union with the invisible,*'—that is the great aim of the Gospel. Therefore it speaks of life, eternal life, which is enjoyed even here."[69] The phrase reappears, in a similar context, in an 1870 treatise by James M. Hoppin on *The Office and Work of the Christian Ministry.* Hoppin, "Professor of Homiletics and Pastoral Theology in Yale College," addresses the "Care of the Sick and the Afflicted": he finds it "needful for the pastor to stimulate the mind, 'to raise the spirit above the dust,' to fix it upon the invisible and eternal—upon that 'everlasting life,' which a true hope in Christ gives" (557). "The spirit above the dust" circulates as a commonplace of pastoral care, and Melville draws from this ministerial model to form his closing homiletics of encouragement and hope.[70]

A similar impulse to enlist ministerial wisdom found expression during the composition of *Billy Budd.* A passage flagged for inclusion by Elizabeth Melville—marked, with a note, by her prioritizing "fist" or manicule symbol—but excised from authoritative editions of the text, makes a plea to seek guidance beyond the purview of secular expertise (see fig. 4).

Under the manuscript heading of "Lawyers, Experts, Clergy," in a passage omitted from the chapter 11 discussion of "the mystery of iniquity" (*Billy Budd, Sailor,* 1384), Melville writes with an urgency, even impatience. He targets procedural limitations (such as those that hamstring Captain Vere, in his failure to permit Justice and Mercy to kiss) that confine courtroom counsel to "the prolonged contentions of lawyers and their fees" and the "yet more perplexing strife of medical experts with theirs" (1475). He turns, sharply, to an untapped third vocation for guidance: "But why leave it to them? why not subpoena as well the clerical proficients? Their vocation bringing them into peculiar contact with so many human beings, and sometimes in their least guarded hour, in interviews very much more confidential than those of physician and patient; this would seem to qualify them to know something about those intricacies involved in the question of moral responsibility" (1475). The clergy, though identified by critical consensus as the targets of Melville's satire from *Typee* (1846) to *Pierre* (1852) and onward, here emerge as sources of potentially valuable spiritual perspective.[71]

Melville's personal discourse also bears the inflections of this turn to the ministerial. The man who in 1851 made the suggestion to "take

God out of the dictionary" (*Correspondence, NN* 14:186) was, in later years, not above invocations of the Deity to close his correspondence. Writing in 1874 to Peter Gansevoort regarding the death of Peter's wife, Susan, Melville presents both the quiet reserve of unspoken sympathy while offering a traditional word of comfort on Holy Dying: "We share in feelings which on such an occasion it is hardly for words to express.— May God keep you, and console you. H. Melville" (*Correspondence,* 427). On June 5, 1876, two days after the publication of *Clarel,* Melville responds to Catherine Gansevoort Lansing in connection with a conversation they had shared at the funeral of Melville's sister, Augusta, and in grateful acknowledgment of Susan's consoling note and commitment to cover the remaining costs of Herman's *Poem and Pilgrimage* (*Correspondence,* 436). Melville writes, as he does for the poem itself, a closing that would offset any absence of warmth in the foregoing composition. He does so with an explicit turn to that form with which the minister brings a worship service to a close, sending forth the congregation with a charge of benediction:

> And now—with my heart upbraiding me for writing so cold a response to so cousinly a note as yours—I hasten to end the sheet—and let it be with a benediction:—
>
> God bless you!
> H. Melville.

Notes

CHAPTER ONE

1. The *OED* gives the earliest sense of "literature" as an "Acquaintance with 'letters' or books; polite or humane learning; literary culture. Now *rare* and *obs.*": a historical usage beginning in the fifteenth century and petering out by the nineteenth. The second sense, "Literary work or production; the activity or profession of a man of letters," arises at the end of the eighteenth century and subsequently becomes dominant after a relatively brief period of coexistence with the initial sense.

2. Cotton Mather, "Nehemias Americanus: The Life of John Winthrop, Esq. Governor of the Massachusetts Colony," *Magnalia Christi Americana* (1702). Initially published in England in 1702, Mather's text received its first American edition in 1820. This passage on the life of Winthrop appears in book 2 of the *Magnalia Christi Americana; or, The Ecclesiastical History of New England* (Russell & Russell, 1967; reprinted from the 1852 edition) 120.

3. Emory Elliott (Princeton UP, 1975). The first metaphorical shift Elliott traces is the transformation from the commemoration of the founding New England ministers as wise fathers to the celebration of their successors as good and faithful sons. In his subsequent contribution to the *Cambridge History of American Literature,* Elliott underscores "the language of witchcraft" as the first (and decisive) challenge in the public sphere to ministerial authority. This may indeed have been the beginning of the end; joining the narrative much later, my project portrays ministerial authority in Emerson's time as overtaken in the literary and intellectual sphere by the language of prophecy.

4. The famous exchange follows Franklin's offer of accommodations to Whitefield: "He reply'd, that if I made that kind Offer for Christ's sake, I should not miss of a Reward. And I return'd, 'Don't let me be mistaken; it was not for Christ's sake, but for your sake.'" From *The Autobiography* in the Library of America *Writings,* ed. J. A. Leo Lemay (Literary Classics of the United States, 1987), 408.

5. "F. O. Matthiessen: Authorizing an American Renaissance" in *The American Renaissance Reconsidered,* ed. Walter Benn Michaels and Donald E. Pease (Johns Hopkins UP, 1985).

6. For some years, the figure of a distinct "late Emerson" has been emerging within Emerson studies (with Robinson's 1993 book on *Emerson and the Conduct of Life: Pragmatism and Ethical Purpose in the Later Work* as a clarion call that continues to echo); more recently, "late Hawthorne" has become a subject of renewed interest to Hawthorneans—see, for example, the 2009 special issue of the *Nathaniel Hawthorne*

Review (Fall, 35.2) on "The Later Works of Nathaniel Hawthorne," especially the essay by Magnus Ullén and David Greven, "Late Hawthorne: A Polemical Introduction" (1–25). The 2007 special issue of *Leviathan* (October, 9.3) on "Melville the Poet" might be thought of analogously as drawing attention to a neglected body of work produced by Late Melville (i.e., the poetry makes up the bulk of the later work, and the prose exception, *Billy Budd,* has not been neglected). Understandably, these relatively new configurations have been established so far mostly separately. The current project seeks the next step of bringing together Late Emerson, Late Hawthorne, and Late Melville's perspective on both.

7. *The Minister's Wooing* (Sampson Low, 1859), 160–61. That Burr mistakes *homo theologicus* for a new species testifies to an unevenness of cultural topography; Stowe portrays the cosmopolitan Burr, sophisticated and decadent, as surprised by the persistent Puritan New England seriousness of Dr. H. and the Scudders. Elsewhere in the novel Stowe will emphasize a different newness attributable to Dr. H.: his radical antislavery stance.

8. *Minister's Wooing,* 163–64.

9. *OED.*

10. Simon & Schuster, 1990. See esp. pp. 23–24 for Bloom's alignment of Emerson with Nietzsche and as originary post-Christian prophet.

11. Ross C Murfin highlights this fact, recorded by Hawthorne himself in "The Old Manse," in his introduction to *The Scarlet Letter* (Bedford Books, 1991), 7.

12. Emerson, *Nature,* "Introduction" and "Language."

13. *The Harper American Literature,* vol. 2 (Harper & Row, 1987), 1510. If the ministers initially furnished the ladder for the post-Christians' declarations from new literary heights, the ministers' removal by this very process disconcerted some, but not all, of the new prophets. Thinkers from Thoreau to Wittgenstein can write with equanimity of liberated vistas—"he must so to speak throw away the ladder, after he has climbed up on it"; but near the end of the day, others might like to be more sure of their footing. Frost continues: "I am overtired / Of the great harvest I myself desired." Again, the mood evoked might be applied to the reflection of Aftermath upon Saturnalia; the wearying task may be thought of as the midcentury outpouring of confident writing.

14. *Against Interpretation and Other Essays* (Dell, 1966), 250. A recent portrayal of Hawthorne as holding onto a Calvinistic vision without faith content in an ambivalent evasion of the Puritan past may be found in Agnes McNeill Donohue's *Hawthorne: Calvin's Ironic Stepchild* (Kent State UP, 1985).

15. *EJ,* 495.

16. *EJ,* 440. In *Emerson and the Climates of History* (Stanford UP, 1997), Eduardo Cadava follows "Emerson's analysis of the political climate of the 1850s and 1860s" (17). While working from the premise that "no sentence in Emerson . . . is not touched

by the weather" (1) in terms of the writing's variability and unpredictable movement, Cadava particularly takes as his point of departure Emerson's declaration that "it is impossible to extricate oneself from the questions in which your age is involved. . . . You can no more keep out of politics than you can keep out of the frost" (17). Cadava begins by quoting an 1863 instance of this declaration in the journals, but he works backward to consider "the specificity of such an entanglement" between the meteorological and the historical (19). Cadava finds it "no surprise" that the statement first appeared in a journal entry for 1851 associated with the Fugitive Slave Law (23). That is, beyond the mere scholarly consideration of historical context for Emerson, the instances of Cadava's key quotation bracket a later period which may be associated with Emerson's own more conscious attunement to historical specificity. For more on Emerson's attunement to the Fugitive Slave Law as registered in the *Conduct of Life,* see Barbara L. Packer, "History and Form in Emerson's 'Fate'" in *Emerson: Bicentennial Essays,* ed. Ronald A. Bosco and Joel Myerson (: Massachusetts Historical Society, 2006).

17. Maurice Gonnaud, *An Uneasy Solitude: The Individual and Society in the Work of Ralph Waldo Emerson,* trans. Lawrence Rosenwald (Princeton UP, 1987), 62.

18. *EJ,* 38.

19. *The CEA Critic,* 49.2–4 (1986) 71. Joanna Brooks has recently taken the bearings of what she terms "the post-Edwards-to-Emerson era," beginning with a reflection on the durability of the old dispensation: "Perhaps, the true power of Miller's 'From Edwards to Emerson' is . . . its redemption of continuities from discontinuities, its salvific narrative of American secularization. For Perry Miller gave us the gentlest and most elegant way of telling the children that at some point even the best and brightest Puritans could keep it up no longer, that they stopped believing what their grandfathers believed, and that it was, finally, really, *okay* because it gave us *literature*"; "From Edwards to Baldwin: Heterodoxy, Discontinuity, and New Narratives of American Religious-Literary History," *American Literary History* 22.2 (March 2010) 440. Brooks announces, ably and inarguably, that a "working narrative of religion and American literature in the post-Edwards-to-Emerson era would need to have multiple origins" (441). The present study, while acknowledging that Brooks issues a worthy invitation to narrate multiplicity, pursues a more modest and yet direct revision to the old Edwards-to-Emerson paradigm: namely, that even starting from and dwelling upon the given endpoint—that of Emerson and his immediate familiar peers—one may discover a new story that challenges the "salvific narrative of American secularization."

20. Discussed by Wesley T. Mott, *"The Strains of Eloquence" : Emerson and His Sermons* (Pennsylvania State UP, 1989), 4–8. Mott mentions William Emerson's (RWE's father) distaste for Whitefield revivalism.

21. The August 28, 1823, journal entry: "'Where are you going, Mr. Whitefield?' said Dr. Chauncy. "I'm going to Boston, sir.'—'I'm very sorry for it,' said Dr. C. 'So is the Devil' replied the eloquent preacher" (*EJ,* 38). Joel Porte's annotation provides useful

emphasis: "Emerson's approval of the great eighteenth-century evangelical preacher George Whitefield seems to have personal significance, since the rationalist Charles Chauncy, who opposed Whitefield, was pastor of Boston's first Church, where Emerson's father succeeded him in 1799. William Emerson admired Chauncy and named his youngest son after him." Maurice Gonnaud (6–8) notes that Emerson's great grandfather, Joseph Emerson, was a friend of Whitefield's.

22. "Eloquence" (1867 Chicago lecture) in *Letters and Social Aims, W,* VIII, 127–28. The "Eloquence" which appears in *Society and Solitude* is based upon an 1847 Boston lecture; *W,* VII, 364.

23. "On the Death of the Rev. Mr. George Whitefield 1770" (lines 5–8); *The Heath Anthology of American Literature,* vol. 1 (D.C. Heath, 1990), 714.

24. *Essays Moral & Political* (1741).

25. *EJ,* 26. Another (American) version of the Whitefield/Hume division, still evident in *The Conduct of Life,* is the contest between Edwards and Franklin. Evelyn Barish's chapter "Hume" in *Emerson: The Roots of Prophecy* (Princeton UP, 1989) details Emerson's early encounter with this "Goliath" figure and the contest between the influence of Mary Moody Emerson's piety and Hume's skepticism.

26. *EJ,* 257.

27. I will refer to the third edition (Edward Moxon, 1853). The book, a series of seven "Letters on the Inspiration of the Scriptures," opens with Coleridge's declaration that he is responding to the section labeled *The Confessions of a fair Saint* in Carlyle's translation of Goethe's *Wilhelm Meister.* The discussion of 2 Tim. 3:16 begins on p. 93.

28. Coleridge instances a number of historical translations corresponding to each side of the argument. On the *verbum plenum* side we find the Dutch Reformed Church (think Melville ancestry) and Diodati (think Emerson's rival moralist, Milton); among those translators omitting the "and" (though not necessarily endorsing the Romantic interpretation) we find the Vulgate and Luther. As far as applied hermeneutics are concerned, Emerson makes clear his personalized inclination toward the latter reading in his "Lord's Supper" (1832) insistence that "there is no other measure of the value of any one form than the measure of its use" *and* that Christ's teachings are invalid if "not suitable to me" (Library of America *Essays and Lectures,* 1983 ed., 1140, 1138). Unless otherwise noted, citations of Emerson's writings will refer to this edition, by page number, in the body of the text.

29. Coleridge, *Confessions of an Inquiring Spirit,* 3rd ed. (Edward Moxon, 1853) 36.

30. *CW* 1:84, 90.

31. "The Method of Nature," *CW* 1:120. Emerson's bold use of biblical language here—"the foundations of the earth"—is typical of Emerson's inhabitation of a scriptural voice, as he positions the scholar priest as Creator (e.g. Job 38:4, "Where wast thou when I laid the foundations of the earth?"; Isaiah 48:13, "Mine hand also hath laid the foundation of the earth") and Messianic expounder of mystery (e.g., Matthew 13:35,

"I will open my mouth in parables; I will utter things which have been kept secret from the foundation of the world").

32. Robert D. Richardson, *First We Read, Then We Write: Emerson on the Creative Process* (U of Iowa P, 2009) 2. Richardson notes that "Emerson's immodest—almost indecent—ambition seems both too high and too abstract to be real, or to be believed; but there was always another side to the man, a side where both his feet are planted in everyday reality, a side of him that often sounds overwhelmed, sometimes desperate, always determined. A person, he wrote, 'must do the work with that faculty he has now. But that faculty is the accumulation of past days. . . . Work and learn in evil days, in insulted days, in days of debt and depression and calamity'" (3). Richardson's "always" is well noted—there may indeed "always" be another side to Emerson, even at the height of his prophetic intensity. Nevertheless, this other side of Emerson becomes more evident after the work of prophecy. Hitting the keynote of "work" (rather than, say, inspiration or intuition), the passage Richardson cites bears strong affinities with "Worship" in *The Conduct of Life* (1860). In fact, it appears in a journal entry for 1847 (*JMN* 10:40) and subsequently in "The Tendencies and Duties of Men of Thought" (*LL* 1:186), which Emerson drew upon for both "Worship" and "Immortality" (*LL* 1:174).

33. *The Trial of Curiosity: Henry James, William James, and the Challenge of Modernity* (Oxford UP, 1991), 9.

34. *Dial* 2, July; cited by James Duban in his discussion of *Pierre* in *Melville's Major Fiction: Politics, Theology, and Imagination* (Northern Illinois UP, 1983), 150.

35. *New England Literary Culture: From Revolution through Renaissance* (Cambridge UP, 1986). Buell—after citing Bronson Alcott, Thoreau, Jones Very, Whitman, and Melville—concludes that by insisting on the double bind of originality and model-following, "Literary scripturism, then, was a vastly exciting project doomed, by definition, to failure" (183).

36. *Anatomy of Melancholy,* III.II.III.i (1651, *OED*).

37. Introduction to *Selected Tales and Sketches* (Penguin, 1987), xxi.

38. *Novels* (Library of America, 1983), 127.

39. *The Correspondence of Henry David Thoreau,* ed. Walter Harding and Carl Bode (New York UP, 1958), 249.

40. Louise L. Stevenson, *Scholarly Means to Evangelical Ends: The New Haven Scholars and the Transformation of Higher Learning in America 1830–1890* (Johns Hopkins UP, 1986), 172.

41. Cited in Carl J. Guarneri, *The Utopian Alternative: Fourierism in Nineteenth-Century America* (Cornell UP, 1991), 400.

42. From "No. VI. 'The Pious Editor's Creed,'" in *The Biglow Papers [First Series]: A Critical Edition,* ed. Thomas Wortham (Northern Illinois UP, 1977), 101–2. We might compare to Parson Wilbur's sermon an 1850 letter from Lowell himself: "I have preached sermons enow, and now I am going to come down out of the pulpit and

go about among my parish" (emphasis his; xxxiii). In one sense Lowell is descending from the heights of his greatest work, which came a bit too early to fit into the 1850–55 Matthiessen heyday; but his accomplishments as a powerful editor are just beginning.

43. This quotation appears in a college essay Thoreau wrote in 1837, shortly before he entered the public stage via the local newspaper. Cited in Steven Fink, *Prophet in the Marketplace: Thoreau's Development as a Professional Writer* (Princeton UP, 1992), 13; Thoreau adds that the preacher's despotism is "narrow and circumscribed." Wesley Mott, for instance, notes the declining clerical influence specifically of the *liberal* clergy favored by intellectuals in "Power in the Pulpit: The Unitarian Problem of Vocation": "The cost of social prestige without power, however, was what continued to bother the most discerning of the new generation of liberal ministers" ("*The Strains of Eloquence,*" 41).

44. *The Feminization of American Culture* (Alfred A. Knopf, 1977), 306.

45. *W,* VI, 213, 217, 212.

46. *CW* 1:201, 206. The Library of America *Essays and Lectures* gives the date as January 1842, while the *Collected Works* reports December 1841. Emerson's address opens with a reference to "Idealism as it appears in 1842."

47. Perry Miller, *The Transcendentalists* (Harvard UP, 1950), 335; emphasis Fuller's.

48. "Aftermath" (lines 1–9); *The Heath Anthology of American Literature,* vol. 1, 2708.

49. *CE* 18:355.

50. Cited in Robert D. Richardson, "Beyond Transcendentalism: The Natural History Projects," *Henry Thoreau: A Life of the Mind* (U of California P, 1986), 382.

51. *CW* 6:455.

52. In his discussion of the Melville-Hawthorne relationship, Robert K. Martin makes the connection between the "cloistral vine" in "Monody" and the "cloister" imagery of *Clarel;* see *Hero, Captain, and Stranger: Male Friendship and Literary Form in the Sea Novels of Herman Melville* (U of North Carolina P, 1986), 98.

53. For an energetic contextualization of *Clarel* with respect to nineteenth-century comparative religion, see William Potter, *Melville's* Clarel *and the Intersympathy of Creeds* (Kent State UP, 2004). Potter finds that in "*Clarel* the eternal need for faith is projected against the backdrop of . . . the spiritual crisis of the nineteenth century, where Western Protestantism—rejecting mysticism and embracing reason—is left in a spiritually vapid materialism largely of its own rational devising. Faith, the poem asserts, remains a fundamental and indispensable aspect of the human mind and imagination" (xiii). For Potter, "Clarel is nothing less than a hugely conceived study of the very nature of all belief. As such, it succeeds in transcending the relatively parochial concerns of the faith and doubt genre to discover what the poem calls, 'The intersympathy of creeds / Alien or hostile tho' they seem' (I.5.207–8), that is, those eternal truths shared by all religions beneath their orthodox differences" (xiii). While

I agree that Clarel's encounters with seemingly alien faith practices do serve effectively to parochialize his own protestant-materialist hand wringing, I would note that the poem retains an interest in how a renewed faith, "*the spirit above the dust*"(498), might still be communicated in the edified minister-pilgrim's local idiom—in Clarel's case, a Christian one, "The sign o' the cross" (498)—as the "creeds," however intersympathetic, remain plural rather than superseded by the universalism of an intersympathetic creed. In any case, Potter's study pursues, with admirable specificity, the implications of Robert Penn Warren's intuition that Melville could not "rest with the humanistic philosophy recurrent in *Battle-Pieces:* though there are no values supernaturally delivered, man may create his own values and in them find self-definition and moral peace. To however noble and grandly tragic a plane this conception of life might be elevated, and however courageously it might be used as a justification for action, the conception was not quite enough to satisfy his eschatological appetite. So we have *Clarel.* ([Introduction to *Selected Poems*] 34–35)," (xvii). In "'Crack'd Archangel': Sir Thomas Browne's *Religio Medici,* the Bible, and Religious Difference in Melville's Fiction and Poetry," Brian Yothers finds in *Clarel* a "congruence of Browne's efforts toward understanding religious difference in seventeenth-century England with Melville's own project of giving expression to the whole range of religious difference in nineteenth-century America, and indeed the 'whole worshipping world'"; Yothers presented this paper at the 2009 MLA in Philadelphia; his abstract appears in *Leviathan* 12.2 (June 2010) 112. Peter Norberg has made with greatest clarity what I take to be a needed complement to claims for Melville's religious "intersympathy": "One will not find in the many sided argument of *Clarel* positive affirmation of religious heterodoxy that the poem presents as the result of modern globalization. Through the mediation of its protagonist Clarel, the poem consistently presents readers with a desire for orthodox belief"; "The sort of orthodoxy Melville would have his readers retain is an *Imitatio Christi* that heeds the suffering of others. Exploring Melville's criticisms of democracy in the context of the poem's running theological debate enables us to gauge the extent to which the poem's Christian framework can help us imagine genuine interreligious dialogue"; "Comparative Religion and Competing Orthodoxies in Melville's *Clarel*" [abstract], *Leviathan* 12.3 (October 2010) 133–34. Charles Taylor offers a model that I find attractive in many ways: "I think what we badly need is a conversation between a host of different positions, religious, nonreligious, antireligious, humanistic, antihumanistic, and so on, in which we eschew mutual caricature and try to understand what 'fullness' means for the other" ("Afterword" to *Varieties of Secularism,* 318). Taylor has many reasons for extolling the virtues of such conversation, not least, as Michael Warner and others have noted, that "Taylor hopes by stressing the cross-pressures attending each position to induce modesty" in each position ("Editors' Introduction" to *Varieties of Secularism,* 23). While wary of "triumphalism," Taylor does confess that a theological position motivates his preference for this form of discourse: "Now, what has that got to do with

Christianity? Everything, to me: that is what it's all about. It's about reconciliation. It's all about reconciliation between human beings" ("Afterword," 320).

54. The other two dissertations listed in Dissertation Abstracts International for 1861 were awarded to Eugene Schuyler, for philosophy (no title given), and Arthur Williams Wright, for physics (he presented a solution to an idealized, that is, greatly simplified, Newtonian problem: "Having given the velocity and direction of motion of a meteor on entering the atmosphere of the Earth, to determine its orbit about the sun, taking into account the attractions of both of these bodies"). The rise of doctor of philosophy marks very directly the continued eclipse of the degree in divinity. That Whiton (1833–1920) also was a reverend may further illustrate this moment as one of transition, one during which distinct intellectual forms of labor could openly compete to recruit minds of similar disposition.

55. *American Renaissance* (Oxford UP, 1941), 6, 6n. The Emerson lecture, finally given in 1880 as his one hundredth appearance before the Concord Lyceum, draws upon notes largely synthesized in 1867 from entries going back twenty years and more. Perry Miller's two Transcendentalist anthologies (1950, 1957) basically recapitulate Matthiessen's judgment on the value of these accounts.

56. For, roughly speaking, an account of the second wave of books about the "American Renaissance," see Robert D. Habich, *Building Their Own Waldos* (U of Iowa P, 2011), in which he tracks how "the decade of the 1880s witnessed the wholesale reinterpretation of American Renaissance writers" (xiv). For subsequent waves, the next arriving with Van Wyck Brooks's search for a "usable past," see Randall Fuller, *Emerson's Ghosts: Literature, Politics, and the Making of Americanists* (Oxford UP, 2007).

57. *Memorial of the Commemoration of the Church of the Disciples, of the Fiftieth Birth-day of their Pastor, James Freeman Clarke, April 4, 1860* (Prentiss & Deland, printers, 1860).

58. Literary historians have variously registered a sense of transition following the "Renaissance," accommodating some view of literary succession of major authors to some version of the contours of history. The Bercovitch *Cambridge History of American Literature* implicitly leaves the timing question open: volume 2 on prose ends at 1865, but volume 3 begins at 1860. This invitation to dissensus contains its own chronological inevitability, of course; a reversed configuration of endpoint and new beginning would have admitted an embarrassing gap in historical coverage. We may also note the reassuring presence of our favorite fiction, the familiar literary thing in itself, "the American Renaissance," albeit with the promise of robust contextualization: the press publicity for volume 2 proclaims, "This is the fullest and richest account of the American Renaissance available." *The Cambridge Handbook of American Literature* (1986) concludes with a two-column chronology: American History on the left and American Literature on the right. The most strikingly asymmetrical years fall between 1849 and

1869. From 1849 to 1855, apparently nothing historical happened. From 1856 to 1869, nothing literary happened. First a block on the right (Thoreau, Hawthorne, Melville, Stowe, Whitman); then a block on the left (1857 Dred Scott to 1865 Reconstruction). After this lapse of the literary, the next block includes, true to Spillers's "cycle," Twain, James, and Howells.

Van Wyck Brooks places the break between New England's "Flowering" and its "Indian Summer" at 1865: which is to say, without opening either of these volumes, that there is no getting around the Civil War as a divider (the division is sufficiently standard to mark the line between "Romanticism" and "Realism" in M. H. Abrams's glossary entry on American Literature, to cite but one example). Yet beyond its title, Brooks's *New England: Indian Summer 1865–1915* does allow the passing of literary generations significant independent, if anecdotal, place. He defers a confrontation with "Cambridge after the Civil War" until the second chapter of the story; the first chapter gives us William Dean Howells's quiet entry into Oliver Wendell Holmes's hub of the universe. Brooks's opening words—"In the early spring of 1866"—select a convenient postwar moment, but the fussy reader may notice Brooks's retreat in paragraph 2 to an incident "six years before," Howells's first pilgrimage to the "holy city" of Boston in 1860. The story, both in Brooks's retelling and in the reported language of the 1860 participants, speaks through religious metaphors in a charged secular context. Howells has come to visit the "high priests" (6), those who, living in "the Boston of 1860 . . . wrote with a certain authority and not as the scribes" (13); that is, those who were carrying on the unmistakably Emersonian task of literary scripturism. Howells meets with James Russell Lowell, James T. Fields, and Holmes in a four-hour dinner conversation, which culminates with Holmes's "prophetic" announcement to Lowell: "Well, James, this is something like the apostolic succession. This is the laying on of hands" (2).

For Brooks, this incident "foreshadowed" Howells's and Boston's future. The account of Howells' second coming gives the effects of the tribulation their proper due, within a perspective of generational succession:

> The aspirant from the West had arrived at the psychological moment. Ten years before, the city of light and learning could scarcely have offered a foothold to the stoutest invader. Dominant, abundant, efflorescent, it was all too well supplied by its own New England, as twenty years hence the stout invader might not have cared to scale the Boston wall. At present, with the breach the war had made, and with all the treasure still within the city, Boston was ripe for invasion, and most of the younger writers throughout the country shared Howell's feeling about it. New England ideals and examples had a commanding influence wherever people cared for thought and writing, and eastern Massachusetts was hallowed ground for thousands of the rising generation.

> Many a pilgrim . . . walked to Concord for a glimpse of Emerson's woodpile, wishing they had the courage to knock at the door. (5)

"Twenty years hence" : Brooks's full titular season doesn't arrive until chapter 16, when we learn that "in the mild air of the early eighties, a haze of Indian summer hung over New England" (330). "Ten years before . . . efflorescent": Brooks's early chapters treat the transitional period when, while it was true that the "flowering" of volume 1 had ended, even so "the day had not yet come when all men said, the Bostonians most of all, 'Ichabod, the glory is departed'" (13). "The treasure": how did the objects of this cultural reverence feel about their achieved literary value? How did they experience the "psychological moment"?

CHAPTER TWO

1. As we will note briefly below, with reference and debt to Len Gougeon's work on Emerson's antislavery commitments, this return to the importance of worship has a particular political as well as generally practical dimension: Emerson's desire to speak on the slavery issue corresponds with a project to reunite religion and morality as a basis for powerful mobilization of effective action.

2. Lawrence Buell's magisterial *Emerson* (Harvard UP, 2003; just about my favorite title ever, perhaps second to Daniel Hoffman's *POE POE POE POE POE POE POE*) emphasizes a related turn when discussing *The Conduct of Life* and "Worship" in particular, which he categorizes as Emerson's "last major completed essay on the nature of religious experience": "Emerson still prizes Religion as the 'flowering and completion' of culture; but 'the moral' tends to replace 'the visionary as the operative religious category'" (37); granting more weight to the "social," "the later moral essays testify to Emerson's increasing attunement to pragmatic realities" (283). Buell's synthesis thus tends to confirm Robinson's thesis on pragmatism and ethical purpose, which Buell explicitly draws upon in both of these passages. I might add that insofar as the "visionary" persists, it also takes on an increasingly social dimension, as Emerson's "we" attends to the visions of others.

3. Emerson scholar Jonathan Bishop endows this phrase with religious significance in his (post-Emersonian) book of that title. Independently, Randall Fuller places these words in italics when describing Emerson's "aesthetic surplus": "a *something else* that evades or extends beyond that which can be categorized"; *Emerson's Ghosts* (Oxford UP, 2007), 5.

4. Albert J. von Frank, in *An Emerson Chronology,* indexes two lectures under this name, which he designates as "Worship" and "Worship" (Conduct of Life Ser.). The degree to which the texts are separate remains undetermined. I am not aware of any manuscripts that exist for either; and von Frank has explained that no positive

evidence is available to distinguish the content of the two, so the separate indexing is based on the chronological separation of delivery dates. Barbara Packer, the editor for the Harvard *Conduct,* has expressed the opinion that Emerson composed only a single "Worship." In the entry for May 9, 1847, von Frank notes that on this Sunday, Emerson "delivers 'Worship' as a sermon at Nantucket" (217). His citation leads to the addendum of Eleanor M. Tilton's "Emerson's Lecture Schedule—1837–1838" which she concludes in a footnote: "Without giving evidence and argument, I note here some other additions and corrections of Charvat" (Tilton refers to William Charvat's *A Chronological List of Emerson's American Lecture Engagements*). Among the items noted are that the 1847 Nantucket series took place "May 4–14, not April" (5279.399). This would accord with the *Journals* and the *Letters,* rather than with the account books (the original discrepancy which led to Charvat's uncertainty as to whether the series was given in April or May). Charvat lists "six lectures (probably from 'Representative Men')" plus "an extra lecture on a Sunday, *Worship.*" Von Frank's chronology, citing Tilton, states that "while on Nantucket RWE gives a course of four lectures (5279.399)" (217); Tilton, however, does not mention the reduction of probable lectures from six to four as one among her corrections to Charvat. There are several possible reasons for von Frank's descriptive assertion that "Worship" was given "as a sermon"; it could be because of the day, or in accordance with the memoirist Cabot, or for some other reason (it may have been given at a church and not at the new Athenaeum).

I have looked for accounts of this event in various newspapers. By checking the *Nantucket Inquirer,* I was able to (re)confirm that the lecture was not given in April, but unfortunately, the May issues are missing from the Library of Congress's bound copies, and I have been unable to get to anywhere that might have these issues. (Boston Public Library may have the issues, but it will not loan them interlibrary. And even if I could see the issues in question, the *Inquirer* does not seem to be among the newspapers that gave generous descriptions of Emerson's performances, as was sometimes the case elsewhere—the *Nantucket Inquirer* typically just ran ads listing the title and speaker for upcoming lectures.) Professor von Frank has been generous in responding to my queries about this lecture. *The Later Lectures of Ralph Waldo Emerson, 1843–1871,* vol. 1, 1843–54, ed. Ronald A. Bosco and Joel Myerson (U of Georgia P, 2001; *LL*), helpfully gathers the known extant materials for the Conduct series, but these do not include "Worship."

5. In Robinson's argument, this waning motivates a developing "pragmatism and ethical purpose in the later work."

6. *Strains of Eloquence,* 133; here Mott draws upon sermon 70, which he notes Emerson used between 1830 and 1836. Similarly in sermon 29 (March 15, 1829), Emerson "hopes to be regarded . . . as 'the mild & blameless friend who would win you to a life of purity by the shining example of his own'" (Mott, *Strains of Eloquence,* 50).

7. The date of "Days'" composition is disputed: 1846 or 1852, according to *The Po-*

etry Notebooks. The disputed dates roughly bookend the period during which Emerson worked on the bulk of the material for *The Conduct of Life.*

8. For a reading of "Days" that incorporates biography, see Matthiessen, 59–60, 63, 68. For a sampling of views on Emerson's vocational crises, see Henry Nash Smith, Mary Kupiec Cayton, and Maurice Gonnaud

9. Though he responds here primarily to the didactic force of Emerson's *Conduct,* E. A. Robinson finds the stern Yankeeism of the collection to be not entirely unleavened: "If you will read this book carefully you will get changed ideas about Emerson's humanity and humor"—I find this latter observation applicable especially to "Worship," as in the rueful mirth of Emerson's already remarked comments on the human reluctance to concede the spiritual superiority of another. David Robinson gathers the Edwin Arlington Robinson comment, originally from the *Yale Review* 25.4 (June 1936) 861, for his entry on "Emerson" in *Nineteenth-Century Literature Criticism,* vol. 1 (Gale Research, 1981) 290.

10. Richard Lee Francis, "Necessitated Freedom: Emerson's *The Conduct of Life,*" in *Studies in the American Renaissance,* ed. Joel Myerson (G. K. Hall, 1980), 75.

11. Hughes emphasizes that she has deliberately chosen a representative example to examine for its form: "The relationship between the essay's ["Behavior"'s] beginning and its end is characteristic of the other chapters in *The Conduct of Life*" (5).

12. Though this sentence refers to "*the* Emersonian essay," one should understand that Hughes's examples of this characteristic form come from *The Conduct of Life* (including, but not limited to, the call to action in "Worship") and that these observations appear in her essay "Cost as Confirmation: *The Conduct of Life.*"

13. Wesley T. Mott, "'An Etching of Emerson' (1853) and the Problem of Attribution" *Emerson Society Papers* 6.1 (1995) 1–4. Mott's note includes the full text of the "Etching," which originally appeared as a chapter in the anonymous *Transatlantic Tracings and Popular Pictures from America* (W. Tweedie, 1853). The critic reports having heard "Fate," whose "attempted reconciliation of fate with liberty was an undeniable piece of Emersonian mystification." He then describes his preference for the "Culture" lecture which presented the doctrine that "the world was one great school of Culture, where a man soon found out what was *real.* Some thought the Lecture conflicted with the previous one [on Fate], though perhaps Mr. E would say he was presenting but two sides of the same truth." His censure then falls upon what is surely the text of "Worship"—though he refers to it once as "Fate"—which he remembers mostly for Emerson's opening "remarks on scepticism, and his fearlessness of the imputation of it" and his initial grouping of "all religions, from Oloff [*sic*] and Hengist, down as common superstitions." The opening paragraph of the published text of "Worship" contains the assurance, "Nor do I fear skepticism for any good soul. A just thinker will allow full swing to his skepticism. I dip my pen in the blackest ink, because I am not afraid of falling into my inkpot." The essay then proceeds to examples of how "absolute truth" is always "speedily dragged down" by the earthly tendencies of the worshippers.

"Religion cannot rise above the state of the votary," Emerson observes, with King Olaf and Hengist appearing early on his list of unworthies (*W*, VI, 201, 205–6). The textual highlights are unmistakable; moreover, it seems unlikely that Emerson on this occasion was simply shuffling titles, as Dix has treated the lectures in order and given sufficient description to make the "Fate" and "Culture" lectures recognizable as versions of their final correspondingly titled essay forms.

14. This period of Sunday silence was established by comparing Charvat's dated list against a perpetual calendar to determine days of the week.

15. July–Oct. 1851; *EJ*, 429.

16. See C. J. Wasung, "Emerson Comes to Detroit," *Michigan History Magazine* 29.1 (1945) 59–72 (see 63–64). Though Wasung does not identify the Sunday discourse by name, the description quoted from the *Detroit Daily Advertiser* matches the contents (in order) of "Worship" as it was published. Samples of the newspaper's transcription include, "Man is born believing, and bears belief as naturally as a tree bears apples. Religion cannot rise above the votary. . . . No sane mind can fear infidelity as a permanent state—that would be like saying in a cloudy weather, there is no sun. . . . Religion is the source of intellect; great ages have always been religious ages. . . . It is pleasant to die if there be a God, and a misery to live if there be none."

17. Page 361, manuscript B; though the sermon was originally delivered May 30, 1830, I quote here from Emerson's extensively revised version delivered for the first time April 1, 1832.

18. Emerson will nevertheless draw upon the strength of these theological arguments to say some rather uncomfortable things about actual Unitarian worship practice; for example, a critique of substitutionary atonement may sound fine in theory to a Unitarian until that same Unitarian is challenged to say what exactly *is* meant by the communion elements.

19. René Girard, *A Theater of Envy: William Shakespeare* (Oxford UP, 1991) 4.

20. A compatible Girardian approach to Emerson had been suggested by Eric Selinger in his essay "'Too Pathetic, Too Pitiable': Emerson's Lessons in Love's Philosophy," *ESQ* (formerly *Emerson Society Quarterly*) 40 (2nd Quarter 1994). Selinger reads an earlier sermon, 104 (first written in January of 1831; see *Sermons* 3:84), as Emerson's retreat "from his strongest assertions, based on a God that dwells in the human heart, to a comforting rhetoric of father and child" (1/1). Selinger reads this move as an attempt to defuse the danger that may arise from the dynamics of "triangular desire" that Girard first outlined in *Deceit, Desire, and the Novel.* What I take to be the definitive statement on "the struggle between Emerson and Jesus" appeared in Jonathan Bishop's "Emerson and Christianity," *Renascence* 38 (Spring 1986) 183–200 (see esp. 191–95). The present crux under examination is but one illustration of the self/Other problematic Bishop identifies in Emerson's positioning of Divinity.

21. Fuller recounts that "Religion was early awakened in my soul,—a sense that what the soul is capable to ask it must attain, and that, though I might be aided and

instructed by others, I must depend on myself as the only constant friend" (*Woman in the Nineteenth Century* [Greeley & McElrath], 1845).

22. We should note that Daniel in fact sees his project as dissociating Edwards's philosophy from the "subjectivism" of "Emersonian Romanticism" and bringing Edwards more into alignment with C. S. Peirce (3, 65). One might respond that work by West, Poirier, Jacobson, Robinson, Lopez, and others has attempted a similar job of dissociation and realignment for Emerson himself. See Cornel West, *The American Evasion of Philosophy: A Genealogy of Pragmatism* (U of Wisconsin P, 1988), Richard Poirier, *Poetry & Pragmatism* (Harvard UP, 1992), David Jacobson, *Emerson's Pragmatic Vision: The Dance of the Eye* (U of Pennsylvania P, 1993), David M. Robinson, *Emerson and the Conduct of Life: Pragmatism and Ethical Purpose in the Later Work* (Cambridge UP, 1993), Michael Lopez, *Emerson and Power: Creative Antagonism in the Nineteenth Century* (Northern Illinois UP, 1996), and the entire volume 43 of *ESQ* (1997), a special collection on Emerson and Nietzsche edited by Lopez. More recently, Neal Dolan, in *Emerson's Liberalism* (U of Wisconsin P, 2009), has offered resistance to what he calls the "Nietzschean-pragmatist monolith" that strikes him as a new "tradition" that threatens to constrain and distort our view of Emerson (10); as a corrective offered in the name of valuing Emerson's "otherness" to contemporary consensus, Dolan emphasizes an Emerson who grew up "attempting to reconcile an idiosyncratic form of radical Christian spirituality with Enlightenment rationalism . . . an unlikely marriage, resulting in a strange hybrid neither recognizably Christian nor strictly rationalist in the Enlightenment sense of the word, but nevertheless distinctively marked by both legacies" (10). In what might be taken as implicit evidence for the existence of the alleged "monolith," Dolan interchanges the bibliographic information for Jacobson's and Robinson's 1993 books (Dolan, 304n15, 330n12). *Emerson's Liberalism* also issues a strong rejoinder to Christopher Newfield's *The Emerson Effect* (Chicago UP, 1996), which Dolan acknowledges as having indicated a "central problem" in Emerson, namely the "puzzling conjunction of liberation and submission" (12).

23. Cf. Daniel Walker Howe, *The Unitarian Conscience: Harvard Moral Philosophy, 1805–1861* (Wesleyan UP, 1988).

24. As, in the culmination of *Nature,* Emerson offers the sacramental message that the world exists "for you."

25. Hence, for example, his objection to the crucifixion (in the conclusion of "Character").

26. *The Betrothed* (London, 1834). Emerson refers to "the English translation" (347), and the most widely circulated English edition to predate Emerson's lecture was Richard Bentley's 1834 edition. Its title page bills it as "The Betrothed. Complete in one volume. Standard Novels. No XLIII. London: Richard Bentley, 1834." But at 432 pages, as Emerson notes, it is not "complete." A New York edition issued by George Dearborn, *Lucia, The Betrothed,* also in 1834, relied upon the same translation and was further

truncated. Though no translator (or even author) is listed on the title page, these editions include "Critical Remarks on Manzoni's Betrothed: By The Count O'Mahony." These remarks constitute a defense of the novel, "recommending its perusal to the good and pious"(v). Emerson, instead, retrieves a Manzoni to inspire the heroic and the holy.

Two other English translations predate Emerson's 1838 lecture on "Holiness": an 1828 Pisa edition of *The Betrothed Lovers,* published by Niccolo Capurro, which omits the passage Emerson recovers, and an 1834 Washington D.C. edition published by Duff Green, which includes the passage Emerson highlights but renders it less directly and makes other omissions. A subsequent translation of *The Betrothed* (London: George Bell, 1844), announces that "the English reader is here, for the first time, presented with a translation of the whole, unmutilated work of Manzoni" as opposed to previous efforts, each of which "omits or alters . . . to bring down its high religious and moral tone more nearly to the level of common taste" (v). Emerson's 1838 intervention seeks to restore that lost tone.

27. The paragraph quoted above is omitted in its entirety from the 1834 edition. Emerson retranslates most of the other material included in the English edition, generally favoring a fairly close word-by-word approach. One exception occurs in this final passage, with Emerson's description of the master (*il padrone*) as thinking "with emotion he had never before known." The original "tutto commosso" does suggest an intense experience of being "very" or "wholly" "moved, touched, or shaken"; Emerson emphasizes the intensity by suggesting that it is completely unprecedented, and he leaves the content of the emotion somewhat more mysterious (through these choices, especially the emphasis on absolute newness, Emerson renders the feeling as something more akin to a moment of religious conversion). The bit about the "devil of a Father!" is indeed a rather precise transcription, and a probable reason for the excision of the passage from the Bentley edition, with its emphasis on pious didacticism. Emerson, with a different ideal of piety, restores the passage for the same reason of emphasis.

28. For commentary with particular attention to these lines, see Maurice Gonnaud, *An Uneasy Solitude: The Individual and Society in the Work of Ralph Waldo Emerson,* trans. Lawrence Rosenwald (Princeton UP, 1987) 241. See also Kenneth W. Cameron, "Early Background for Emerson's 'The Problem,'" *ESQ* 27.2 (1962) 37–46.

29. René Girard, with Jean-Michel Oughourlian and Guy Lefort, *Things Hidden since the Foundation of the World,* trans. Stephen Bann and Michael Metteer (Stanford UP, 1987) 297.

30. On this restless pursuit, see also Donald Gelpi, *Endless Seeker : The Religious Quest of Ralph Waldo Emerson* (UP of America, 1991).

31. Thus far, Robert Hudspeth's thematically focused essay "Later Emerson: 'Intellect' and *The Conduct of Life*" is the only study of Conduct to have appeared subse-

quent to the publication of the Packer edition in the Collected Works. Hudspeth's study appears in *Emerson: Bicentennial Essays,* ed. Ronald A. Bosco and Joel Myerson (Massachusetts Historical Society, 2006), 405–31, and that volume also includes an essay by Packer on "Fate" ("History and Form in Emerson's 'Fate'"), the chapter of Conduct which still seems destined to command the lion's share of critical attention.

32. Ellison apparently makes this nomination independently, as she does not cite Hughes's earlier study; nor do Ellison or Hughes cite Francis.

33. Cf. Barbara Packer on this point of unoriginality; she likewise notes the affinity between "Worship" and the Divinity School Address—("Emerson" in *Columbia Literary History of the United States [subsequently referred to as LHUS]).*

34. Emerson confesses at the outset of "Fate," "We are incompetent to solve the times"(*CW* 6:1). As "literature becomes criticism" (as Emerson had noticed in his 1847 journal), this regret may be taken as a palinode of, among other things, his 1841 "Introductory Lecture on the Times" (*CW* 1:167).

35. Various more or less plausible schemes have been proposed somewhat impressionistically, based upon interpretative arrangements of the essays' main ideas or of other inferential criteria. For one of the more complete pictures, see Francis, "Necessitated Freedom" (80–81).

36. Regarding the book's structure, Neal Dolan has similarly observed that "the sequencing in Emerson's collections is often significant . . . but never so pointed as in 'Power,' 'Wealth,' 'Culture,' and 'Worship' in *The Conduct of Life.* The first two present the strongest endorsement anywhere in Emerson's writing of the modern liberal emancipation of material self-interest from long-standing Christian stricture. The latter two then present a rhetorically stirring summation of Emerson's long-nourished conception of how a civilization based upon such emancipated self-interest can avoid moral and spiritual shallowness"; *Emerson's Liberalism* (288). Gathering the first essay, "Fate," into the sequence, Dolan concludes that Emerson "traverses two opposite poles in these five major essays in *The Conduct of Life*. . . . The first three embrace the historically unprecedented freedom, dynamism, and sheer material abundance of modern liberal society, while the latter two acknowledge and propose a means for overcoming moral and spiritual deficiencies intrinsic to its productive dynamism" (296). Dolan sets up this compositional performance as a kind of vocational inevitability: "a scion of ministers who was himself initially trained to be a minister could not help but wonder about the symbolic sustenance of such an untethered society. What symbolic structures would provide moral inspiration. . . . What would be the source of social cohesion? 'How is it people manage to live on,' Emerson asks in *The Conduct of Life* [and, I would note, in "Worship"], 'so aimless as they are?'(E&L 1059)" (283).

37. A reading of Twain by way of Emerson in some ways anticipates the findings of *Writing beyond Prophecy;* in *Mark Twain and the Limits of Power: Emerson's God in Ruins* (U of Tennessee P, 1982), James L. Johnson gives us a Twain who shared in the

desire of the Andersonian Emerson's *Imperial Self*: "He poured much of his creative energies into dramatizing such power at large in the world, and in the end he found himself in near despair over the implications he discovered in it" (9). That despairing Emersonian individual is the "god in ruins," and from those ruins arises the call to "Worship."

38. Though the issue of retaining wealthy members would become a more urgent one after the "disestablishment" of the clergy (when pastorships ceased to be tax-supported offices), Stowe makes clear that Dr. H depends upon his flock's patronage for important projects such as the publication of his theological treatises.

39. The *OED* gives the traditional line on this nonpredictive, nonwillful use of shall: "In the first person, *shall* has, from the early ME. period, been the normal auxiliary for expressing mere futurity, without any adventitious notion"; *shall* may refer to "events conceived as independent of the speaker's volition" (definition 8b).

40. He delivers his most caustic remarks with a deliberately blithe diction. In reviewing the history of how "absolute truths . . . are speedily dragged down into savage interpretation," he includes some harrowing examples: "Among our Norse forefathers, King Olaf's mode of converting Eyvind to Christianity was to put a pan of glowing coals on his belly, which burst asunder. 'Wilt thou now, Eyvind, believe in Christ?' asks Olaf, *in excellent faith. Another argument* was an adder put into the mouth of the reluctant disciple Rand, who refused to believe" (*CW* 6:109; my emphasis on Emerson's sarcastic interpolations between the flatly rendered historical accounts).

41. Earlier in the essay, Emerson provides a fuller echo of this materialist/determinist tradition as adapted to an idealist perspective: "The primordial atoms are prefigured and predetermined to moral issues, are in search of justice, and ultimate right is done. Religion or worship is the attitude of those who see this unity . . . who see that, against all appearances, the nature of things works for truth and right forever" (*CW* 6:116–17). At this and similar points of the essay, Emerson restates worship as an acceptance of his doctrine of Compensation.

42. These concepts may also differ in temporal orientation: voluntary obedience suggests a conscious election to follow the course dictated by fate, but necessitated freedom may involve a realization after the fact, as suggested by an example from Haruki Murakami's *Wind-Up Bird Chronicle:* "On occasion, after the momentary satisfaction of having decided something of his own free will, he would see that things had been decided beforehand by an external power cleverly camouflaged as free will, mere bait thrown in his path to lure him into behaving as he was meant to behave"(513–14).

43. See Francis for a philosophical consideration of this paradoxical concept; see Newfield and Prettyman for a political criticism of it.

44. Reading these tendencies with a somewhat different emphasis, John T. Lysaker argues that at "such points, friendship and self-culture meet in what is really a double consciousness, wherein we side with our emerging selves against the inertia of

our foregoing hour, alert to the prophecy of one another and loyal to our prospects. But because this is friendship, we owe the same to our companions, and thus must side with their emerging selves as well, come what may. In *Conduct of Life,* Emerson celebrates self-culture because it unlocks us from our 'mastertones,' which I read as native genius or temperament (*CW* 6:72). It even 'succors us against ourselves' so that we might develop a catholicity that reaches beyond our normal ken"; "On the Faces of Emersonian 'Friendship,'" in *Emerson & Thoreau: Figures of Friendship* (Indiana UP, 2010) 97. Lysaker compellingly observes a dynamic whereby Emerson's *Conduct of Life* calls upon us to seek outside ourselves, but to my mind, it seems curious to insist upon calling this interpersonal process a celebration of *self*-culture. Along these lines, Branka Arsić notes that her reading differs from that of Lysaker, who says, "We may rely upon others along the way, whether for illumination or support. . . . But no one can play our part in individuation"; Arsić comments, "It seems to me that for Emerson, rather, individuation is made by others, by friends"; *On Leaving: A Reading in Emerson* (Harvard UP, 2010), 360n25. See also Lysaker's *Emerson & Self-Culture* (Indiana UP, 2008) for a valuable discussion of how Emerson turns from prayer to "the practice of worship, and from an isolated activity toward one synonymous with the conduct of life"; "That worship lies at self-culture's summit is clear from both the early lecture 'Private Life' and the later essay 'Worship'" (95, 99). Again, the shift from isolated practice would qualify the emphasis on the word "self," as would Emerson's own wording in speaking of "culture" as such at this point; in support of the claim for worship's preeminence, Lysaker quotes *Conduct*'s declaration on "the question of culture" that "its flowering or completion may described as Religion, or Worship" (*CW* 6:108).

45. William J. Scheick, *The Slender Human Word: Emerson's Artistry in Prose* (U of Tennessee P, 1978) 98.

46. *Doctrine and Difference: Essays in the Literature of New England* (Routledge, 1997) 114.

47. Not that Colacurcio intends to put the question of "personification" to rest with this statement. Colacurcio further notes that "Emerson and the 'language' of persons remains a vital and neglected topic" (*Doctrine and Difference,* 271n19). Also, in light of some recent Emerson criticism, the entirety of Colacurcio's sentence bears repeating: Emerson works toward "what worship might mean in a world in where God no longer figures as a person *and* where veneration of the state (or any other figment of collectivity) is simply unthinkable"(22, my emphasis). The reminder of that "and" serves as a corrective to certain political assaults on Emerson.

48. One consequence of criticism that makes "Behavior" the center of the book is to render *The Conduct of Life* a bit too self-reliant. Hughes (5) and Francis (82) both note that "Behavior" echoes the earlier essay "Self-Reliance." "Self-Reliance" itself is not such a stable or self-evident manifesto: as Colacurcio reminds us, that famous essay fails to recover an "aboriginal Self" upon which to found conduct (*Doctrine and Dif-*

ference, 130). Maybe so. But the Emerson of "Self-Reliance" doesn't seem to think you should waste any time stopping to ask someone *else* for directions. "Worship" actually pauses a moment to consider other-reliance as a live possibility.

49. On the occasion of this vacancy, Emerson's uncle Reverend Samuel Ripley of Waltham makes plans to move back in. The Old Manse, which had, in succession, been the site of literary output from Emerson and then Hawthorne and some of their most assertive "writing after the minister," would revert to being occupied by one of those "ministers, ministers, ministers" Emerson had sought to replace through his own calling.

50. Nearing the publication of *Conduct,* the trend had in some ways been temporarily reversed, but only as prelude to more permanent departures: "Emerson was content to be surrounded once more with his crew of associates—Alcott and Hawthorne dwelling side by side half a mile from his door, Thoreau and Channing available for afternoon walks through the countryside. . . .What he could not have known at the end of 1860 was how soon two of the four would be lost to him. . . .The shark's tooth was not yet fully visible in the gray and wrinkled Hawthorne, but it was already there, and the decade of the 1860s was not yet half over when he followed Thoreau" (Carlos Baker, *Emerson among the Eccentrics: A Group Portrait* [Viking, 1996],427).

51. *EJ,* 444.

52. March–April 1843; *EJ,* 302.

53. *Emerson: The Mind on Fire* (U of California P, 1995) 389. Richardson notes that the Fuller connection correlates to Emerson's veneration of Dante's *Vita nuova* (which he translated), which he praised as "the Bible of Love." For a fascinating consideration of what the Emerson-Fuller-Dante nexus meant to Hawthorne—as generative for "Rappacini's Daughter"—see Thomas R. Mitchell, *Hawthorne's Fuller Mystery* (U of Massachusetts P, 1998) 94–95. Richardson further observes that both Emerson's first wife, Ellen, and his aunt Mary Moody Emerson also occupied privileged positions at this nexus of visionary faith associated with Dante: "Years earlier he had idealized his first wife, Ellen, until she became a sort of Beatrice. Now, in a final reckoning, he set his aunt even higher—if such a thing is possible—recognizing in her some of the qualities of the creator of Beatrice. In an astonishing and moving passage, he said, 'When I read Dante the other day, and his paraphrases to signify with more adequateness Christ or Jehovah, whom do you think I was reminded of? Whom but Mary Emerson and her eloquent theology.' . . . She stands, finally, said her nephew, apart from works, even from her own works, for 'faith alone; faith alone'" (560–61). For Emerson's allusional debt to Dante, specifically Virgil's "angelic butterfly," in imagining the American Scholar, see Randall Fuller, *Emerson's Ghosts* (Oxford UP, 2007) 16, 161n26.

54. *EJ,* 414.

55. See esp. pp. 39–40 for Taylor's comments on the self of American Transcendentalism. In "The Widening Gyre: Out from Emerson," Philip Gura emphasizes the

"selfhood-in-relation" that emerges as an ideal in Lidian Emerson's letters; *Emersonian Circles: Essays in Honor of Joel Myerson,* ed. Wesley T. Mott and Robert E. Burkholder (U of Rochester P, 1997) 264. Gura thus points to a congruence between the work of Phyllis Cole, "'Men and Women Conversing': The Emersons in 1837," and Albert J. von Frank, "'Build Therefore Your Own World': Emerson's Constructions of the 'Intimate Sphere,'" whose essays appears in the same volume and which value "the opportunity to hear an author in dialogue with those who made up his private world" (264, 128). More recently, Jennifer Gurley has recovered an Emerson "with a new understanding of himself as not merely an interested 'ego' but an 'individual with [a] world,' and within a 'system' ('Fate,' in *W,* 6:4)"; "Emerson's Politics of Uncertainty," *ESQ* 53.4 (2007) 323–59. Gurley concludes that "Emerson's social dialogue, like the universal conversation, requires as much humility as conviction" (349). See also 341 and 358n42, for Gurley on Emerson as other than a resolute loner: "Certainly he did not prefer group work, but he joined and even formed more than his share of groups."

CHAPTER THREE

1. Cf. Richard Brodhead's "Hawthorne, Melville, and the Fiction of Prophecy," in his *The School of Hawthorne* (Oxford UP, 1986); also Teresa Toulouse's *The Art of Prophesying* (U of Georgia P, 1987), a study of New England preaching that, in its concluding pages, gestures toward Hawthorne's and Melville's writings as (revisionary) extensions of that tradition.

2. He did famously read *The Scarlet Letter* aloud to his wife, reporting that it "broke her heart"—an achievement that a Puritan divine in the Thomas Hooker tradition might have envied (Hooker, as mentioned below, insisted that the soul's preparation for salvation required that the heart must be broken.)

3. The captain is identified by name only in the notebooks.

4. It appears the minister, a Dr. Richards, had spent a week, and all his cash, at a Liverpool brothel. The Reverend never did repay Hawthorne for money advanced toward a return ticket to America (James R. Mellow, *Nathaniel Hawthorne in His Times* [Houghton Mifflin, 1980] 433, 455). See *CE,* vol. 18, *The Letters, 1857–1864,* ed. Thomas Woodson et al. (1987), for an 1857 letter to Ticknor enlisting his help in recovering the funds, 73.

5. *CE,* vol. 17, *The Letters, 1853–1856,* ed. Fredson Bowers, James A. Rubino, L. Neal Smith, James Kayes (1987), 347; discussed by Mellow, 433. Additional comment on the incident appears in *The English Notebooks* for May 24, 1855, *CE* 21:171–73.

6. See Norman Pettit, *The Heart Prepared: Grace and Conversion in Puritan Spiritual Life,* Second Edition (Wesleyan UP, 1989).

7. The situation whereby Hawthorne replaces the errant pastor bears certain structural similarities to Emerson's analysis of what has caused religion to stumble: both

authors point to the minister's failure of duty. On Emerson's account, ministers across America had abdicated their posts, fallen into "supine" attitudes—Emerson issues a call for the ministerial role to be filled by those who would stand tall, speaking a language of prophecy unfettered by tradition. But one key distinguishing factor between Emerson's and Hawthorne's replacement scenarios lies in their attitudes toward the status of the profession in general. Those practitioners Emerson would replace appear to their colleagues to remain in perfectly good faith and appropriate comportment. In the case of Hawthorne and the "desecrated" Doctor, the dereliction of duty may be measured according to the profession's normative standards, rather than as a failure to meet the criteria of Emerson's revisionary call.

8. *English Notebooks, CE,* vol. 21, May 31, 1855, 175.

9. In his chapter on the *Elixir* manuscripts in *Tradition and Revolution* (Cambridge UP, 1991), Charles Swann provides a textual rationale for privileging *Septimius Felton,* while making judicious comparative use of the *Septimius Norton* manuscript—*Norton* significantly amplifies and revises *Felton,* but breaks off in mid-narrative, whereas *Felton* tells a complete plot. For purposes of the present study, *Septimius Felton* has the additional attraction that Melville had in his library the posthumous edition.

10. "Feathertop" recounts the misadventures of a scarecrow, animated by witchery to pass for a man. The attempt having ultimately failed, the witch, Mother Rigby, concludes, "Well, well! I'll make a scarecrow of him after all. 'Tis an innocent and useful vocation." Perhaps being a minister (of the warnings of hellfire garden variety, frightening souls away from where they ought not to go) might be seen to have certain similarities to this cornfield work. Early in the tale, the narrator declares that Mother Rigby "might, with very little trouble, have made a scarecrow ugly enough to frighten the minister himself"—one implication being that to do so would be to beat the minister at his own game. If the tale satirizes the rhetoric of vocational utility, "Feathertop" makes us not less wary of placing faith in literary illusions: the tale repeatedly tropes on the word "composition" in describing the process of Feathertop's creation. The narrator makes sure the reader does not miss the potential self-deprecation of this metaphor: "Shall I confess the truth? At its present point of vivification, the scarecrow reminds me of some of the lukewarm and abortive characters, composed of heterogeneous materials, used for the thousandth time, and never worth using, with which romance-writers (and myself, no doubt, among the rest) have so over-peopled the world of fiction." Feathertop's moment of undoing is likewise a moment of crisis for the fictional enterprise:

> Feathertop likewise had looked towards the mirror, and there beheld, not the glittering mockery of his outside show, but a picture of the sordid patchwork of his real composition, stript of all witchcraft.
>
> The wretched simulacrum! We almost pity him. He threw up his arms,

> with an expression of despair that went further than any of his previous manifestations, towards vindicating his claims to be reckoned human. For perchance the only time, since this so often empty and deceptive life of mortals began its course, an illusion had seen and fully recognized itself.

"Feathertop" is the last of the "adult" tales. Composed the same year as *The Blithedale Romance* was published, 1852, "Feathertop" was first published in the 1854 edition of *Mosses.* In terms of composition date, what follows are *The Tanglewood Tales* for children, the nonfiction prose of "Chiefly about War Matters" and *Our Old Home,* and, in terms of fiction, only *The Marble Faun* and the late manuscripts.

The scarecrow recurs as a figure of comparative utility in *Septimius Felton,* but the satire works a bit differently, perhaps more conventionally than in "Feathertop." In the passage that follows the narrator's conclusion that Septimius as a preacher might have been of "great usefulness to his generation," we learn that not only has Septimius failed to pursue the ministry, he has neglected to cultivate the field by his house: "Unwilling to spare the time to plough, to plant, to hoe it, himself, [Septimius] had hired a lazy lout of the village, when he might just as well have employed and paid wages to the scarecrow which Aunt Zezia dressed out in ancient habiliments, and set up in the midst of the corn"(53–54). Here the figure of the scarecrow serves as a satiric comment upon the laziness of the "lout" and Septimius himself: both of whom clearly ought to be making themselves more useful, the narrative suggests. The satire of Feathertop's return to the inanimate vocation of scarecrow is more cynical, unsettling the rhetoric of usefulness and the justification of *any* active vocation whatsoever: "Tis an innocent and useful vocation, and will suit my darling well; and, if each of his human brethren had as fit a one, 'twould be the better for mankind."

11. Quoted in Albert Gelpi, *The Tenth Muse* (Cambridge UP, 1975) 1.

12. See Charvat, "The Condition of Authorship in 1820," in *The Profession of Authorship in America 1800–1870,* ed. Matthew J. Bruccoli (Columbia UP, 1992). Charvat points out that the lack of international copyright protection could work both ways, but explains further factors which contributed to the fact American authors suffered more (31–32). Before 1790 there was no copyright law even to prevent piracy of American originals within America; no international copyright law would be enacted until 1891; see Michael Davitt Bell, "Conditions of Literary Vocation," in *The Cambridge History of American Literature,* ed. Sacvan Bercovitch, vol. 2, *Prose Writing 1820–1865* (Cambridge UP, 1995), 14.

13. Commenting upon the dialectic of "Quotation and Originality" in Emerson's method of "creative reading," Joseph Riddel proposes that "only God does not quote," and thus "man, who is condemned to quotation," must realize an "inventive originality" through a writing that is reading, or rather misreading; *Purloined Letters: Originality and Repetition in American Literature* (Louisiana State UP, 1995) 29. "Literature,"

achieved through creative quotation, "mimes our desire to be original"; at this turn in *Septimius Felton,* it mimes the Devil's desire to be like God. As Jean-Michel Oughourlian puts it in *The Puppet of Desire* (Stanford UP, 1991), there is no "original" sin; there are only imitations, envious acts of rebellion driven by a felt lack of being (72, 25–26).

14. Few readers can have overlooked the ironic ambiguity introduced by the scholarly practice of referring to the final cluster of Hawthorne's unfinished romances as the "elixir of life manuscripts"; the last word of the phrase could denote either the materiality of the incomplete Hawthornean artifacts (the *Elixir of Life* manuscripts), or the subjects of the stories and thus part of the title of their compilation (*The Elixir of Life Manuscripts*). These are unfinished "manuscripts" from Hawthorne's hand, telling and retelling a fictional character's attempt to fix the meaning of fragmentary manuscripts.

15. Some commentators have noted that the remarkably compact narrative required the additional breadth of the "Custom-House" sketch in order to physically stand on its own without toppling—and to fulfill the print market's expectations for the length of a novel; few have doubted its metaphysical substance.

16. *Our America: Nativism, Modernism, and Pluralism* (Duke UP, 1995), 15; Michaels also connects the tradition of "wordless eloquence" to a discussion of Faulkner on 4–5.

17. Granted, by almost any standard the "sad and passionate" moments of "love, and anguish" shared by Arthur and Hester in the dim forest dell would seem elevated when compared to the sad and tawdry adventures of the "desecrated" American reverend in Liverpool. But however "true" the love between the novel's pastor and his parishioner may have been, the perspective from which the Reverend Dimmesdale's *termination* of his affair with Hester Prynne may be deemed a "desecration" is rather far removed from the more traditionally sanctioned position from which Hawthorne later excoriates Richards for his escapades.

18. Much of what I have to say derives from Emily Miller Budick's "Sacvan Bercovitch, Stanley Cavell, and the Romance Theory of American Fiction," *PMLA* 107.1 (January 1992): 78–91. Paul K Johnston's "Killing the Spirit: Anne Hutchinson and the Office of the Scarlet Letter," and Richard Millington's "*The Office of* The Scarlet Letter: An 'Inside Narrative'?" both appeared in a special issue of the *Nathaniel Hawthorne Review,* 22.1 (Spring 1996), devoted to addressing Bercovitch's landmark study of the novel. A relevant essay from Bercovitch himself, "*The Scarlet Letter:* A Twice-Told Tale," appears in the subsequent number of the journal, making volume 22 perhaps the strongest ever for this publication.

19. Millington, 3–4, offers a lucid interpretation of "Hester's Return" as a radical cultural project.

20. *CE* 21:376, *The English Notebooks 1853–1856,* ed. Thomas Woodson and Bill Ellis, 1997.

21. Thomas Woodson and Bill Ellis report on this identification in their notes to *CE*

21:648, 741.

22. In contrast, as *The Marble Faun* will suggest, Hawthorne did find in "The World's Cathedral" an impressiveness appropriate to its scale.

23. Lines 5–6; repeated, with variation, at poem's conclusion.

24. For further discussion of Hawthorne's concern with an Emersonian antagonism to priests, see my "Reading the Bloody 'Face of Nature': The Persecution of Religion in Hawthorne's *The Marble Faun*," *Contagion: Journal of Violence, Mimesis, and Culture* 12–13 (2005–6) 133–45. That essay extends, with specificity to the vocation of preaching, my earlier work on Hawthorne's critique of sacrificial logic.

25. I specify that this account has become traditional, for Ullén and Greven have recently demonstrated that "Hawthorne's last phase was not always known as that record of a dying man's failing imagination we have become accustomed to accept" (5). These scholars read into the record, for example, early appreciative reception of the posthumously published *Septimius: A Romance* (1872).

26. Both James Wallace and Charles Swann, for example, prominently cite this passage; Swann indeed leads his concluding chapter, "*The Elixir of Life Manuscripts:* Had we but world enough and time" (219), with the same juxtaposition of the journal entry and the *Septimius Felton* passage which are foregrounded at the start of the present essay (*CE* 21:153 and 13:12). Both Wallace and Swann supply the single sentence truncation of the journal entry. Edward H. Davidson likely did much to establish this association when, in 1949, he provided a lengthier quotation of this passage near the beginning of his chapter on "Septimius Felton" in *Hawthorne's Last Phase* (Yale UP, 1949) 73.

27. *CE* 16:407; cited in Wineapple, "Nathaniel Hawthorne, 1804–1864: A Brief Biography," *A Historical Guide to Nathaniel Hawthorne,* ed. Larry J. Reynolds (Oxford UP, 2001) 30.

28. Amid Hawthorne's late ponderings of immortality, Samuel Johnson, the figure he referred to as the "English Moralist," looms large (*CE* 5:123). Johnson's prominent appearance in *Our Old Home* (1863) reprises, for an older readership, a didactic episode Hawthorne had crafted for a juvenile audience some twenty years prior. In *Biographical Stories for Children* (1842), he had told the story of young Sam Johnson's filial disobedience and his later penitence. Son of the bookseller Michael Johnson of Lichfield, Sam had refused to go Uttoxeter to spell his father on a day the old man had felt too ill to take his books to market. Having long borne the guilt of this failure, the famous Dr. Johnson returned to Uttoxeter some fifty years later to perform a public penance in the marketplace.

Hawthorne, visiting Lichfield during his consulship (1853–57), encounters a strikingly lifelike sculpture of the "colossal" Doctor (131). After replaying a momentary shock of recognition for his readers, Hawthorne breaks the representational illusion and moves closer to examine the iconography of the memorial. Noticing that the pedestal contains a bas-relief of the scene he "long ago tried to tell . . . for the behoof of childish readers," he finds himself spurred to perform a "pious errand" to Uttoxeter and "the holy site where Johnson stood to do his penance" (132, 135–36).

Arriving at the destination of his "pilgrimage," Hawthorne is aghast to discover that there is no "memorial of this incident, as beautiful and touching as can be cited out of any human life; no inscription of it, *almost as sacred as a verse of Scripture,* on the wall of the church" (133, 137, my emphasis). Hawthorne's first telling of the Johnson episode had sprung from the same moment in 1842 when he had testified in his journal to the need for a "new revelation," and he had issued it as a true tale that stands on its own as a new scripture even if a pious one (see "Textual Introduction" to *CE* 6 for a discussion of this tale's circulation as a pamphlet for the Sunday School Society). In the *Our Old Home* retelling twenty years later, Johnson's exemplarity still represents a potential excess of revelation, but only "almost." The sentimental journey takes the reverent pilgrim to a Johnsonian scene just outside the church; Hawthorne wants to move things inside. As he warms to his topic, he voices his feeling that Dr. Johnson's holy wisdom ought to have been brought into alignment with the old revelation through the orthodox medium of the sermon. But based upon the inhabitants' apparent ignorance of the penance, he fears this preaching opportunity has thus far been missed: "If the clergyman of the parish, for example, had ever heard of it, would he not have used the theme, time and again, wherewith to work tenderly and profoundly on the souls committed to their charge?" (137)

In determining the extent of the didactic failure, Hawthorne places great weight on his survey of a local youth "whom I should take to be a clergyman's son" (138). The twelve- or thirteen-year-old boy, who has lived in Uttoxeter all his life, says he has never heard about how Dr. Johnson "stood an hour doing penance near the church, the spire of which rose before us" (138). This youth bears a special emblematic role in Hawthorne's errand. The pilgrimage had begun at Johnson's sculpture with the series of bas-reliefs on its pedestal. In the first scene, "Johnson is represented as hardly more than a baby, bestriding an old man's shoulders . . . listening earnestly to the high-church eloquence of Dr. Sacheverell" (132). In Hawthorne's presentation, the bas-reliefs form a logical sequence that culminates in the third scene, the penance. The infant Sam, initially inspired by an eloquent sermon, eventually matures to perform a deed worthy of inspiring a sermon. From eloquence to eloquence, the word proceeds forward into the world. Hawthorne, in his interview with the Uttoxeter youth, seeks a fourth panel to extend the sequence: the testimony of a child who might well have been inspired in turn by a sermon that incorporated Johnson's repentance of youthful sin. But the "clergyman's son" has not received the word; the kerygmatic cycle has been broken. Hawthorne's text seeks to restore it.

"The hermeneutical situation of Christianity," writes Paul Ricoeur, "is that the relation between speech and writing is constitutive of what we term proclamation, kerygma, preaching. What appears to be primary is the series speech-writing-speech, or else writing-speech-writing, in which at times speech mediates between two writings, as does the word of Jesus between the two Testaments, and at times writing mediates between two forms of speech, as the gospel does between the preaching of the early church and contemporary preaching. This chain is the condition of the possibility of tradition as such, in the fundamental sense of the transmission of a message." Ricoeur develops this idea in the essay "Philosophical and Biblical Hermeneutics," in *From Text to Action: Essays in Hermeneutics, II,* trans. Kathleen Blamey and John B. Thompson (Northwestern UP, 1991), 94, 91.

29. London: Henry S. King & Co., 65 Cornhill, 1872. The "pious" receptions of the text tend to align with the sentiments of the narrator (who laments Septimius's turn to heresy in following his immortality impulse into mad science "instead of interpreting it truly" as theological index), while the "promethean" readings tend to celebrate Septimius's heroic declarations (as in his expression of Nietzschean resolve: "Let other men die if they choose or yield; let him that is strong enough, live!" [*CE* 13:13]).

30. Raymona Hull, "Hawthorne and the Magic Elixir of Life: The Failure of a Gothic Theme," *ESQ* (formerly *Emerson Society Quarterly*) 67 (1972) 97–107.

31. Paul Auster, *The Locked Room,* in *The New York Trilogy* (Penguin, 1990) 235.

32. Brenda Wineapple, *Hawthorne: A Life* (Knopf, 2003) 363. Wineapple also perceptively notes that the Septimius narrative "incorporates elements of almost all of Hawthorne's previous work" (364). It may thus be read, I would add, as a thorough stocktaking in the aftermath of prophecy. Contextualizing Nina Baym's thesis (in *The Shape of Hawthorne's Career*) on *Septimius Felton* as an "antiromance" with recourse to reform writing on the dangers of fiction, James N. Mancall finds that even as Hawthorne's text satirizes these reformers, it "serves also as a critique of the author's vocation"; "*Thoughts Painfully Intense*" (Routledge, 2002), 120. Arguing for an even broader significance, Larry J. Reynolds also takes a minority stance in defending the value of these late fragments: "Though dismissed by most Hawthorne scholars, the 'Elixir of Life' manuscripts, which include 'Septimius,' represent Hawthorne's most sustained, direct, and tortured effort to work through the issues of popular violence, mass hysteria, and partisan politics, especially with regard to natural, ethnic, and racial differences. With great effort and intermittent confidence, he sought to resolve fears about the dissolution of his life and that of his nation, especially the latter's bloody way of addressing the problem of variegated racial identities within the house divided"; *Devils and Rebels: The Making of Hawthorne's Damned Politics* (U of Michigan P, 2008) 232.

33. Hawthorne mentions this fact in "The Old Manse" (*CE* 10:5), as Larry Reynolds has underscored (16). In his useful overview, Reynolds expands upon Colacurcio's above characterization of the Old Manse phase as Emersonian in its provocation: "One result of Emerson's 'attack,' as Sophia calls it, was Hawthorne's decision to write about

contemporary issues and contemporary figures, including Emerson" (17).

34. See, for example, David Van Leer, "The Apocalypse of the Mind: Idealism and Annihilation in the American Renaissance" (Diss., Cornell U, 1978).

35. Reynolds, *Devils and Rebels*, 72. Reynolds subsequently develops the Thoreauvian resonances of "Septimius Felton" (228–29).

36. James Mellow's biography (*Nathaniel Hawthorne in His Times* [Houghton Mifflin, 1980]) gives the details of Hawthorne's first visit to the Peabody home (101). Klaus P. Stich ("The Saturday Club as Intertext in Hawthorne's *The Elixir of Life Manuscripts*," *Nathaniel Hawthorne Review* 20.2 [Fall 1994] 11–20) supplies links to Cornelius Felton (as well as to Charles Eliot Norton and Oliver Wendell Holmes). In *The Transcendentalists: An Anthology* (Harvard UP, 1950), Perry Miller refers to the Menzel project and also gives a biographical sketch of Felton (369, 294, 98). Details of Felton's and Hawthorne's mutual membership and participation in "The Saturday Club" appear in Edward Waldo Emerson, *The Early Years of the Saturday Club, 1855–1870* (Houghton Mifflin, 1918); Cornelius Felton is counted among the original fourteen members (20) and is credited for involvement in its forming (162); Hawthorne was "apprised of his election to the club" in 1859, and began to attend upon his 1860 return to America (206).

37. Barbara Packer reports that Felton wrote to Emerson asking him to give the annual address to Phi Beta Kappa Society ("The Transcendentalists," in *The Cambridge History of American Literature, Volume Two: Prose Writing 1820–1865* [Cambridge UP, 1995], 396). Kenneth Sacks (*Understanding Emerson* [Princeton UP, 2003]) cites Felton's "significant influence in determining the choice of speaker" for the annual address (179n2). His invitation does not mean that Felton endorsed all things Emersonian, and, in fact, he delivered a rather negative review of *Essays, First Series* in 1841; cf. Hutchinson, 192. But in an 1856 letter to The Saturday Club, he offers this toast: "May the fruits be as rich as Emerson's philosophy" (Edward Emerson, 15).

38. Cited in Brooks Atkinson's introduction to *The Selected Writings of Ralph Waldo Emerson*, xv; alternatively, Edward Emerson reports the dictum as "our literary Declaration of Independence" (53).

39. Sacrifice implicitly pervades Septimius's quest for the elixir of life: Septimius obtains the elixir manuscript from a man he has killed; the life of "his victim" (*CE* 13:32) is subsequently referred to as having been "sacrificed" (35); and the crucial ingredient for the elixir itself appears to be a plant that springs up from the man's grave. A legend surrounding the elixir secret makes the sacrificial connection even more directly. The mysterious Sybil Dark (or Dacy) tells Septimius that the elixir quest began "long ago" with an English "noble" who was a "man of science" (90–93):

> You see, the object of the Lord of Smithills Hall was, to take a life from the course of Nature, and Nature did not choose to be defrauded; so that, great

> as was the power of this scientific man over her, she would not consent that he should escape the necessity of dying at the proper time; except upon the condition of sacrificing some other life for his; and this was to be done, for every thirty years that he chose to live, thirty years being the account of a generation of man; and if, in any way, in that time, the lord could be the death of a human being, that satisfied the requisition; and he might live on. There is a form of the legend which says, that one of the ingredients of the drink, which the nobleman brewed by his science, was the heart's blood of a pure young boy or girl; but this I reject as too coarse an idea. (94)

Though Sybil's narrative equivocates as to the literal truth of the elixir tradition, the legend suggests that, however ostensibly scientific the quester's dedication to discovering the mechanistic nature of life, at the heart of the immortality impulse lies a recurrent appetite for sacrifice.

To head a survey of Renaissance concepts of sacrifice—her chapter on "The Key to All Mythologies" from *The Renaissance Bible: Scholarship, Sacrifice, and Subjectivity* (U of California P, 1994)—Debora Shuger quotes a nineteenth-century assertion: "The real religion of nature is not to be found in the optimistic platitudes of Deism but in the dark and bloody superstitions of the heathen" (54). Hawthorne's text intimates that these two sides, the optimistic and the bloody, may coexist in the same ambitious person. In the elixir legend, the assiduous scholar who seeks to comprehend and to manipulate the laws of the clockwork universe—who would cause the hands of time to stop—finds himself bound to placate Nature with cyclical acts of bloody propitiation.

40. By "strong reading," I refer to the concept of inventive interpretation popularized by Harold Bloom and referred to more or less interchangeably as "creative misprision," a set of terms initially derived from Bloom's reading of Emerson's "The American Scholar," specifically the passage (quoted somewhat more briefly above) advocating the need for a "strong head" when confronting the "printed page" and proclaiming that "one must be an inventor to read well. . . . There is then creative reading as well as creative writing" (*CW* 1:58). Bloom derives his key revisionary move from this passage in *A Map of Misreading* (Oxford UP, 1975), 24, and revisits it, for instance, in *How to Read and Why* (Scribner, 2000), 25.

41. Miller summarizes the controversy and excerpts Norton's *A Discourse on the Latest Form of Infidelity* in *The Transcendentalists*, 210–13. James Turner, author of *Without God, Without Creed: The Origins of Unbelief in America*, subsequently published a biography of Charles Eliot Norton, presenting the educator as an epitome of the secularizing cultural movement outlined in his earlier study: *The Liberal Education of Charles Eliot Norton.*

42. See also Walls's subsequent book, *Emerson's Life in Science: The Culture of Truth* (2003). Lee Rust Brown, in a book-length study that appeared simultaneously with the

Walls article, has entitled this integrative project *The Emerson Museum: Practical Romanticism and the Pursuit of the Whole* (1997). The argument for Emerson's scientific religion has been anticipated by earlier scholars, including Leon Chai in *The Romantic Foundations of the American Renaissance* (1987). An emphatic development of this conjunction appears in Eric Wilson's *Emerson's Sublime Science* (1999). For a refreshing account of Emerson—and much else—within the larger context of a "desecularized Enlightenment history," see Kris Fresonke's *West of Emerson: The Design of Manifest Destiny* (U of California P, 2003), which describes "the theological lineage of Manifest Destiny, or the quasi-sacred explanation for the way America looked to Americans in the nineteenth century" and then sees "key texts of our nature canon, *Nature* and *Walden*, in this new line of descent" (28, 2).

43. As it tends to do in Sharon Cameron's reading of "Fate" and Emerson's "impersonal." Even so, Branka Arsić acknowledges Cameron's productive step toward the "impersonal" as one away from sovereign identity: "from a totally enclosed willful individuality to a self with a fragile identity or in fact lacking in it, Emerson criticism has traveled a long way"; *On Leaving: A Reading in Emerson* (Harvard UP, 2010) 9.

CHAPTER FOUR

1. Walker Cowen, *Melville's Marginalia,* vol. 1 (Garland Publishing, 1987), 520.

2. Rowland A. Sherrill, *The Prophetic Melville: Experience, Transcendence, and Tragedy* (U of Georgia P, 1979) 236, 3–4.

3. The chapter on the "fiction of prophecy" appears in Brodhead's *The School of Hawthorne* (Oxford UP, 1986) 27.

4. In this same 1849 letter, Melville refers to Emerson as "more than a brilliant person," although he mixes this praise with some rather humorous qualifications. Melville detects a "flaw" in Emerson: "It was, the insinuation, that had he lived in those days when the world was made, he might have offered some valuable suggestions." Reviews of Melville's relation to Emerson typically begin with this letter as primary evidence of a principally critical and even antithetical stance; see, for example, William Braswell, "Melville as a Critic of Emerson," *American Literature* 9.3 (November 1937) 317–34, and Merton Sealts, "Melville and Emerson's Rainbow," in *Pursuing Melville, 1940–1980: Chapters and Essays* (U of Wisconsin P, 1982). In *White Fire: The Influence of Emerson on Melville* (California State U, Long Beach P, 1991), John B. Williams offers a revisionary account of Melville as "critic" by expanding upon the typical archive to include Emerson's unpublished lectures of 1848–50—the logic being that Melville attended an Emerson lecture in 1849 and was also likely aware of this phase of Emerson's thinking via the Concord Sage's increasing media saturation in this period. The present study likewise looks to Melville's unexplored affinities with the *Later Lectures*—whether through direct influence or a developed intellectual kinship—including "Tendencies

and Duties of Men of Thought," to which Williams also gives prominence. By reading these later lectures alongside *Clarel*, we may discern how an antithetical relationship might move towards synthesis. Matthiessen famously structured *American Renaissance* on the dialectic: Emerson and Thoreau as optative Thesis, Hawthorne and Melville as thunderously naysaying Antithesis, and Whitman as multitudinous Synthesis. Yet Melville's poetry may partake of its own synthesis. Even the structure of antithesis requires a productive relation, as Williams notes in crediting Charles Feidelson's early insight on the "interdependence" of Emerson and Melville (6). As Feidelson puts it in *Symbolism and American Literature* (U of Chicago P, 1953), "Their methods were reciprocal, and each entailed the other. . . . Melville assumed the ambient idea that Emerson made explicitly, and if we feel Melville as one of ours, we must take Emerson into the bargain, whether we like it or not" (120). Gregg Crane restates the point more recently, in *The Cambridge Introduction to the Nineteenth-Century American Novel* (Cambridge UP, 2007): "While Melville appears to be uncertain whether Emerson dives deep enough, even the implicit criticism (more explicitly stated elsewhere) suggests Melville's recognition of the connection in their speculative ventures" (213n9).

5. For a recent important intervention on the use of the term "American Renaissance," see Joe B. Fulton, "Reason for a Renaissance: The Rhetoric of Reformation and Rebirth in the Age of Transcendentalism," *New England Quarterly* 80.3 (September 2007) 383–407. Fulton seeks to overturn the traditional anecdotal account that the use of the "Renaissance" concept to describe this literary period derives entirely retrospectively from Matthiessen's title, showing instead the term's currency in Transcendentalist circles and also (in what Fulton argues is a distortion of the Transcendentalist usage) among critics who precede Matthiessen. Though Fulton, among other acts of recovery, usefully emphasizes the neglected reformative meaning of the concept, I find that the allegedly distorted usage, with special comparison to the Elizabethan age, remains descriptively appropriate, justified by documents such as Melville's "Hawthorne and Its Mosses" (1850) and Margaret Fuller's *Woman in the Nineteenth Century* (Greeley & McElrath,1845). Fuller, in citing "prophetic" indications of the age of new "revelation," declares that "the reigns of Elizabeth of England and Isabella of Castile foreboded this era. They expressed the beginning of the new state; while they forwarded its progress" (52). For Fuller as for Melville, Shakespeare appears to provide a key analogy; Fuller, for example, adopts the name "Miranda" for her alter ego. Fulton's work adds balance by highlighting the concurrent reformation-minded celebration of Milton (402).

6. See also Wyn Kelley on "Writing New Gospel in *Moby-Dick* and *Pierre*," part 3 of *Herman Melville: An Introduction* (Blackwell, 2008) 57–93; and, especially for its modification of the typical understanding of Melville's "wicked" book of prophecy, see Zachary Hutchins, "*Moby-Dick* as Third Testament: A Novel 'Not Come to Destroy But to Fulfill' the Bible," *Leviathan* 13.2 (June 2011) 34–35.

7. Sealts, *Melville's Reading: Revised and Enlarged Edition* (U of South Carolina P, 1988), 119.

8. For example, Rolfe, the character commonly thought to be a version of the older Melville, asks Clarel if he knows anything about the "prior life" of one of the other pilgrims: "Nothing," said Clarel.—"I recall," / Said Rolfe, a mariner like him" (1.37.10, 11–12). One might note that it is the "Melville" character who steps in to supply the link of memory, invoking a literary type from his earlier career. Later in the pilgrimage, Clarel catches an enigmatic eye: "'Twas a glance / Clarel did many a time recall, / Though its unmeant significance—/ That was the last thing learned of all" (3.24.20–23). This use of recall, in the sense of a recurring, haunting, inexplicable memory, defines the tone of much of the poem. Clarel recalls and *Clarel* recalls—as Samuel Otter observes, "Memories saturate the landscapes of Melville's poetry," as in the melancholy, barren scenes of 'Jerusalem' and 'The Wilderness'" [i.e., the first half of *Clarel*]; *Melville's Anatomies* (U of California P, 1999) 307n10.

9. Sealts, *Reading,* 120, 183.

10. Emerson, in his 1855 "Address to the Inhabitants at Concord, at the Consecration of Sleepy Hollow," similarly argues that "life is not long enough for art, nor long enough for friendship." For Emerson, this shortness points to "Immortality" (and indeed parts of this address were used for the essay of that title in *Letters and Social Aims*): "The evidence from intellect is as valid as the evidence from love. . . . Our dissatisfaction with any other solution is the blazing evidence of immortality" (*LL* 2:34). Emerson well understands the basis of the Septimius impulse: "Why is the fable of the Wandering Jew agreeable to men, but because they want more time and land to execute their thoughts in?" (34).

11. For important exceptions to this neglect of the narrator, see Stan Goldman, *Melville's Protest Theism* (Northern Illinois UP, 1993) 11; Douglas Robillard, *Melville and the Visual Arts* (Kent State UP, 1997), on "Melville's most carefully considered book," 123, 156–57; and John T. Shawcross, "'Too intellectual a poet ever to be popular': Herman Melville and the Miltonic Dimensions of *Clarel,*" in *Melville and Milton* (Duquesne UP, 2004) 86. In each case, this greater attention to the persona of narrator leads to a greater appreciation for the poem's "Epilogue": as Shawcross puts it, "The distance between the Clarel of Canto 34 and the narrative voice of Canto 35 is the difference between the Melville of the past and the Melville who has learned the efficacy of conscience" (86). For a connection to the *Divina Commedia* as well as brilliant consideration of the *ottava rima* in the last "resurrectional" stanza, see Shawcross, 83.

12. The line scans in regular iambic hexameter, presuming a clipped poetic "heav'n." Another (rare) exception to the rule of tetrameter is the pentameter of "Reproaching him: *Dost tarry, tarry yet?*" (3.24.104), in which the repetition of "tarry" may be seen to account for (and thematize) the extra syllables.

13. *Looking Awry* (MIT Press, 1991), 5–8.

14. Quoted in Carlos Baker, *Emerson among the Eccentrics,* 424. Cf. Jay Leyda, *The*

Melville Log: A Documentary Life of Herman Melville, 1819–1891 (Gordian P, 1969), 2:617, 621.

15. See David M. Robinson, "Poetry, Poetic Perception, and Emerson's Spiritual Affirmations," in *Shaping Belief: Culture, Politics, and Religion in Nineteenth-Century Writing,* ed. Victoria Morgan and Clare Williams (Liverpool UP, 2008) 95.

16. The difficulty of the poem is legendary; Walter Bezanson, before undertaking the heroic work of making the poem available in a modern edition, had been warned that *Clarel* was "un-readable" ; "Letter," *Leviathan* 12.1 (March 2010), 77. It seems that some of the greatest scholar-heroes of the present study—Bezanson for editing *Clarel* and Edward H. Davidson for co-editing *The Elixir of Life* manuscripts—begin rather modestly when donning the cap of critic, as if shy to protest too fervently on behalf of the objects of love's labor. Bezanson and Davidson clearly did find these late works readable and worthy of attention, but they sometimes adopt an apologetic tone when discussing the works' poetic and narrative craft. Of the later works featured in *Writing beyond Prophecy,* Emerson's *Conduct of Life* has occasioned the fewest apologies for linguistic artistry; rather, apologetics for his politics—and the difficulty of their legibility—have seemed more in order. For a contextualization of that question, see Barbara Packer's "History and Form in Emerson's 'Fate'" in *Emerson: Bicentennial Essays,* ed. Ronald A. Bosco and Joel Myerson (Massachusetts Historical Society, 2006), and her "Historical Introduction" to *The Collected Works of Ralph Waldo Emerson, volume 6: The Conduct of Life* (Harvard UP, 2003). Packer finds it "ironic that *The Conduct of Life,* born of Emerson's involvement in one of the most turbulent decades of the nation's history, should have acquired in our own day a reputation for aloofness and unconcern with events. . . . For his contemporaries, who understood his political references, who had heard him openly declare his political convictions on the lecture platform, Emerson's book was easy enough to decode. To modern readers, *The Conduct of Life* can sometimes seem as puzzling as an edition of Dryden's *Absalom and Achitophel* without a key to the historical characters" (*CW* 6:lxvi–lxvii). Perhaps most powerfully, Packer keys "Fate" to the figure of John Brown: "The composition of 'Fate' spanned the unquiet decade between the compromise of 1850 and the execution of John Brown, and Emerson had no desire to . . . mute the declarations of faith that 'Fate' also contains: 'A breath of will blows eternally through the universe of souls in the direction of the Right and Necessary. It is the air which all intellects inhale and exhale, and it is the wind which blows the worlds into order and orbit' (*CW* 6:15). When Emerson heard that John Brown had been captured, he mocked any slaveholder foolish enough to think that by chaining up Brown he was getting rid of his tormentors; such a man 'does not see that the air which this man breathed is liberty, & is breathed by thousands and millions; . . . and therefore no matter how many Browns he can catch & kill, he does not make the number less, for the air breeds them' (*JMN* 14:329–330). Nature's name may be fatal, but everywhere 'The air is full of men' (*CW* 6:9)" ("History and Form,"

446). Evan Carton is at work on a promising study that links the prophetic impulses in Brown and Emerson, an extension of his award-winning *Patriotic Treason: John Brown and the Soul of America* (Free Press, 2006).

17. For rich illumination of how a book *can* be a pilgrimage, see Gregory S. Jackson, *The Word and Its Witness: The Spiritualization of American Realism* (U of Chicago P, 2009), esp. "Journeying to Jerusalem: Pilgrimages Old and New" (116–25), "Homiletic Fiction and the Novelization of Progress" (125–33), and "Narrative Incrementalism" (133–43).

18. See also the Prodigal's education of Clarel on reading more fully the poetry of David, as he "turn(s)" (as in verse) "to be rid / Of further prosing" (475)—here the turn on the word "rid" rids the sentence of prosing lineation. Substantively, the Prodigal teaches Clarel to read the Song of Songs as embodied and not purely symbolic, as denoting physical love and not merely connoting metaphysical abstraction; compatibly with this hermeneutics, the Prodigal's poetics call attention to the materiality of language itself. Cf. William Spengemann's frustration with readings of Melville's poetry that "treat it not as poetry but as (inconveniently) versified information about the 'mind' of the novelist"; "Melville the Poet," *American Literary History* 11.4 (Winter 1999) 606. Cf. also the true public service performed by Robert D. Madison and Gordon M. Poole in "CLAR-el or cla-REL: Pronouncing Melville's Clarel," *Leviathan* 12.1 (March 2010) 21–24. Madison and Poole cite more recent attention to the poem, such as Samuel Otter's, as indicating that "we need no longer apologize for Melville's poetics: his poems should be read as poetry, with prosodic considerations brought to bear on their interpretation" (21). For the record, it is CLAR-el, and Madison and Poole have the prosodic considerations to prove it.

19. Dennis Donoghue, *Connoisseurs of Chaos: Ideas of Order in Modern American Poetry, 2nd ed.* (Columbia UP, 1984), 93.

20. William Potter finds a "withering critique of America throughout *Clarel,* where it is asserted that America's emphasis on independence, self-reliance, and a sense of mission have led, ironically enough, to the almost pathological self-consciousness and spiritual sterility that so paralyze the main characters, each of whom is essentially trapped within what might be called a tyranny of self"; *Melville's* Clarel *and the Intersympathy of Creeds* (Kent State UP, 2004) 32.

21. Dennis Berthold, *American Risorgimento: Herman Melville and the Cultural Politics of Italy* (Ohio State UP, 2009) 227; *Moby-Dick,* "The Gilder."

22. David M. Robinson, "Experience, Instinct, and Emerson's Philosophical Reorientation," in *Emerson: Bicentennial Essays,* ed. Ronald A. Bosco and Joel Myerson (Massachusetts Historical Society, 2006) 392.

23. Spengemann adds that this vacuation of the volitional self extends even to the production of the verse: "On the few occasions when Melville says anything at all about his poems . . . he does so mainly to say that he himself does not seem to have written them" (605).

24. William Ellery Sedgwick, *Herman Melville: The Tragedy of Mind* (Harvard UP, 1944) 202.

25. On such hauntings within modernity, see Vincent Pecora, *Secularism and Cultural Criticism: Religion, Nation, & Modernity* (U of Chicago P, 2006). More generally, see Charles Taylor, *A Secular Age* (Cambridge, Mass.: Harvard UP, 2007) and the discussions thereof in *Varieties of Secularism in a Secular Age,* ed. Michael Warner, Jonathan VanAntwerpen, Craig Calhoun (Harvard UP, 2010).

26. Alfred Kazin notes that, despite Clarel's "archaic form and diction," "somehow it works," in part due to a dialogic structure: "Clarel vocalizes in dialectic all the residual certainties and uncertainties possible to men making their way past sacred surroundings"; *God and the American Writer* (Knopf, 1997) 101.

27. Both Robert Penn Warren and Hilton Obenzinger comment upon the Pentecostal significance of this occasion; *Selected Poems of Herman Melville* (Random House, 1970), 410, and *American Palestine: Melville, Twain, and the Holy Land Mania* (Princeton UP, 1999), 75–76.

28. Larry Wegener, *A Concordance to Herman Melville's* Clarel (Edwin Mellen P, 1997) 1:xxiii.

29. Robinson, "Poetry, Poetic Perception, and Emerson's Spiritual Affirmations," 108.

30. Cited in Goldman, *Theism,* 13. Goldman, also deriving a dialectic, calls this dual motion the "operational, all-pervasive idea that actualizes *Clarel*'s narrative" (13).

31. Goldman usefully enumerates key related stumbling blocks for prior interpretations of *Clarel:* most studies focus on the character of Clarel, at the expense of attention to the *narrator*'s voice throughout, and, consequently, "most critics also read the Epilogue of the poem as a tacked-on afterthought. . . . The hope and faith depicted in the Epilogue are, however, present throughout the poem" (11). See also Goldman, 174n18, on the "recent dismissal of the Epilogue" as "misdirection," and the preceding note for an excellent *Clarel* bibliography. Goldman's study has influenced the direction of *Clarel* studies, but for a post-Goldman insistence upon reading the Epilogue as ironically "facile," see Edgar Dryden, *Monumental Melville* (Stanford UP, 2004) 144–45, 213. For other helpful reviews of the literature, see Vincent Kenny's contribution on "*Clarel*" to *A Companion to Melville Studies,* ed. John Bryant (Greenwood P, 1986) and the notes to Shirley Dettlaff's " 'Counter Natures in Mankind': Hebraism and Hellenism in *Clarel,*" in *Melville's Evermoving Dawn: Centennial Essays,* ed. John Bryant and Robert Milder (Kent State UP, 1997). See especially Dettlaff's evenhanded treatment of both the strengths and limitations of Baym's and Ra'ad's important articles on, respectively, the erotic motif and death plot of *Clarel* (219–20). Ra'ad's study also stands out as taking seriously the premise of the poem's coherence all the way to the end: "My interpretation of the plot within the death scheme places the 'Epilogue' solidly as a final statement to-

ward which the poem develops rather than, as has been concluded by some critics, a theoretical expression of optimism which contradicts the poem's movement"; see Basem L Ra'ad, "The Death Plot in Melville's *Clarel*," *ESQ* 27.1 [102] (1st Quarter 1981) 26.

32. Hilton Obenzinger, focusing on *Clarel* and "Failure," considers that "the writing of Melville's customs house poem was itself a discipline of intense meditation, a 'rosary' and a pilgrimage simultaneously. . . . For Melville, his release from the bounds of value, circulation, and exchange was acted out in the poem as a system of sacred journey, as indicated in Clarel's subtitle—the book is not just a 'Poem' but also a 'Pilgrimage'"; *American Palestine*, 65, 70. This faithful labor from the pen of the New York Customs House inspector—hence Obenzinger's description of it as Melville's customs house poem—marked the "failure of a literary career, of an intensely prophetic, 'masculine' calling to literature" (69, 65), an account much in keeping with my sense of Melville in *Writing beyond Prophecy*. And to step back to the greater context of Obenzinger's analysis, to a significant extent *Clarel*'s "Failure" in Obenzinger's account should be classed a political victory—a failure to ratify the covenantal understanding of America as the New Jerusalem (65, 79, x). Obenzinger has examined the poem within the context of "Holy Land books seeking to appropriate Palestine for the American imagination" and finds Melville's text as among the "the *least* representative while yet the most expressive and revelatory" in its "counternarratives" to "America's narrative of settlement as divine errand" (x). John Davis, in *The Landscape of Belief: Encountering the Holy Land in Nineteenth-Century American Art and Culture* (Princeton UP, 1996) likewise observes that "Melville's extreme response to the Holy Land placed him far outside the circle of conventional American Visitors" (45). William Spanos has notably valued in "Melville's novels" his "decisive critiques of the myth of American exceptionalism," critiques delivered from an "exilic global perspective"; *Herman Melville and the American Calling* (SUNY Press, 2008) 20. In Michael Paul Rogin's view, "*Clarel*, a meditation on Christianity, also contains Melville's reflections on the failure of the political spirit world . . . like the wandering Jew, [Clarel] finds no spiritual home. . . . Young Melville embraced that fate, for it bonded him with other victimized outcasts in America. . . . *Clarel* imagined one fate for Melville's youthful rover, the fate of a self-aware outcast"; *Subversive Genealogy: The Politics and Art of Herman Melville* (U of California P, 1983) 283–4. *Clarel*'s affinities with the political outcast author Dante, also noted by Obenzinger (68), might be enlisted in resonance with "exilic global" readings of the poem. See, for example, Wai Chee Dimock's valuation of Dante in "Literature for the Planet," *PMLA* 116.1 (January 2001) 173–88.

33. Though mostly indexed to ascent, "win" may also signify traversal, as in the most typologically freighted passage, when the pilgrims "win the hither side" of the river Jordan (208), an action that recalls the Israelites' delivery into Canaan, that allegorically figures Christ's cleansing of the soul in salvation, and that anagogically an-

ticipates the soul's entry into heaven. Most of the uses of "win" in the poem emphasize a steady effort toward all such goals, yet, sometimes, a pilgrim gains such footing as if by a kind of grace: "By chance Rolfe won the rocky stair" (372).

34. In a poem of 150 cantos, the verb "to win" occurs 144 times (67 instances for "win," 68 for "won," 9 for "winning"). "Lose" occurs only once, and "losing" twice. The forms "loss" or "lost" occur relatively more frequently (15 and 22 times, respectively—but even adding these in, all possible forms of "lose" occur at less than one-third the frequency of forms of "win"), but in reference to an event or object externalized, as loss is for Emerson in "Experience": he reports that in the death of a loved one he "seem[s] to have *lost*" something, but that *loss* is something that he cannot get "nearer" to himself. To adopt an alternative distinction for Clarel's pilgrimage: to experience a loss, at whatever distance, is not necessarily *to lose,* as an intransitive verb reflecting an absolute subjective state.

35. Robert Milder, *Exiled Royalties: Melville and the Life We Imagine* (Oxford UP, 2006) 194.

36. Jenny Franchot, "Melville's Traveling God," in *The Cambridge Companion to Herman Melville,* ed. Robert S. Levine (Cambridge UP, 1998) 182. For another reading that extends a "thematics of form" to *Clarel* (to use Edgar Dryden's phrase for the prose career), see Bryan C. Short, "Form as Vision in Herman Melville's *Clarel,*" *American Literature* 50.4 (January 1979) 553–69. Though, more persuaded by Franchot and Goldman, I differ from Short in my reading of the Epilogue, I respect his attention to Melville's structure and versification, by which he earns conclusion that "*Clarel* can be called America's greatest Victorian poem" (569).

37. Clark Davis, *After the Whale: Melville in the Wake of* Moby-Dick (U of Alabama P, 1995) 144.

38. Davis, like Goldman, takes a minority position on the ending of *Clarel* as prepared for by the rest of the poem: "It reflects an impulse present at various moments in the work to find in the desert and death some manner of redemption" (150).

39. J. Chesley Mathews reports Lowell's description of the *Divine Comedy* as sermon and song in "James Russell Lowell's Interest in Dante," *Italica* 36.2 (June 1959) 82. Matthew Pearl, acknowledging the work of Mathews, incorporates this phrasing into *The Dante Club* (Random House, 2003), 65, 372; Pearl's novel brings Dante's sermonic potential imaginatively to life, as George Washington Greene preaches out of cantos from the *Inferno* (273–74).

40. Edward Said, "Introduction to the Fiftieth-Anniversary Edition" of Erich Auerbach, *Mimesis: The Representation of Reality in Western Literature* (Princeton UP, 2003) xi.

41. Lawrence Buell, "Melville the Poet," in *The Cambridge Companion to Herman Melville,* ed. Robert S. Levine (Cambridge UP, 1998) 147.

42. At such junctures of epistemological strain, I detect affinities between *Writing beyond Prophecy* and Joseph Millichap's recent book, *Robert Penn Warren after*

Audubon: *The Work of Aging and the Quest for Transcendence in His Later Poetry* (Louisiana State UP, 2009). Robert Penn Warren was one of the first to recognize the achievement of Melville's later poetry, a fact which takes on further significance in light of Millichap's study of Warren's quest for transcendence (by the way, Millichap's choice of milestone for "later" Warren, *Audubon,* appeared in 1969, and Warren's edition of Melville's poetry appeared in 1970; See Millichap, 20ff, for further career context). For example, Millichap, in discussing a biblical echo in a Warren poem, notes that "the text proves a helpful one for a meditative review of life as the work of age, and Warren develops this one in the imagery of the sea and shore he knew from Melville" (137).

43. *The Vision; or Hell, Purgatory, and Paradise. Translated by the Rev. Henry Francis Cary, M.A.* (Bohn, 1847), autographed, marked, and annotated by Herman Melville; Collection of Mr. William Reese. I am most grateful to Steven Olsen-Smith for providing me with an early glimpse of Melville's Dante marginalia—including an enhanced image of the endpaper, with transcriptions—which should be freely available at "Melville's Marginalia Online" before the present study arrives in print. Olsen-Smith also graciously offered this guidance in interpreting the marginalia of interest here: "One of the problems we're dealing with in the Dante volume is that the annotations in the Paradise section do not conform in all respects with Melville's hand, raising the possibility that some marginalia in the volume are not Melville's. The convoluted character of the markings also (particularly in portions of Paradise) depart from HM's normally neat and precise manner of inscription [MK: hence I use language such as "bracketed in Melville's copy" rather than unambiguously "bracketed by Melville"]. However, in regards to the heavily marked conclusion you'll be delighted to learn about newly recovered rough notes on the rear endpaper of the book that are clearly Melville's, and that appear directly related to Dante's image of the trinity on p. 527 and Cary's accompanying footnote. See the enhanced endpaper image for 'three spheres insphered'" (personal e-mail correspondence, June 1, 2011). Many thanks also to Peter Norberg for connecting me to this resource.

44. For the importance of Dante to *Moby-Dick,* see Christopher Sten, *Sounding the Whale:* Moby-Dick *as Epic Novel* (Kent State UP, 1996), viii, 1–2, 5–7. In diagnosing the difficulties of critics in categorizing the genre *Moby-Dick,* Sten demonstrates that Melville in this work "brings together two epic traditions rather than one: the ancient or primitive national epic of combat or conflict, as in the *Iliad* or *Beowulf,* and the modern universal epic of spiritual quest, of the search for a transcendent order or significance to human life, as in the *Divine Comedy* or *Paradise Lost*" (2). In *Moby-Dick,* Sten suggests, Melville weaves the two strands together, with the former primarily tracking Ahab and the latter, in the ascendant, primarily tracking Ishmael. In *Clarel,* I would add, what Sten calls the "modern" epic of spiritual quest, indebted to the example of Dante, predominates to an even greater degree. I note that Christopher N. Phillips will soon be gracing us with a new book-length study on *The Course of Epic in American*

Culture: From Settlement to Reconstruction, which will include a consideration of new evidence for Melville's sources for *Moby-Dick* and, more generally, will argue—against the assumption of the epic's demise in modernity—for the cultural pervasiveness of the epic as a mode for giving meaning to modernity. For a prior study that tracks the epic into even more modern instances, picking up, with overlap at Whitman, close to where Phillips leaves off, see Jeffrey Walker, *Bardic Ethos and the American Epic Poem: Whitman, Pound, Crane, Williams, Olson* (Louisiana State UP, 1989).

45. Discussed by August J. Nigro in "Squaring the Circle in *Moby-Dick,*" in *The Diagonal Line: Separation and Reparation in American Literature* (Association of University Presses, 1984), 77–84. Nigro also here compares Ishmael to Dante. I here cite the *LCRE* of *Moby-Dick* in preference to the *NN,* which amends "false bow" to "false brow"; see *LCRE,* 593, for the "Revision Narrative" of this passage. *NN* assumes "bow" as a typo, and, as LCRE notes, one could argue that "brow" accords better with the phrenological associations of the chapter. To my mind, "false bow" fits better with the "geometrical" context of failed attempts to square the circle using a compass and straight edge. The arc of the bow also evokes the "rainbow" that Dante describes in the context of this geometrical conundrum. I further suggest, below, that Melville uses the image of the "fog-bow" in *Clarel* (261) to return to Dante's geometry problem and perhaps to echo the "false bow" of *Moby-Dick.*

46. In viewing Melville as one "vers'd in geometric lore" (Cary translation), we may consider Ishmael in "The Try-Works" : " . . . with the soapstone diligently circling round me. . . . I was first indirectly struck by the remarkable fact, that in geometry all bodies gliding along the cycloid . . . will descend from any point in precisely the same time" (*Moby-Dick,* chap. 96; *LCRE,* 373).

47. The poem also seems hostile to the stern Elder who would "try disprove / Legend and sire by square and line" (135).

48. Even so, intimations of faith and spirit also cluster around these silences. We may find the traditional association of silence and the brush with spirit inscribed even in the Dantean geometry considered above. The circle cannot be squared because π is an irrational number, also known as a "surd." Etymologically, the "surd" is also "silent"; Dante's vision of the unsquareable, celestial rain-bowed circle delivers the poetry into silence. Melville's mid-poem vision of a "thing of heaven," the oval fog-bow, also appears in "silence" (261).

49. Bezanson cites Leon Howard's conclusion that, by *Clarel,* "Melville had learned to 'face uncertainty without despair'"(551).

50. I here endorse Vincent Kenny's insight that we find in Mortmain a figure "anticipating the Epilogue"—though I do not agree that Melville "suggests emotional tranquility for him but without intimation of transcendent redemption" (*Herman Melville's* Clarel*: A Spiritual Autobiography* [Archon Books / Shoe String P, 1973], 193). Surely no promise thereof, but, at least, intimation. Hopeful readings for Mortmain's death

have often given emphasis to the eagle's feather that has fluttered to the lips: Merlin Bowen in 1960 takes this object, "wafted from the skies," "as token, it would seem, of a higher wisdom than earth's" (*The Long Encounter* [U of Chicago P, 1960] 271); Joseph G. Knapp in 1971 similarly finds here a "symbol of a wisdom that this world cannot give," while making the qualification that Mortmain's "wisdom has remained speculative" (*Tortured Synthesis* [Philosophical Library, 1971] 74); Stan Goldman in 1993 cites and modifies Bowen, adding that "the symbolic scene of a feather on the lips that completes the images and allusions of the spirit-breath of God would indicate that the experience of death is compared to being breathless," yet in a "breathless death sleep . . . related to Jacob's dream vision" (124), and argues that Mortmain's death and its accompanying record of the inner voice as a psychological revelation of the Spirit of God best illuminate the nature of the other side of death" (*Protest Theism,* 121); Laurence Stapleton in 1995 likewise finds Mortmain's "resolution" to seek the comfort of the Paraclete to be "endorsed by a miraculous detail: when Rolfe finds Mortmain next morning, still lying under the Palm, there is an eagle's feather, a sign of victory, fallen on his mouth. It does not move. Mortmain, like Nehemiah, dies after dreaming of his redemption" ("About Melville and the Angel" in *Some Poets and Their Resources* [UP of America, 1995] 104).

51. See Colacurcio, "'The Corn and the Wine': Emerson and the Example of Herbert," *Nineteenth-Century Literature* 42.1 (1987) 1–28, for Emerson's relation to Herbert's poem about whether or not to wear the priestly collar and administer to sacrament of communion. Melville owned an 1857 edition of Herbert's *The Temple* and corresponded with George L. Duyckinck about that volume in 1859. Coincidentally, Duyckinck published biographies of both George Herbert (in 1858) and Jeremy Taylor (1860), for the General Protestant Episcopal Sunday School Union and Church Book Society (*Correspondence, NN* 14:340, 326).

52. On the largest scale, Goldman's conclusion supports the idea of a Herbertian structure for *Clarel:* "The governing claim of the poem is first to protest God and then to love God" (167).

53. On this symbolic sway, see Wyn Kelley's eloquent and climactic reading of the palm as a "text circulating throughout the poem, taking on new meanings and associations": despite the apparently downbeat plot resolution, the "palm, though, seems to triumph in spite of Clarel's fall into obscurity. Once again, in this celebration of Palm Sunday, it signifies Christ's glory and the pilgrim's devotion. As the harbinger of Easter, where the poem ends, it also suggests the poem *Clarel*'s own death and rebirth as text, its endless circulation through Melville's mind and the minds of readers. The image of the palm is the leaf on which Melville has inscribed his text, and like the palm, his text is both perennially green and subject to decay, fixed and fluid, continuous and discontinuous, original and borrowed, literal and liberal, ancient and ever new"; *Herman Melville: An Introduction,* 159. One might compare here John Bryant's

commentary on the late manuscript prose and poem piece, from *Weeds and Wildings Chiefly: With a Rose or Two,* "Rip Van Winkle's Lilac," which "recasts Rip as an emblem of the artist whose legacy, a single sprig of lilac, has proliferated throughout the land. . . . As prose gives way to poem, Rip's widespread lilac foretells Melville's own resurrection"; *Herman Melville: Tales, Poems, and Other Writings,* ed. John Bryant (Modern Library, 2001) 553–54. As Bryant therein notes, "Melville introduces two new characters, a bohemian who sketches Rip's picturesque lilac and a puritanical villager who disparages all color but the sacred white of his church" (554), and he does so in a way that bears precisely on the writing that emerges *Writing beyond Prophecy.* In the face-off between the "meditative vagabondo" and the stern advocate of "respectable" and "useful" activity (accosting the "idle" artist in tones that recall Hawthorne's ancestors in "The Custom-House"), the churchman accuses the bohemian: "You wrest Holy Writ" by alluding to the verse about creation in God's image (561–62). Yet upon being judged "profane," the artist, rather than musing in a self-authorizing romantic vein or otherwise pursuing an opposition to scriptural tradition, pauses to ruminate: "What is that verse in the Apocalypse? . . . *And I looked, and behold a pale horse, and his name that sat on him was Death*" (562). In critiquing the death in life of the gaunt churchman, the artist does not prophesy anew, but rather points to the applicability of existing prophecy. As Bryant also notes, the "Rose Poems" in this late work offer an alternative to the deadened style of worship here critiqued: "Melville's brilliant but neglected Rose Poems are a set of devotionals in praise of physical and spiritual love. . . . A love letter to his wife, Melville's Rose Poems articulate the writer's life-long quandary over faith and doubt in the wholly new terms of transcendence through physical love" (554). Melville's expression of a "desire / for the garden of God" (572) merits comparison to Dante's final vision of the "Celestial Rose," bound by the love that moves the universe. Melville finds faithful attestation in the Rose, as he does in the Palm: "Flower, voucher of Paradise, visible pledge, / Rose, attesting it spite of the worm" (572).

54. Melville's choice of tetrameter for *Clarel* is often—though not always—adduced as a kind of de facto proof that the poem is hack work. Yet I have never heard the same objection made to "The Problem," which shares this meter (as, incidentally, does Longfellow's "Aftermath," discussed above). On balance, Elizabeth Renker reminds us not to perpetuate solely the mythic "master narrative in the history of the criticism on the poetry, which portrays it as unfortunate, bad, weak, and so on, and not the counter-narratives that are also part of that history, which see it as compelling, deep, difficult, and worthy of study"; "Melville the Poet," *American Literary History* 12.1&2 (Spring/Summer 2000) 349. In that same article, Renker famously predicted "that a revival of Melville's poetry will begin within the next 10 years" (348)—famously, because within that timeframe, the prediction has come true.

55. For instances of Melville's poetics even more self-referentially mimetic, we may consider how Clarel "hugged the wall, / Then turned; in that brief interval / The dust

came on him, powdery light" (128); The hugging of the "wall" and the turn occurs at the turn of the verse, and a brief "interval" likewise occurs across the next turn, an enjambment that suspends the arrival of the dust (occurring between prosodic intervals, the phrase "in that brief interval" may refer to a period of time starting with the semicolon caesura preceding the "in"—indeed, the term interval applies technically: "The caesura is for . . . musical prosody the keystone of the metrical arch, a pure interval"; Phelan, 177). Or, even more playfully, the line "Where Nehemiah slow footed it" (115) violates the usual eight-syllable expectation of the iambic tetrameter, containing an "extra" ninth syllable within what might thus be seen as a "slow foot," an anapestic third foot that bridges the tail end of "Nehemiah" and "slow" (Where **Ne** | hemi**i**|ah slow **foot** |ed **it**).

56. Quoted in *The Recognition of Herman Melville: Selected Criticism Since 1846,* ed. Hershel Parker (Ann Arbor: U of Michigan P, 1967) 112–13. A more sarcastic reviewer, essentially describing the same ruggedness, notes that "the metre selected is the octosyllable, which Scott used in his narrative poems. But from the 'fatal facility' which Byron said inhered in this verse Mr. Melville does not appear to have suffered" (New York *Times,* July 10, 1876, quoted on 109).

57. For dazzling speculation that the silences of grief provided the first articulations of speech, see Robert Pogue Harrison's "The Voice of Grief": "While the vowel-based melodies of the early human voice were continuous, . . . it would seem that the first human consonants arose as the vocal introjections of this void, or effect of interruption, which the death of a loved one brought about" (*The Dominion of the Dead,* 64). For a provocative diagrammatic alignment of *Mardi* with *Clarel,* see Wegener (1997 ed.), vol. 1.

58. Neal Tolchin opens his study of *Mourning, Gender, and Creativity in the Art of Herman Melville* (Yale UP, 1988) by quoting this journal passage regarding the Armenian funeral (xi). With its wailing abandon, the scene Melville witnesses contrasts sharply with the constrained norms of mourning that Tolchin diagnoses in Victorian America, norms which formed a "double bind" as they "at once prolonged the process of mourning and blocked the expression of feeling in bereavement" (xii). It is a contrast that, upon reflection, Melville may have found productive while composing *Clarel* and considering alternatives to what Tolchin calls the "genteel" American style of death (xi).

59. Ali Behdad's work on *Belated Travelers* (Duke UP, 1994) might be used to diagnose Clarel's ungladness within a postcolonial frame: for Behdad, the "melancholy traveler . . . cannot recognize that he is a *stranger* in the familiar field of orientalist discourse; he is, in short, blind to his cognitive blankness, to his asymbolic condition, and to his semantic alienation" (71). Clarel remains blind to the fact that the circumstances of his belated orientalism can only exacerbate the melancholy of the spiritual crisis that he undertakes his travel to resolve; Melville, some twenty years after his own pilgrimage, does not.

I might also diagnose Clarel's provincial Protestant shock on a more personal note. I retain a very early memory of attending an orthodox funeral for a relative on the Armenian side of our family. For my mother, a non-Armenian American Protestant who married into this family, the experience was jarring: "It seemed that there was so little hope." But that "seemed"—I recall her words distinctly—marked an important concession. The style of lamentation may have unsettled, but the endurance of the faith tradition could not be denied. I thus find, in Melville's responses to Armenian funerals, a continuity from the 1970s to the 1870s and, no doubt, long before.

60. The day after observing the Armenian funerals, Melville "remembered that much of the fearful interest of Schiller's Ghost-Seer hands upon being followed in Venice by an Armenian. The mere mysterious, persistant, silent following" (*Journals,* 64). Echoing this memory, Clarel's unshakeable bier partakes of a Romantic mode of the uncanny; *Clarel* places the young student's fantastical fear within a post-Romantic frame that tends to provincialize its orientalism. For a postmodern update on Schiller's *Ghost Seer,* see Michael Dibdin's *Dead Lagoon.*

61. Goldman identifies Psalm 102:7 as a source for this passage (38). The word "forsaken," in this scene of call-without-response modeled upon the Psalms, also recalls the most well-known gospel instance of the pattern, which Melville has adapted to a line of tetrameter earlier in the poem: *"My God, my God, forsakest me?"* (41).

62. In *An Awareness of What is Missing* (Polity, 2010), Jürgen Habermas points to the funeral as a signal instance of how "the enlightened modern age has failed to find a suitable replacement for a religious way of coping with the final *rîte de passage*" (15). While I find here an affinity between Habermas and Melville on the specific question of death and modernity—"to moderns death is drear"—Albert J. von Frank has recently made a more general case for Habermas as diagnosing a contemporary cultural challenge which Emersonian studies might address. In "Batting Oranges on the Beach: And the Way Forward in Emerson Studies," presented at the American Literature Association conference, San Francisco, May 29, 2010, von Frank concluded with a discussion of Jürgen Habermas's *Between Naturalism and Religion: Philosophical Essays* (English translation, 2008):

> In very rough paraphrase, Habermas sees the present East-West political conflict as subsisting in the contrast between an American and Anglo-European secular enlightenment, underpinned by a commitment to the scientific naturalism on which the overwhelming power of modernity rides, and what Habermas tends to totalize on the other side as 'religion,' especially in its fundamentalist or irrationalist rejection of Western secularism. The argument is complex and by no means unsympathetic to the religious impulse. But the diagnosis feels compelling and it encourages us to consider a number of implications, such as, for example, that modern Western political arrogance

> is largely rooted in the nature of its disbelief in spirit—which includes, necessarily, a disbelief in platonic ideas, which in turn, as a cultural matter, directly renders Emerson inaccessible. The point is not, of course, the accessibility of Emerson, but the capacity of the modern Western mind to think at will in alien ways—as in a multicultural world it must increasingly do or die. And this ability—as it has always been—is what an unperverted liberal education promotes.

Emerson—and, perhaps alongside him, the Melville of *Clarel*—stands as "one who can convince us of the power and beauty of an intelligence not in service to the material world, not subservient to bean-counting or getting along or to vocational preparation or the amassing of much money." I am grateful to Professor von Frank for sharing the full text of this presentation. For a recent advocacy of what we might call a "post-detranscendentalized" Emerson, see Jennifer Gurley's "Emerson's Politics of Uncertainty," *ESQ* 53.4 (2007) 323–59. Gurley suggests that "Emerson's moral skepticism—his transcendental attitude—might suggest the appropriate manner in which to court public dilemmas, because it fosters and tempers the human ability to look beyond experience for another view of experience" (349).

63. On this greater allurement that Clarel finds in Vine's silence, we may turn to Christopher Castiglia's hypothesis in *Interior States* (Duke UP, 2008), which, going against long-standing assumptions, refuses to see Hawthorne's famously silent responses to Melville as indexes of a failed relationship: "We might see the Melville-Hawthorne relationship as a successful experiment in queer sociality," one that yields "intimacy without interiority" (286). David Van Leer discovers what one might call a "queer faith" in *Clarel,* noting that "Melville depicts the experience of religion as an overhearing of ghostly whispers by someone in a closet" and that "Clarel looks out on sexuality as a form of belief"; see "A View from the Closet: Reconcilable Differences in Douglass and Melville," in *Frederick Douglass and Herman Melville: Essays in Relation,* ed. Robert S. Levine and Samuel Otter (U of North Carolina P, 2008) 280, 290. We seem to have arrived at a critical dispensation in Melville studies wherein it is possible to consider the erotic and the spiritual together, possibly entwined with yet other discourses, as in Samuel Otter's reference to "the exacting lines of *Clarel*'s spiritual, scientific, and sexual quest" (*Melville's Anatomies* [U of California P, 1999] 255). Robert Milder's *Exiled Royalties* both advocates for and demonstrates the richness of this approach, as in his insistence that "the 'spiritual' in Pierre is not a mere superstructure of illusions reared up from the desires of the unconscious; spiritual drives in the form of impulses toward an enigmatic wonder-world in the self and the universe are *part* of the unconscious, entangled with other drives (the sexual included) but by no means reducible to them" (133). Writing in 1974, Nina Baym could justly comment that "on the whole, following Melville's lead in the matter, critics have tended to assign much more

importance to Melville's metaphysical than his erotic speculations"; "The Erotic Motif in Melville's *Clarel*," *Texas Studies in Literature and Language*, 16.2 (Summer 1974) 315. Seeking to correct that imbalance, Baym's reading tends toward the deterministic reductionism Milder eschews, as when she remarks that "it is not the quest for God that produces a horror of woman so much as a horror of woman that produces the quest for God" (318); here, spirituality appears merely as symptom. Writing thirty-six years later, Jonathan A. Cook observes that given the texture of Melville's "creative vision," "the subject of religion in Melville studies should be one of the most active and exciting; yet academic criticism routinely ignores this dimension to Melville's writing"; "Melville and Religious Experience: A Response"[abstract], *Leviathan* 12.3 (October 2010) 135–36. Of course, even as I write these words, that equation is shifting; Milder's model of non-symptomatic inclusivity seems an excellent one going forward.

64. Charles Olson, *Call Me Ishmael*, with a new afterword by Merton M. Sealts, Jr. (Johns Hopkins UP, 1997 [originally published by City Lights Books, 1947]) 104–5.

65. Olson uses this comment to gloss a work of 1857: "In *The Confidence-Man*, when Melville used Christ himself directly as a character, he clothed him in a white doe-skin—and made him MUTE" (105). The 1869 comment seems at least equally relevant to a reading of *Clarel*.

66. In *Hawthorne's Shyness: Ethics, Politics, and the Question of Engagement* (Johns Hopkins UP, 2005), Clark Davis makes the beautiful remark that "what was important about his personal shyness was the way it clarified his sense of ethical restraint, the way all relationships came to represent the difficulty of knowing others. . . . It had the effect, of course, of making him silent, enigmatic, an attractive walking partner, a good listener—not in spite of his shyness but *because* of it, not to counter distance but to *express* it" (156).

67. E.g., a caesura within a line of tetrameter takes up a larger percentage of the time to read the line than it would within a line of pentameter. Likewise, the shorter lines allow the possibility for enjambment to arise more frequently and tend to increase the number of lines across which a sentence may be suspended.

68. In 1871, Melville acquired Tennyson's *In Memoriam* and marked a stanza resonant with an unseen yet anticipated turn toward heavenly completion: "So here shall silence guard thy fame; / But somewhere, out of human view, / Whate'er thy hands are set to do / Is wrought with tumult of acclaim" (Leyda, *Melville Log*, vol. 2, 718).

69. *The Manse of Mastland*, trans. Thomas Keightley (Bell and Daldy, 1860) 209. Viewing a tombstone, Rolfe comments on the potential value of a deathbed word in season: "I knew thee, and thou hadst small hope. / But if at this spent man's death-bed / Some kind soul kneeled and chapter read—" (122).

70. We may note that, though *Clarel* contains portraits of ministers and religious figures often taken—and rightly so—as satirical (see especially Berthold, *American Risorgimento*, and the brief summary by Emory Elliott in "'Wandering To-and-Fro':

Melville and Religion," 198), in totality the book was deemed an appropriate gift for a minister, a gift graciously acknowledged by the Rev. William B. Thomas in 1876 (Leyda, *Melville Log,* vol. 2, 753). In an appreciation that might explain that fact, Helen Vendler notes *Clarel*'s "respect for genuine faith even while it condemns the rivalries of creeds" (quoted in Buell, "Melville the Poet," 142).

71. Taking a "step beyond" John Samson's study of Melville's missionary satire in *Omoo,* Erin Suzuki contends that the "connections" between Melville's "criticism of missionary and imperial projects in the Pacific and the more metaphysical concerns about the nature of divinity and its relationship to religion . . . not only centrally inform *Omoo* but also directly prefigure the project of unifying political critique and spiritual quest that Melville attempts in *Mardi*"—that is, that Melville's "prophetic and spiritual vision" is inextricable from his attacks on clerics and colonizers; "Frauds and Gods: The Politics of Religion in Melville's *Omoo* and *Mardi,*" *ESQ* 53.4 (4th Quarter 2007) 362–63. Samson's account may be found in *White Lies: Melville's Narratives of Facts* (Cornell UP, 1989). For a richly researched and imagined reconstruction of the "Missionary Talk" behind and in Melville's first six novels, see Mary K. Bercaw Edwards, *Cannibal Old Me: Spoken Sources in Melville's Early Works* (Kent State UP, 2009); see "'Their Gestures Shame the Very Brutes': Missionary Talk," and especially the culminating chapter, "'Cannibal Old Me': The Development of Melville's Narrative Voice," which weaves together the various discourses recovered through the study.

Bibliography

Abrams, M. H. *A Glossary of Literary Terms, Sixth Edition.* San Diego, CA: Harcourt, Brace, 1993.

———. *Natural Supernaturalism: Tradition and Revolution in Romantic Literature.* New York: W. W. Norton, 1971.

Agamben, Giorgio. *The End of the Poem: Studies in Poetics.* Translated by Daniel Heller-Roazen. Stanford, CA: Stanford UP, 1999.

Ahlstrom, Sydney E. *A Religious History of the American People.* 2 vols. Garden City, NY: Image Books, 1975.

Albanese, Catherine. *Nature Religion in America: From the Algonkian Indians to the New Age.* Chicago: U of Chicago P, 1990.

Alighieri, Dante. *The Divine Comedy of Dante Alighieri.* Translated by Henry Wadsworth Longfellow. Boston: Ticknor & Fields, 1867.

———. *The Vision; or Hell, Purgatory, and Paradise. Translated by the Rev. Henry Francis Cary, M.A. A New Edition, Corrected. With the Life of Dante, Chronological View of His Age, Additional Notes, and Index.* London: Bohn, 1847. Sealts number: 174. Autographed, marked, and annotated by Herman Melville; collection of Mr. William Reese. Introduction to Melville's marginalia in this copy by Steven Olsen-Smith. http://melvillesmarginalia.org.

Allen, Gay Wilson. "Emerson's Audiences: American and British." *Ariel* 7.3 (July 1976) 87–108.

Anderson, Quentin. *The Imperial Self; An Essay in American Literary and Cultural History.* New York: Knopf, 1971.

Arac, Jonathan. "F. O. Matthiessen: Authorizing an American Renaissance." In *The American Renaissance Reconsidered.* Ed. Walter Benn Michaels and Donald E. Pease. Baltimore: Johns Hopkins UP, 1985.

Arsić, Branka. *On Leaving: A Reading in Emerson.* Cambridge, MA: Harvard UP, 2010.

Atkinson, Brooks. "Introduction" to *The Selected Writings of Ralph Waldo Emerson.* New York: Modern Library, 1940.

Auster, Paul. *The Locked Room.* In *The New York Trilogy.* New York: Penguin, 1990.

Bailie, Gil. *Violence Unveiled: Humanity at the Crossroads.* New York: Crossroad, 1995.

Baker, Carlos. *Emerson among the Eccentrics: A Group Portrait.* Introduction and epilogue by James R. Mellow. New York: Viking, 1996.

Banta, Martha, et al., eds. *The Harper American Literature*. Vol. 2. New York: Harper & Row, 1987.

Barish, Evelyn. *Emerson: The Roots of Prophecy*. Princeton, NJ: Princeton UP, 1989.

Barszcz, James. "What Happened to Hawthorne? Metaphor versus Narrative in the Unfinished Romances." *Raritan* 12.4 (Spring 1993) 94–108.

Baym, Nina. "Delia Bacon: Hawthorne's Last Heroine." *Nathaniel Hawthorne Review* 20.2 (Fall 1994) 1–10.

———."The Erotic Motif in Melville's *Clarel*." *Texas Studies in Literature and Language* 16.2 (Summer 1974) 315–28.

———. *The Shape of Hawthorne's Career*. Ithaca, NY: Cornell UP, 1976.

Behdad, Ali. *Belated Travelers: Orientalism in the Age of Colonial Dissolution*. Durham, NC: Duke UP, 1994.

Bell, Michael Davitt. "Conditions of Literary Vocation." In *The Cambridge History of American Literature, Volume Two: Prose Writing 1820–1865*. Ed. Sacvan Bercovitch. New York: Cambridge UP, 1995.

Bell, Millicent. *Hawthorne's View of the Artist*. Albany: SUNY Press, 1962.

Bercovitch, Sacvan. *The Office of* The Scarlet Letter. Baltimore: Johns Hopkins UP, 1991.

———. "*The Scarlet Letter*: A Twice-Told Tale." *Nathaniel Hawthorne Review* 22.2 (Fall 1996) 1–20.

Bergland, Renée. "The Puritan Eye-Ball." In *The Puritan Origins of American Sex*. New York: Routledge, 2000.

Berthold, Dennis. *American Risorgimento: Herman Melville and the Cultural Politics of Italy*. Columbus: Ohio State UP, 2009.

Bezanson,Walter. "Letter to the Conference Organizers [Melville and the Mediterranean, Jerusalem, June 2009]." *Leviathan* 12.1 (March 2010) 77–78.

Bible, the Holy, Containing the Old and New Testaments. Translated out of the Original Tongues and with the Former Translations Diligently Compared and Revised, By His Majesty's Special Command, Appointed to be Read in Churches, Authorized King James Version.

Bishop, Jonathan. "Emerson and Christianity." *Renascence* 38 (Spring 1986) 183–200.

———. *Emerson on the Soul*. Cambridge, MA: Harvard UP, 1964.

———. *Something Else*. New York: George Braziller, 1972.

Bloom, Harold. *The American Religion: The Emergence of the Post-Christian Nation*. New York: Simon & Schuster, 1990.

———. *How to Read and Why*. New York: Scribner, 2000.

———. *A Map of Misreading*. New York: Oxford UP, 1975.

———. *Poetics of Influence : New and Selected Criticism.* Edited and with an introduction by John Hollander. New Haven, CT: H. R. Schwab, 1988.

Bosco, Ronald A., and Joel Myerson, eds. *Emerson: Bicentennial Essays.* Boston: Massachusetts Historical Society, 2006.

Boswell, James. *The Life of Samuel Johnson, LL.D.* Chicago: Encyclopædia Britannica, 1952.

Bowen, Merlin. *The Long Encounter: Self and Experience in the Writings of Herman Melville.* Chicago: U of Chicago P, 1960.

Brantley, Richard E. *Anglo-American Antiphony: The Late Romanticism of Tennyson and Emerson.* Gainesville: UP of Florida, 1994.

———. *Coordinates of Anglo-American Romanticism: Wesley, Edwards, Carlyle & Emerson.* Gainesville: UP of Florida, 1993.

Braswell, William. "Melville as a Critic of Emerson." *American Literature* 9.3 (November 1937) 317–34.

Brodhead, Richard. "Hawthorne, Melville, and the Fiction of Prophecy." In *The School of Hawthorne.* New York: Oxford UP, 1986.

Brooks, Joanna. "From Edwards to Baldwin: Heterodoxy, Discontinuity, and New Narratives of American Religious-Literary History." *American Literary History* 22.2 (March 2010) 439–53.

Brooks, Van Wyck. *The Flowering of New England.* New York: Dutton, 1952.

———. *New England: Indian Summer, 1865–1915.* New York: Dutton, 1940.

Brown, Jerry Wayne. *The Rise of Biblical Criticism in America, 1800–1870. The New England Scholars.* Middletown, CT: Wesleyan UP, 1969.

Brown, Lee Rust. *The Emerson Museum: Practical Romanticism and the Pursuit of the Whole.* Cambridge, MA: Harvard UP, 1997.

Brownson, Orestes Augustus. *The Convert: or, Leaves from My Experience.* New York: Edward Dunigan & Brother (James B. Kirker), 1857.

Budick, Emily Miller. "Sacvan Bercovitch, Stanley Cavell, and the Romance Theory of American Fiction." *PMLA* 107.1 (January 1992) 78–91.

Buell, Lawrence. *Emerson.* Cambridge, MA: Harvard UP, 2003.

———. "From Sermon to Scripture." In *Literary Transcendentalism: Style and Vision in the American Renaissance.* Ithaca, NY: Cornell UP, 1973.

———. "Melville the Poet." In *The Cambridge Companion to Herman Melville.* Ed. Robert S. Levine. New York: Cambridge UP, 1998.

———. "*Moby-Dick* as Sacred Text." In *New Essays on* Moby-Dick. Ed. Richard Brodhead. New York: Cambridge UP, 1986.

———. *New England Literary Culture: From Revolution through Renaissance.* New York: Cambridge UP, 1986.

———. "Reading Emerson for the Structures: The Coherence of the Essays." *Quarterly Journal of Speech* 58.1 (February 1972) 58–69.

Burke, Kenneth. *The Rhetoric of Religion: Studies in Logology.* Berkeley: U of California P, 1970.

Cabot, James Eliot. *A Memoir of Ralph Waldo Emerson.* Boston: Houghton Mifflin, 1895.

Cadava, Eduardo. *Emerson and the Climates of History.* Stanford, CA: Stanford UP, 1997.

Cagidemetrio, Alide. *Fictions of the Past: Hawthorne and Melville.* Amherst, MA: Institute for Advanced Studies in the Humanities, 1992.

Calasso, Roberto. *The Ruin of Kasch.* Trans. William Weaver and Stephen Sartarelli. Cambridge, MA: Harvard UP, 1994.

Cameron, Kenneth Walker. *A Commentary on Emerson's Early Lectures, 1833–1836, with an Index-Concordance.* Hartford, CT: Transcendental Books, 1961.

———. "Early Background for Emerson's 'The Problem,'" *ESQ* (formerly *Emerson Society Quarterly*) 27.2 (1962) 37–46.

———. *Ralph Waldo Emerson's Reading.* Raleigh, NC: Thistle Press, 1941.

Cameron, Sharon. *Impersonality: Seven Essays.* Chicago: U of Chicago P, 2007.

Carton, Evan. *The Marble Faun: Hawthorne's Transformations.* New York: Twayne Publishers, 1992.

———. *Patriotic Treason: John Brown and the Soul of America.* New York: Free Press, 2006.

———. *The Rhetoric of American Romance: Dialect and Identity in Emerson, and Dickinson, Poe, and Hawthorne.* Baltimore: Johns Hopkins UP, 1985.

Castiglia, Christopher. *Interior States: Institutional Consciousness and the Inner Life of Democracy in the Antebellum United States.* Durham, NC: Duke UP, 2008.

Cavell, Stanley. *Conditions Handsome and Unhandsome: The Constitution of Emersonian Perfectionism.* Chicago: U of Chicago P, 1990.

———. "Emerson's Constitutional Amending: Reading 'Fate.'" In *Philosophical Passages: Wittgenstein, Emerson, Austin, Derrida.* Cambridge, MA: Blackwell, 1995.

Cayton, Mary Kupiec. *Emerson's Emergence: Self and Society in the Transformation of New England, 1800–1845.* Chapel Hill: U of North Carolina P, 1989.

Chai, Leon. *The Romantic Foundations of the American Renaissance.* Ithaca, NY: Cornell UP, 1987.

Channing, William Ellery. *Selected Writings.* Ed. David Robinson. New York: Paulist Press, 1985.

Charvat, William. "A Chronological List of Emerson's American Lecture

Engagements." *Bulletin of the New York Public Library.* 64.9–12 (September–December 1960) to 65.1 (January 1961).

———. "The Condition of Authorship in 1820." In *The Profession of Authorship in America 1800–1870.* Ed. Matthew J. Bruccoli. New York: Columbia UP, 1992.

Clarke, James Freeman. *Memorial of the Commemoration of the Church of the Disciples, of the Fiftieth Birth-day of their Pastor, James Freeman Clarke, April 4 1860.* Boston: Prentiss & Deland, Printers, 1860.

Colacurcio, Michael J. "The American-Renaissance Renaissance." *New England Quarterly* 64 (1991) 445–93.

———. "'The Corn and the Wine': Emerson and the Example of Herbert." *Nineteenth-Century Literature* 42.1 (1987) 1–28. Reprinted in *Doctrine and Difference.*

———. *Doctrine and Difference: Essays in the Literature of New England.* New York: Routledge, 1997.

———. *Godly Letters: The Literature of the American Puritans.* Notre Dame, IN: U of Notre Dame P, 2006.

———. "Idealism and Independence." In *Columbia Literary History of the United States.* Ed. Emory Elliott et al. New York: Columbia UP, 1988.

———. "Introduction" to *Selected Tales and Sketches.* New York: Penguin, 1987.

———. *The Province of Piety: Moral History in Hawthorne's Early Tales.* Cambridge, MA: Harvard UP, 1984.

Cole, Phyllis. "From the Edwardses to the Emersons." *The CEA Critic* 49.2–4 (Winter–Summer 1986–87) 70–78.

———. "'Men and Women Conversing': The Emersons in 1837." In *Emersonian Circles: Essays in Honor of Joel Myerson.* Ed. Wesley T. Mott and Robert E. Burkholder. Rochester, NY: U of Rochester P, 1997.

Cole, Thomas R. *The Journey of Life: A Cultural History of Aging in America.* New York: Cambridge UP, 1992.

Coleridge, Samuel Taylor. *Confessions of an Inquiring Spirit. 3rd ed.* London: Edward Moxon, 1853.

Conforti, Joseph A. *Jonathan Edwards, Religious Tradition, & American Culture.* Chapel Hill: U of North Carolina P, 1995.

Cook, Jonathan A. "Melville and Religious Experience: A Response" [abstract]. *Leviathan* 12.3 (October 2010) 135–36.

Cook, Joseph. *Orthodoxy: With Preludes on Current Events.* Boston: J. R. Osgood, 1878.

———. *Transcendentalism: With Preludes on Current Events.* Boston: J. R. Osgood, 1878.

Cowen, Walker. *Melville's Marginalia.* New York: Garland Publishing, 1987.

Crane, Gregg. *The Cambridge Introduction to the Nineteenth-Century American Novel.* Cambridge: Cambridge UP, 2007.

Crews, Frederick. *The Sins of the Fathers: Hawthorne's Psychological Themes. With a New Afterword.* Berkeley: U of California P, 1989.

Daniel, Stephen H. *The Philosophy of Jonathan Edwards: A Study in Divine Semiotics.* Bloomington: Indiana UP, 1994.

Davidson, Edward H. *Hawthorne's Last Phase.* New Haven, CT: Yale UP, 1949.

Davis, Clark. *After the Whale: Melville in the Wake of* Moby-Dick. Tuscaloosa: U of Alabama P, 1995.

———. *Hawthorne's Shyness: Ethics, Politics, and the Question of Engagement.* Baltimore: Johns Hopkins UP, 2005.

Davis, John. *The Landscape of Belief: Encountering the Holy Land in Nineteenth-Century American Art and Culture.* Princeton, NJ: Princeton UP, 1996.

De la Carrera, Rosalina. *Success in Circuit Lies: Diderot's Communicational Practice.* Stanford, CA: Stanford UP, 1991.

Delbanco, Andrew. *Melville: His World and Work.* New York: Vintage, 2005.

Dettlaff, Shirley. "'Counter Natures in Mankind': Hebraism and Hellenism in *Clarel.*" In *Melville's Evermoving Dawn: Centennial Essays.* Ed. John Bryant and Robert Milder. Kent, OH: Kent State UP, 1997.

Dimock, Wai Chee. "Literature for the Planet." *PMLA* 116.1 (January 2001) 173–88.

Dolan, Neal. *Emerson's Liberalism.* Madison: U of Wisconsin P, 2009.

Donoghue, Dennis. *Connoisseurs of Chaos: Ideas of Order in Modern American Poetry.* 2nd ed. New York: Columbia UP, 1984.

Donohue, Agnes McNeill. *Hawthorne: Calvin's Ironic Stepchild.* Kent, OH: Kent State UP, 1985.

Douglas, Ann. *The Feminization of American Culture.* New York: Alfred A. Knopf, 1977.

Dryden, Edgar A. *Melville's Thematics of Form: The Great Art of Telling the Truth.* Baltimore: Johns Hopkins UP, 1968.

———. *Monumental Melville: The Formation of a Literary Career.* Stanford, CA: Stanford UP, 2004.

Duban, James. *Melville's Major Fiction: Politics, Theology, and Imagination.* DeKalb: Northern Illinois UP, 1983.

———. "The Skeptical Context of 'Mr. Higginbotham's Catastrophe.'" *American Literature* 48.3 (1976) 292–301.

———. "The Triumph of Infidelity in Hawthorne's *The Story Teller.*" *Studies in American Fiction* 7 (1979) 49–60.

Edwards, Jonathan. *Basic Writings*. Ed. Ola Elizabeth Winslow. New York: Meridian, 1978.

Edwards, Mary K. Bercaw. *Cannibal Old Me: Spoken Sources in Melville's Early Works*. Kent, OH: Kent State UP, 2009.

Elliott, Emory. "New England Puritan Literature." In *The Cambridge History of American Literature, Volume One: 1590–1820*. Ed. Sacvan Bercovitch. New York: Cambridge UP, 1994.

———. *Power and the Pulpit in Puritan New England*. Princeton, NJ: Princeton UP, 1975.

———. "'Wandering To-and-Fro': Melville and Religion." In *A Historical Guide to Herman Melville*. Ed. Giles Gunn. Oxford: Oxford UP, 2005.

Ellison, Julie. *Delicate Subjects: Romanticism, Gender, and the Ethics of Understanding*. Ithaca, NY: Cornell UP, 1990.

———. *Emerson's Romantic Style*. Princeton, NJ: Princeton UP, 1984.

———. "The Gender of Transparency: Masculinity and the Conduct of Life." *American Literary History* 4.4 (Winter 1992) 584–606.

Emerson, Edward Waldo. *The Early Years of the Saturday Club, 1855–1870*. Boston: Houghton Mifflin Company, 1918.

Emerson, Ralph Waldo. *The Collected Works of Ralph Waldo Emerson* [*CW*]. Ed. Robert Spiller, Alfred Ferguson, et al. Cambridge, MA: Harvard UP, 1971– .

———. *The Complete Sermons of Ralph Waldo Emerson* [*CS*]. Chief ed. Albert J. von Frank. 4 vols. Columbia: U of Missouri P, 1989–1992. Vol. 2: Ed. Teresa Toulouse and Andrew Delbanco. Columbia: U of Missouri P, 1990. Sermon 76. Vol. 3: Ed. Ronald A. Bosco. Columbia: U of Missouri P, 1991. Sermon 104. Vol. 4: Ed. Wesley T. Mott. Columbia: U of Missouri P, 1992. Sermons 155–58, 162.

———. *The Complete Works of Ralph Waldo Emerson* [*W*]. Ed. Edward Waldo Emerson. 12 vols. Centenary Edition. Boston: Houghton Mifflin, 1903–4.

———. *The Early Lectures of Ralph Waldo Emerson* [*EL*]. Ed. Stephen Whicher, Robert Spiller, et al. 3 vols. Cambridge, MA: Harvard UP, 1960–72.

———. *Emerson in His Journals*. Ed. Joel Porte. Cambridge, MA: Harvard UP, 1982.

———. *Essays and Lectures*. Ed. Joel Porte. New York: Literary Classics of the United States, Library of America, 1983.

———. *The Journals and Miscellaneous Notebooks of Ralph Waldo Emerson* [*JMN*]. Ed. William Gilman et al. Cambridge, MA: Harvard UP, 1960–82.

———. *The Letters of Ralph Waldo Emerson*. Ed. Ralph L. Rusk. 6 vols. New York: Columbia UP, 1939.

———. *The Poetry Notebooks of Ralph Waldo Emerson*. Ed. Ralph H. Orth et al. Columbia: U of Missouri P, 1986.

———. *The Topical Notebooks of Ralph Waldo Emerson.* Ed. Ralph H. Orth et al. Columbia: U of Missouri P, 1990–94.

Feidelson, Charles. *Symbolism and American Literature.* Chicago: U of Chicago P, 1953.

Fink, Steven. *Prophet in the Marketplace: Thoreau's Development as a Professional Writer.* Princeton, NJ: Princeton UP, 1992.

Firkins, O. W. *Ralph Waldo Emerson.* Boston: Houghton Mifflin, 1915.

Franchot, Jenny. "Melville's Traveling God." In *The Cambridge Companion to Herman Melville.* Ed. Robert S. Levine. New York: Cambridge UP, 1998.

Francis, Richard Lee. "Necessitated Freedom: Emerson's *The Conduct of Life.*" In *Studies in the American Renaissance.* Ed. Joel Myerson. Boston: G. K. Hall, 1980.

Franklin, Benjamin. *The Autobiography* in the Library of America *Writings.* Ed. J. A. Leo Lemay. New York: Literary Classics of the United States, 1987.

Freccero, John. *Dante: The Poetics of Conversion.* Ed. Rachel Jacoff. Cambridge, MA: Harvard UP, 1986.

Frei, Hans W. *The Eclipse of Biblical Narrative: A Study in Eighteenth- and Nineteenth-Century Hermeneutics.* New Haven, CT: Yale UP, 1974.

Fresonke, Kris. *West of Emerson: The Design of Manifest Destiny.* Berkeley: U of California P, 2003.

Frothingham, Octavius Brooks. *Transcendentalism in New England: A History.* Intro. Sydney E. Ahlstrom. New York: Harper & Brothers, 1959.

Fuller, Randall. *Emerson's Ghosts: Literature, Politics, and the Making of Americanists.* New York: Oxford UP, 2007.

Fuller, S. Margaret. *Woman in the Nineteenth Century.* New York: Greeley & McElrath, 1845.

Fulton, Joe B. "Reason for a Renaissance: The Rhetoric of Reformation and Rebirth in the Age of Transcendentalism." *New England Quarterly* 80.3 (September 2007) 383–407.

Gans, Eric. *Originary Thinking: Elements of Generative Anthropology.* Stanford, CA: Stanford UP, 1993.

———. "The Victim as Subject: The Esthetico-Ethical System of Rousseau's *Rêveries.*" *Studies in Romanticism* 21.1 (1982) 3–31.

Gates, Henry Louis, Jr. "Good-bye, Columbus? Notes on the Culture of Criticism." In *The* American Literary History *Reader.* Ed. Gordon Hutner. New York: Oxford UP, 1995.

Gelpi, Albert. *The Tenth Muse* [with a new preface]. New York: Cambridge UP, 1991.

Gelpi, Donald. *Endless Seeker: The Religious Quest of Ralph Waldo Emerson.* Lanham, MD: UP of America, 1991.

Girard, René. *A Theater of Envy: William Shakespeare.* New York: Oxford UP, 1991.

———. *Things Hidden since the Foundation of the World.* With Jean-Michel Oughourlian and Guy Lefort. Trans. Stephen Bann and Michael Metteer. Stanford, CA: Stanford UP, 1987.

Goldman, Stan. *Melville's Protest Theism: The Hidden and Silent God in* Clarel. DeKalb: Northern Illinois UP, 1993.

Gonnaud, Maurice. *An Uneasy Solitude: The Individual and Society in the Work of Ralph Waldo Emerson.* Trans. Lawrence Rosenwald. Princeton, NJ: Princeton UP, 1987.

Gougeon, Len. *Virtue's Hero: Emerson, Antislavery, and Reform.* Athens: U of Georgia P, 1990.

Green, Martin. *The Problem of Boston; Some Readings in Cultural History.* New York: W. W. Norton, 1966.

Grusin, Richard A. *Transcendentalist Hermeneutics: Institutional Authority and the Higher Criticism of the Bible.* Durham, NC: Duke UP, 1991.

Guarneri, Carl J. *The Utopian Alternative: Fourierism in Nineteenth-Century America.* Ithaca, NY: Cornell UP, 1991.

Gumbrecht, Hans Ulrich. "After Learning from History." In *In 1926: Living at the Edge of Time.* Cambridge, MA: Harvard UP, 1997.

———. "Who were the *Philosophes?*" In *Making Sense in Life and Literature.* Trans. Glen Burns. Minneapolis: U of Minnesota P, 1992.

Gunn, Giles. "Beyond Transcendence or Beyond Ideology: The New Problematics of Cultural Criticism in America." *American Literary History* 2.1 (Spring 1990) 119–30.

———. *F. O. Matthiessen: The Critical Achievement.* Seattle: U of Washington P, 1975.

Gura, Philip. "The Widening Gyre: Out from Emerson." In *Emersonian Circles: Essays in Honor of Joel Myerson.* Ed. Wesley T. Mott and Robert E. Burkholder. Rochester, NY: U of Rochester P, 1997.

Gurley, Jennifer. "Emerson's Politics of Uncertainty." *ESQ* 53.4 (4th Quarter 2007) 323–59.

Habermas, Jürgen. *An Awareness of What Is Missing.* Cambridge: Polity, 2010.

Habich, Robert D. *Building Their Own Waldos: Emerson's First Biographers and the Politics of Life-Writing in the Gilded Age.* Iowa City: U of Iowa P, 2011.

Harding, Walter Roy. *Emerson's Library.* Charlottesville: UP of Virginia, 1967.

Haroutunian, Joseph. *Piety versus Moralism: The Passing of the New England Theology.* New York: Henry Holt, 1932.

Hastings, Louise. "Emerson in Cincinnati." *New England Quarterly* 21.3 (September 1938) 443–69.

Hatch, Nathan O. *The Democratization of American Christianity.* New Haven, CT: Yale UP, 1989.

Hawthorne, Julian. *Hawthorne Reading.* Cleveland, OH: Rowfant Club, 1902.

Hawthorne, Nathaniel. *The Centenary Edition of the Works of Nathaniel Hawthorne, vol. 1, The Scarlet Letter.* Ed. William Charvat et al. Columbus: Ohio State UP, 1962.

———. *The Centenary Edition of the Works of Nathaniel Hawthorne, vol. 5, Our Old Home.* Ed. Claude M. Simpson et al. Columbus: Ohio State UP, 1970.

———. *The Centenary Edition of the Works of Nathaniel Hawthorne, vol. 6, True Stories from History and Biography.* Ed. Fredson Bowers, L. Neal Smith, John Manning. Columbus: Ohio State UP, 1972.

———. *The Centenary Edition of the Works of Nathaniel Hawthorne, vol. 8, The American Notebooks.* Ed. Claude M. Simpson et al. Columbus: Ohio State UP, 1973.

———. *The Centenary Edition of the Works of Nathaniel Hawthorne, Vol. 9, Mosses from an Old Manse.* Ed. J. Donald Crowley et al. Columbus: Ohio State UP, 1974.

———. *The Centenary Edition of the Works of Nathaniel Hawthorne, vol. 12, The American Claimant Manuscripts.* Ed. Edward H. Davidson, Claude M. Simpson, and L. Neal Smith. Columbus: Ohio State UP, 1977.

———. *The Centenary Edition of the Works of Nathaniel Hawthorne, vol. 13, The Elixir of Life Manuscripts.* Ed. Edward H. Davidson, Claude M. Simpson, and L. Neal Smith. Columbus: Ohio State UP, 1977.

———. *The Centenary Edition of the Works of Nathaniel Hawthorne, vol. 17, The Letters, 1853–1856.* Ed. Fredson Bowers, James A. Rubino, L. Neal Smith, and James Kayes. Columbus: Ohio State UP, 1987.

———. *The Centenary Edition of the Works of Nathaniel Hawthorne, vol. 18, The Letters, 1857–1864.* Ed. Thomas Woodson et al. Columbus: Ohio State UP, 1987.

———. *The Centenary Edition of the Works of Nathaniel Hawthorne, vol. 21, The English Notebooks 1853–1856.* Ed. Thomas Woodson and Bill Ellis. Columbus: Ohio State UP, 1997.

———.*The Centenary Edition of the Works of Nathaniel Hawthorne, vol. 22, The English Notebooks 1856–1860.* Ed. Thomas Woodson and Bill Ellis. Columbus: Ohio State UP, 1997.

———. *Novels.* Ed. Millicent Bell. New York: Library of America, 1983.

———. *Septimius: A Romance.* London: Henry S. King & Co., 65 Cornhill, 1872.

———. *Tales and Sketches.* Ed. Roy Harvey Pearce. New York: Library of America, 1982.

Hayford, Harrison. *Melville's 'Monody': Really for Hawthorne?* Evanston, IL: Northwestern UP, 1990.

Herbert, T. Walter. "Calvinist Earthquake: *Moby-Dick* and Religious Tradition." In *New Essays on* Moby-Dick. Ed. Richard Brodhead. New York: Cambridge UP, 1986.

———. *Dearest Beloved: The Hawthornes and the Making of the Middle-Class Family.* Berkeley: U of California P, 1995.

Hoeltje, Hubert. *Inward Sky: The Mind and Heart of Nathaniel Hawthorne.* Durham, NC: Duke UP, 1962.

Hoffman, Daniel. *POE POE POE POE POE POE POE.* Baton Rouge: Louisiana State UP, 1998.

Hopkins, Louisa Payson. *The Guiding Star; or, The Bible God's Message.* Dayton, OH: United Brethren Publishing House, 1874 [orig. Boston: 1851].

Hopkins, Mark. *Science and Religion. A sermon delivered in the Second Presbyterian church, Albany, on Sabbath afternoon, August 24, 1856.* Albany, NY: Van Bethuysen, 1856.

Hoppin, James M. *The Office and Work of the Christian Ministry.* New York: Sheldon and Co., 1870.

Houghton, Walter E. *The Victorian Frame of Mind, 1830–1870.* New Haven, CT: Yale UP, 1957.

Howe, Daniel Walker. *The Unitarian Conscience: Harvard Moral Philosophy, 1805–1861.* With a new introduction. Middletown, CT: Wesleyan UP, 1988.

Hudspeth, Robert. "Later Emerson: 'Intellect' and *The Conduct of Life.*" In *Emerson: Bicentennial Essays.* Ed. Ronald A. Bosco and Joel Myerson. Boston: Massachusetts Historical Society, 2006.

Hughes, Gertrude Reif. *Emerson's Demanding Optimism.* Baton Rouge: Louisiana State UP, 1984.

Hull, Raymona. "Hawthorne and the Magic Elixir of Life: The Failure of a Gothic Theme." *ESQ* 67 (1972) 97–107.

Hutchins, Zachary. "*Moby-Dick* as Third Testament: A Novel 'Not Come to Destroy but to Fulfill' the Bible." *Leviathan* 13.2 (June 2011) 18–37.

Hutchinson, William R. *The Transcendentalist Ministers.* New Haven, CT: Yale UP, 1959.

Jackson, Gregory S. *The Word and Its Witness: The Spiritualization of American Realism.* Chicago: U of Chicago P, 2009.

Jacobson, David. "The Fatal Event and the Birth of Agency." In *Emerson's Pragmatic Vision: The Dance of the Eye.* University Park: Pennsylvania State UP, 1993.

Jager, Colin. "This Detail, This History: Charles Taylor's Romanticism." In

Varieties of Secularism in a Secular Age. Ed. Michael Warner, Jonathan VanAntwerpen, and Craig Calhoun. Cambridge, MA: Harvard UP, 2010.

Jeffrey, David Lyle. *People of the Book: Christian Identity and Literary Culture*. Grand Rapids, MI: William B. Eerdmans, 1996.

———, ed. *Dictionary of Biblical Tradition in English Literature*. Grand Rapids, MI: William B. Eerdmans, 1992.

Johnson, James L. *Mark Twain and the Limits of Power: Emerson's God in Ruins*. Knoxville: U of Tennessee P, 1982.

Johnston, Paul K. "Killing the Spirit: Anne Hutchinson and the Office of the Scarlet Letter." *Nathaniel Hawthorne Review* 22.1 (Spring 1996) 26–35.

Kazin, Alfred. *God and the American Writer*. New York: Knopf, 1997.

Kelley, Wyn. *Herman Melville: An Introduction*. Oxford: Blackwell, 2008.

Kenny, Vincent. "*Clarel*." In *A Companion to Melville Studies*. Ed. John Bryant. New York: Greenwood P, 1986.

———. *Herman Melville's* Clarel*: A Spiritual Autobiography*. Hamden, CT: Archon Books / Shoe String P, 1973.

Kesselring, Marion L. *Hawthorne's Reading: 1828–1850: A Transcription and Identification of Title Recorded in the Charge-Books of the Salem Athenaeum*. New York: New York Public Library, 1949.

Kevorkian, Martin. "Reading the Bloody 'Face of Nature': The Persecution of Religion in Hawthorne's *The Marble Faun*." *Contagion: Journal of Violence, Mimesis, and Culture* 12–13 (2005–6) 133–45.

———. "'Within the domain of Chaos': Nathaniel Hawthorne, Lucretian Physics, and Martial Logic." *Studies in the Novel* 31.2 (Summer 1999) 178–201.

Knapp, Joseph G. *Tortured Synthesis: The Meaning of Melville's* Clarel. New York: Philosophical Library, 1971.

Kovacs, George. *The Question of God in Heidegger's Phenomenology*. Evanston, IL: Northwestern UP, 1990.

Kristeva, Julia. *Black Sun*. New York: Columbia UP, 1992.

Kuklick, Bruce. *Churchmen and Philosophers: From Jonathan Edwards to John Dewey*. New Haven, CT: Yale UP, 1985.

Lacoue-Labarthe, Philippe. *Musica Ficta (Figures of Wagner)*. Trans. Felicia McCarren. Stanford, CA: Stanford UP, 1994.

Lauter, Paul, ed. *The Heath Anthology of American Literature*, vol. 1. Lexington, MA: D.C. Heath, 1990.

Levine, Robert S. "'Antebellum Rome' in *The Marble Faun*." *American Literary History* 2.1 (Spring 1990) 19–38.

Leyda, Jay. *The Melville Log: A Documentary Life of Herman Melville, 1819–1891, vol. 2, With a New Supplementary Chapter*. New York: Gordian P, 1969.

Lopez, Michael. *Emerson and Power: Creative Antagonism in the Nineteenth Century*. DeKalb: Northern Illinois UP, 1996.

Lowell, James Russell. *The Biglow Papers [First Series]: A Critical Edition.* Ed. Thomas Wortham. DeKalb: Northern Illinois UP, 1977.

Lysaker, John T. *Emerson & Self-Culture.* Bloomington: Indiana UP, 2008.

———. "On the Faces of Emersonian 'Friendship.'" In *Emerson & Thoreau: Figures of Friendship.* Ed. John T. Lysaker and William Rossi. Bloomington: Indiana UP, 2010.

Madison, Robert D., and Gordon M. Poole. "CLAR-el or cla-REL: Pronouncing Melville's Clarel." *Leviathan* 12.1 (March 2010) 21–24. [Madison's name corrected from Robert K. to Robert D. in *Leviathan* 12.2 (June 2010) 2.]

Mancall, James N. *"Thoughts Painfully Intense": Hawthorne and the Invalid Author.* New York: Routledge, 2002.

Manzoni, Alessandro. *The Betrothed.* London: Richard Bentley, 1834.

———. *The Betrothed.* London: George Bell, 1844.

Martin, Robert K. *Hero, Captain, and Stranger: Male Friendship and Literary Form in the Sea Novels of Herman Melville.* Chapel Hill: U of North Carolina P, 1986.

Mason, Ronald. *The Spirit above the Dust: A Study of Herman Melville.* London: John Lehmann, 1951.

Mather, Cotton. *Magnalia Christi Americana; or, The Ecclesiastical History of New England.* New York: Russell & Russell, 1967; reprinted from the 1852 edition.

———. *Magnalia Christi Americana,* vol. 2. Hartford: Silas Andrus & Son, 1853.

Mathews, J. Chesley. "James Russell Lowell's Interest in Dante." *Italica* 36.2 (June 1959) 77–100.

Matthiessen, F. O. *American Renaissance: Art and Expression in the Age of Emerson and Whitman.* New York: Oxford UP, 1941.

McAleer, John. *Ralph Waldo Emerson: Days of Encounter.* Boston: Little, Brown, 1984.

Mellow, James R. *Nathaniel Hawthorne in His Times.* Boston: Houghton Mifflin, 1980.

Melville, Herman. *Clarel: A Poem and Pilgrimage in the Holy Land.* The Northwestern-Newberry Edition, vol. 12. Ed. Harrison Hayford et al. Historical and Critical Note by Walter E. Bezanson. Evanston/Chicago: Northwestern UP and Newberry Library, 1991.

———. *Billy Budd, Sailor.* Ed. Harrison Hayford and Merton M. Sealts, Jr. In *Pierre, Israel Potter, The Piazza Tales, The Confidence Man, Uncollected Prose, Billy Budd.* New York: Literary Classics of the United States/Library of America, 1984.

———. *Billy Budd, Sailor (An Inside Narrative). Reading Text and Genetic Text, Edited from the Manuscript with Introduction and Notes.* Ed. Harrison Hayford and Merton M. Sealts, Jr. Chicago: U of Chicago P, 1962.

———. *Herman Melville: Tales, Poems, and Other Writings.* Ed. John Bryant. New York: Modern Library, 2001.

Memorial of the Commemoration of the Church of the Disciples, of the Fiftieth Birth-day of their Pastor, James Freeman Clarke, April 4, 1860. Boston: Prentiss & Deland, printers, 1860.

Michaels, Walter Benn. *Our America: Nativism, Modernism, and Pluralism.* Durham, NC: Duke UP, 1995.

Milder, Robert. *Exiled Royalties: Melville and the Life We Imagine.* Oxford: Oxford UP, 2006.

Miller, Edwin Haviland. *Salem Is My Dwelling Place: A Life of Nathaniel Hawthorne.* Iowa City: U of Iowa P, 1991.

Miller, Perry. "From Edwards to Emerson." In *Errand into the Wilderness.* Cambridge, MA: Harvard UP, 1956.

———. *The New England Mind: From Colony to Province.* Cambridge, MA: Harvard UP, 1953.

———. *The Transcendentalists: An Anthology.* Cambridge, MA: Harvard UP, 1950.

Millichap, Joseph R. *Robert Penn Warren after* Audubon*: The Work of Aging and the Quest for Transcendence in His Later Poetry.* Baton Rouge: Louisiana State UP, 2009.

Millington, Richard. "*The Office of* The Scarlet Letter: An 'Inside Narrative'?" *Nathaniel Hawthorne Review,* 22.1 (Spring 1996) 1–8.

Mitchell, Thomas R. *Hawthorne's Fuller Mystery.* Amherst: U of Massachusetts P, 1998.

Mizruchi, Susan L. *The Science of Sacrifice: American Literature and Modern Social Theory.* Princeton, NJ: Princeton UP, 1998.

Montgomery, Marion. *Why Hawthorne Was Melancholy.* La Salle, IL: Sherwood Sugden, 1984.

Moore, Margaret. *The Salem World of Nathaniel Hawthorne.* Columbia: U of Missouri P, 1998.

Mott, Wesley T. "'An Etching of Emerson' (1853) and the Problem of Attribution." *Emerson Society Papers* 6.1 (1995) 1–4.

———. *"The Strains of Eloquence": Emerson and His Sermons.* University Park: Pennsylvania State UP, 1989.

Mumford, Lewis. *The Conduct of Life.* New York: Harcourt, Brace, 1951.

———. *The Golden Day; A Study in American Literature and Culture. With a New Introduction.* Boston: Beacon, 1957.

Murakami, Haruki. *The Wind-Up Bird Chronicle.* Trans. Jay Rubin. New York: Alfred A. Knopf, 1997.

Murfin, Ross C. "Introduction: The Biographical and Historical Background" to *Nathaniel Hawthorne: The Scarlet Letter.* New York: Bedford Books, 1991.

Newfield, Christopher. *The Emerson Effect: Individualism and Submission in America.* Chicago: U of Chicago P, 1996.

Nigro, August J. "Squaring the Circle in *Moby-Dick.*" In *The Diagonal Line: Separation and Reparation in American Literature.* Cranbury, NJ: Association of University Presses, 1984.

Norberg, Peter. "Comparative Religion and Competing Orthodoxies in Melville's *Clarel*" [abstract]. *Leviathan* 12.3 (October 2010) 133–34.

Norton, Andrews. *A Discourse on the Latest Form of Infidelity.* Cambridge, MA: John Owen, 1839.

Nuttall, Geoffrey. *The Holy Spirit in Puritan Faith and Experience.* London: Oxford UP, 1946.

Obenzinger, Hilton. *American Palestine: Melville, Twain, and the Holy Land Mania.* Princeton, NJ: Princeton UP, 1999.

Olson, Charles. *Call Me Ishmael.* With a new afterword by Merton M. Sealts, Jr. Baltimore: Johns Hopkins UP, 1997 [originally published San Francisco: City Lights Books, 1947].

Otter, Samuel. "An Aesthetics in All Things." *Representations* 104.1 (Fall 2008) 116–25.

———. *Melville's Anatomies.* Berkeley: U of California P, 1999.

Oughourlian, Jean-Michel. *The Puppet of Desire.* Stanford, CA: Stanford UP, 1991.

Packer, Barbara L. *Emerson's Fall: A New Interpretation of the Major Essays.* New York: Continuum, 1982.

———. "Historical Introduction." *The Collected Works of Ralph Waldo Emerson, volume 6: The Conduct of Life.* Ed. Barbara L. Packer, Joseph Slater, and Douglas Emory Wilson. Cambridge, MA: Harvard UP, 2003.

———. "History and Form in Emerson's 'Fate.'" In *Emerson: Bicentennial Essays.* Ed. Ronald A. Bosco and Joel Myerson. Boston: Massachusetts Historical Society, 2006.

———. "Origin and Authority: Emerson and the Higher Criticism." In *Reconstructing American Literary History.* Ed. Sacvan Bercovitch. Cambridge, MA: Harvard UP, 1986.

———. "Ralph Waldo Emerson." In *Columbia Literary History of the United States.* Ed. Emory Elliott et al. New York: Columbia UP, 1988.

———. "The Transcendentalists." In *The Cambridge History of American Literature, Volume Two: Prose Writing 1820–1865.* Ed. Sacvan Bercovitch. New York: Cambridge UP, 1995.

Page, Frances. "The Great Hall: Fond Memories Are Brought to Life by the Atheneum Restoration." *Historic Nantucket* 4.4 (April 1957) 13–20.

Pardes, Ilana. *Melville's Bibles*. Berkeley: U of California P, 2008.

Parker, Hershel. *Melville: The Making of the Poet*. Evanston, IL: Northwestern UP, 2008.

———, ed. *The Recognition of Herman Melville: Selected Criticism since 1846*. Ann Arbor: U of Michigan P, 1967.

Parker, Theodore. "A Discourse on the Transient and Permanent in Christianity." Pages 259–83 in *The Transcendentalists*. Ed. Perry Miller. Cambridge, MA: Harvard UP, 1950.

———. *Theodore Parker's Experience as a Minister, with some account of his early life, and education for the ministry: contained in a letter from him to the members of the twenty-eighth Congregational society of Boston*. Boston: R. Leighton, Jr., 1859.

Parrington, Vernon Louis. *Main Currents in American Thought. An Interpretation of American Literature from the Beginnings to 1920*. New York: Harcourt, Brace, 1930.

Paul, Sherman. *Emerson's Angle of Vision; Man and Nature in American Experience*. Cambridge, MA: Harvard UP, 1952.

Pearl, Matthew. *The Dante Club*. New York: Random House, 2003.

Pecora, Vincent. *Secularism and Cultural Criticism: Religion, Nation, & Modernity*. Chicago: U of Chicago P, 2006.

Pettit, Norman. *The Heart Prepared: Grace and Conversion in Puritan Spiritual Life*. 2nd ed. Middletown, CT: Wesleyan UP, 1989.

Phelan, Joseph Patrick. "Radical Metre: The English Hexameter in Clough's *Bothie of Toper-na-Fuosich*." *Review of English Studies*, new series 50 [198] (1999) 166–87.

Phillips, Christopher N. *The Course of Epic in American Culture: From Settlement to Reconstruction*. Baltimore: Johns Hopkins UP, forthcoming 2012.

Poirier, Richard. *Poetry & Pragmatism*. Cambridge, MA: Harvard UP, 1992.

Posnock, Ross. *The Trial of Curiosity: Henry James, William James, and the Challenge of Modernity*. New York: Oxford UP, 1991.

Potter, William. *Melville's* Clarel *and the Intersympathy of Creeds*. Kent, OH: Kent State UP, 2004.

Prettyman, Gib. "'Working after His Thought': The Signification of Industry in Emerson's *The Conduct of Life*." *American Transcendentalist Quarterly*, new series 7.1 (March 1993) 45–64.

Ra'ad, Basem L. "The Death Plot in Melville's *Clarel*." *ESQ* 27.1 [102] (1st Quarter 1981) 14–27.

Radicalism in religion, philosophy, and social life: four papers from the Boston Courier for 1858. Boston: Little, Brown, 1858.

Renker, Elizabeth. "Melville the Poet: Response to William Spengemann." *American Literary History* 12.1–2 (Spring/Summer 2000) 348–54.

Reynolds, Larry J. *Devils and Rebels: The Making of Hawthorne's Damned Politics.* Ann Arbor: U of Michigan P, 2008.

———. "Hawthorne's Labors in Concord." Pages 10–34 in *The Cambridge Companion to Nathaniel Hawthorne.* Ed. Richard H. Millington. Cambridge: Cambridge UP, 2004.

Richardson, Robert D. *Emerson: The Mind on Fire.* Berkeley: U of California P, 1995.

———. *First We Read, Then We Write: Emerson on the Creative Process.* Iowa City: U of Iowa P, 2009.

———. *Henry Thoreau: A Life of the Mind.* Los Angeles: U of California P, 1986.

Ricoeur, Paul. "Philosophical and Biblical Hermeneutics." In *From Text to Action: Essays in Hermeneutics, II.* Trans. Kathleen Blamey and John B. Thompson. Evanston, IL: Northwestern UP, 1991.

Riddel, Joseph. *Purloined Letters: Originality and Repetition in American Literature.* Baton Rouge: Louisiana State UP, 1995.

Roberson, Susan L. *Emerson in His Sermons: A Man-Made Self.* Columbia: U of Missouri P, 1995.

Robillard, Douglas. *Melville and the Visual Arts: Ionian Form, Venetian Tint.* Kent, OH: Kent State UP, 1997.

Robinson, David M. *Apostle of Culture: Emerson as Preacher and Lecturer.* Philadelphia: U of Pennsylvania P, 1982.

———. "Emerson." In *Nineteenth-Century Literature Criticism.* Vol. 1. Detroit: Gale Research, 1981.

———. *Emerson and the Conduct of Life: Pragmatism and Ethical Purpose in the Later Work.* New York: Cambridge UP, 1993.

———. "Experience, Instinct, and Emerson's Philosophical Reorientation." In *Emerson: Bicentennial Essays.* Ed. Ronald A. Bosco and Joel Myerson. Boston: Massachusetts Historical Society, 2006.

———. "Poetry, Poetic Perception, and Emerson's Spiritual Affirmations." In *Shaping Belief: Culture, Politics, and Religion in Nineteenth-Century Writing.* Ed. Victoria Morgan and Clare Williams. Liverpool: Liverpool UP, 2008.

———. "The Road Not Taken: From Edwards, through Chauncy, to Emerson." *Arizona Quarterly* 48.1 (Spring 1992) 45–62.

Rogin, Michael Paul. *Subversive Genealogy: The Politics and Art of Herman Melville.* Berkeley: U of California P, 1983.

Rusk, Ralph L. *The Life of Ralph Waldo Emerson.* New York: C. Scribner's Sons, 1949.

Sacks, Kenneth. *Understanding Emerson.* Princeton, NJ: Princeton UP, 2003.

Said, Edward. "Introduction to the Fiftieth-Anniversary Edition" of Erich Auerbach, *Mimesis: The Representation of Reality in Western Literature.* Princeton, NJ: Princeton UP, 2003.

Salzman, Jack, ed. *The Cambridge Handbook of American Literature.* New York: Cambridge UP, 1986.

Samson, John. *White Lies: Melville's Narratives of Facts.* Ithaca, NY: Cornell UP, 1989.

Scheick, William J. *The Slender Human Word: Emerson's Artistry in Prose.* Knoxville: U of Tennessee P, 1978.

Scorza, Thomas J. *In the Time before Steamships:* Billy Budd, *The Limits of Politics, and Modernity.* DeKalb: Northern Illinois UP, 1979.

Scott, Donald. *From Office to Profession: The New England Ministry, 1750–1850.* Philadelphia: U of Pennsylvania P, 1978.

Scudder, Townsend, III. "Emerson's British Lecture Tour, 1847–1848" [in two parts]. *American Literature* 7 (March 1935), 15–36, and 8 (May 1936) 166–80.

Sealts, Merton, Jr. *Emerson on the Scholar.* Columbia: U of Missouri P, 1992.

———. "Melville and Emerson's Rainbow." In *Pursuing Melville, 1940–1980: Chapters and Essays.* Madison: U of Wisconsin P, 1982.

———. *Melville's Reading; Revised and Enlarged Edition.* [Columbia]: U of South Carolina P, 1988.

Sedgwick, William Ellery. *Herman Melville: The Tragedy of Mind.* Cambridge, MA: Harvard UP, 1944.

Selinger, Eric. "'Too Pathetic, Too Pitiable': Emerson's Lessons in Love's Philosophy." *ESQ* 40 (2nd Quarter 1994) 139–82.

Shawcross, John T. "'Too intellectual a poet ever to be popular': Herman Melville and the Miltonic Dimensions of *Clarel.*" In *Melville and Milton: An Edition and Analysis of Melville's Annotations on Milton.* Ed. Robin Grey. Pittsburgh: Duquesne UP, 2004.

Sherrill, Rowland A. *The Prophetic Melville: Experience, Transcendence, and Tragedy.* Athens: U of Georgia P, 1979.

Short, Bryan C. "Form as Vision in Herman Melville's *Clarel.*" *American Literature* 50.4 (January 1979) 553–69.

Shuger, Debora Kuller. *The Renaissance Bible: Scholarship, Sacrifice, and Subjectivity.* Berkeley: U of California P, 1994.

Shurr, William H. *The Mystery of Iniquity: Melville as Poet, 1857–1891.* Lexington: UP of Kentucky, 1972.

Smith, Henry Nash. "Emerson's Problem of Vocation: A Note on 'The

American Scholar.'" *New England Quarterly* 12 (1939) 59–67.

Sontag, Susan. *Against Interpretation and Other Essays*. New York: Dell, 1966.

Spanos, William. *Herman Melville and the American Calling*. Albany: SUNY Press, 2008.

Spengemann, William. "Melville the Poet." *American Literary History* 11.4 (Winter 1999) 571–609.

Spiller, Robert. *The Cycle of American Literature: An Essay in Historical Criticism*. New York: Macmillan, 1955.

———. "Ralph Waldo Emerson." In *The Literary History of the United States: History. Fourth Edition: Revised*. Ed. Robert Spiller et al. New York: Macmillan, 1974.

Spitzer, Leo. "American Advertising Explained as Popular Art." In *Leo Spitzer: Representative Essays*. Ed. Alban K. Forcione, Herbert Lindenberger, and Madeline Sutherland; foreword by John Freccero. Stanford, CA: Stanford UP, 1988.

Stapleton, Laurence. "About Melville and the Angel." In *Some Poets and Their Resources, The Future Agenda: Lawrence, Emerson, Heaney, Bishop, Muir, Thomas, Melville, Wilbur*. Lanham, MD: UP of America, 1995.

Sten, Christopher. *Sounding the Whale:* Moby-Dick *as Epic Novel*. Kent, OH: Kent State UP, 1996.

Stern, Milton. *The Fine Hammered Steel of Herman Melville*. Urbana: U of Illinois P, 1957.

Stevenson, Louise L. *Scholarly Means to Evangelical Ends: The New Haven Scholars and the Transformation of Higher Learning in America 1830–1890*. Baltimore: Johns Hopkins UP, 1986.

Stich, Klaus P. "The Saturday Club as Intertext in Hawthorne's *The Elixir of Life Manuscripts*." *Nathaniel Hawthorne Review* 20.2 (Fall 1994) 11–20.

Stoehr, Taylor. *Hawthorne's Mad Scientists: Pseudoscience and Social Science in Nineteenth-Century Life and Letters*. Hamden, CT: Archon Books, 1978.

Stowe, Harriet Beecher. *The Minister's Wooing*. London: Sampson Low, 1859.

———. *Oldtown Folks*. Ed. Dorothy Berkson. New Brunswick, NJ: Rutgers UP, 1987.

Suzuki, Erin. "Frauds and Gods: The Politics of Religion in Melville's *Omoo* and *Mardi*." *ESQ* 53.4 (4th Quarter 2007) 361–86.

Swann, Charles. *Nathaniel Hawthorne: Tradition and Revolution*. New York: Cambridge UP, 1991.

Taylor, Charles. "Afterword: Apologia pro Libro suo." In *Varieties of Secularism in a Secular Age*. Ed. Michael Warner, Jonathan VanAntwerpen, and Craig Calhoun. Cambridge, MA: Harvard UP, 2010.

———. *A Secular Age*. Cambridge, MA: Harvard UP, 2007.

———. *Sources of the Self: The Making of Modern Identity*. Cambridge, MA: Harvard UP, 1989.

Taylor, Jeremy. *The Rule and Exercise of Holy Dying*. Boston: Little, Brown, [1864?]. Sealts number: 495a.

Thoreau, Henry David. *The Correspondence of Henry David Thoreau*. Ed. Walter Harding and Carl Bode. Washington Square: New York UP, 1958.

———. *Walden*. In *The Writings of Henry D. Thoreau*. Ed. J. Lyndon Shanley; intro. Joyce Carol Oates. Princeton, NJ: Princeton UP, 1989.

Tilton, Eleanor M. "Emerson's Lecture Schedule—1837–1838—Revised." *Harvard Library Bulletin* 21.4 (October 1973) 382–99.

Tolchin, Neal. *Mourning, Gender, and Creativity in the Art of Herman Melville*. New Haven, CT: Yale UP, 1988.

Tomc, Sandra. "'The Sanctity of the Priesthood': Hawthorne's 'Custom-House.'" *ESQ* 39 (1993) 161–83.

Toulouse, Teresa. *The Art of Prophesying: New England Sermons and the Shaping of Belief*. Athens: U of Georgia P, 1987.

Turner, James. *The Liberal Education of Charles Eliot Norton*. Baltimore: Johns Hopkins UP, 1999.

———. *Without God, Without Creed: The Origins of Unbelief in America*. Baltimore: Johns Hopkins UP, 1985.

Ullén, Magnus, and David Greven. "Late Hawthorne: A Polemical Introduction." *Nathaniel Hawthorne Review* 35.2 (Fall 2009) 1–25.

Van Koetsveld, Cornelis Elisa. *The Manse of Mastland*. Trans. Thomas Keightley. London: Bell & Daldy, 1860.

Van Leer, David. "The Apocalypse of the Mind: Idealism and Annihilation in the American Renaissance." Diss. Cornell U, 1978.

———. *Emerson's Epistemology: The Argument of the Essays*. New York: Cambridge UP, 1986.

———. "Hester's Labyrinth: Transcendental Rhetoric in Puritan Boston." In *New Essays on the Scarlet Letter*. Ed. Michael J. Colacurcio. New York: Cambridge UP, 1985.

———. "A View from the Closet: Reconcilable Differences in Douglass and Melville." In *Frederick Douglass and Herman Melville: Essays in Relation*. Ed. Robert S. Levine and Samuel Otter. Chapel Hill: U of North Carolina P, 2008.

Von Frank, Albert J. "Batting Oranges on the Beach: And the Way Forward in Emerson Studies." American Literature Association conference, San Francisco, May 29, 2010.

———. "'Build Therefore Your Own World': Emerson's Constructions of the

'Intimate Sphere.'" In *Emersonian Circles: Essays in Honor of Joel Myerson*. Ed. Wesley T. Mott and Robert E. Burkholder. Rochester, NY: U of Rochester P, 1997.

———. *An Emerson Chronology*. New York: G. K. Hall, 1994.

———. *The Trials of Anthony Burns: Freedom and Slavery in Emerson's Boston*. Cambridge, MA: Harvard UP, 1997.

Waggoner, Hyatt. *Hawthorne*. Cambridge, MA: Harvard UP, 1955.

Walker, Jeffrey. *Bardic Ethos and the American Epic Poem: Whitman, Pound, Crane, Williams, Olson*. Baton Rouge: Louisiana State UP, 1989.

Wallace, James D. "Immortality in Hawthorne's *Septimius Felton*." *Studies in American Fiction* 14.1 (Spring 1986) 19–33.

Walls, Laura Dassow. "The Anatomy of Truth: Emerson's Poetic Science." *Configurations* 5.3 (Fall 1997) 425–61.

———. *Emerson's Life in Science: The Culture of Truth*. Ithaca, NY: Cornell UP, 2003.

Ware, Henry, Jr. "The Personality of Deity." In *An American Reformation: A Documentary History of Unitarian Christianity*. Ed. Sydney E. Ahlstrom and Jonathan S. Carey. Middletown, CT: Wesleyan UP, 1985.

Warner, Michael, Jonathan VanAntwerpen, and Craig Calhoun. "Editors' Introduction." In *Varieties of Secularism in a Secular Age*. Ed. Michael Warner, Jonathan VanAntwerpen, and Craig Calhoun. Cambridge, MA: Harvard UP, 2010.

Warren, Robert Penn. "Introduction" and notes. *Selected Poems of Herman Melville*. New York: Random House, 1970.

Wasung, C. J. "Emerson Comes to Detroit." *Michigan History Magazine* 29.1 (1945) 59–72.

Wegener, Larry Edward. *A Concordance to Herman Melville's* Clarel: *A Poem and Pilgrimage in the Holy Land*. 4 vols. Lewiston, NY: Edwin Mellen P, 1997.

Weinsheimer, Joel C. *Eighteenth-Century Hermeneutics: Philosophy of Interpretation in England from Locke to Burke*. New Haven, CT: Yale UP, 1993.

Wendell, Barrett. *A Literary History of America*. New York: Scribner, 1905.

West, Cornel. "Emerson on Power (and Tradition)." In *The American Evasion of Philosophy: A Genealogy of Pragmatism*. Madison: U of Wisconsin P, 1989.

Whicher, Stephen E. *Freedom and Fate; An Inner Life of Ralph Waldo Emerson*. Philadelphia: U of Pennsylvania P, 1971.

———, ed. *Selections from Ralph Waldo Emerson*. Boston: Houghton Mifflin, 1972.

Wider, Sarah. "What Did the Minister Mean? Emerson's Sermons and Their Audience." *ESQ* 34 (1988) 1–22.

Williams, John B. *White Fire: The Influence of Emerson on Melville.* Long Beach: California State U, Long Beach P, 1991.

Wilson, Eric. *Emerson's Sublime Science.* New York: St. Martin's, 1999.

Wineapple, Brenda. *Hawthorne: A Life.* New York: Knopf, 2003.

———. "Nathaniel Hawthorne, 1804–1864: A Brief Biography." Pages 13–45 in *A Historical Guide to Nathaniel Hawthorne.* Ed. Larry J. Reynolds. New York: Oxford UP, 2001.

Wortham, Thomas. "Recent Books" [Emerson]. *Nineteenth-Century Literature* 46.1 (June 1991) 139–43.

———. "Recent Books." *Nineteenth-Century Literature* 48.4 (March 1994) 549–56.

Yothers, Brian. "'Crack'd Archangel': Sir Thomas Browne's *Religio Medici,* the Bible, and Religious Difference in Melville's Fiction and Poetry" [abstract]. *Leviathan* 12.2 (June 2010) 111–12.

Žižek, Slavoj. *Looking Awry.* Cambridge, MA: MIT Press, 1991.

Index